MW00644130

Melville's Bibles

The publisher gratefully acknowledges the generous support
of Loren and Frances Rothschild as members of the Publisher's
Circle of the University of California Press Foundation.

Melville's Bibles

Ilana Pardes

UNIVERSITY OF CALIFORNIA PRESS
Berkeley · Los Angeles · London

University of California Press, one of the most
distinguished university presses in the United States,
enriches lives around the world by advancing
scholarship in the humanities, social sciences, and
natural sciences. Its activities are supported by the UC
Press Foundation and by philanthropic contributions
from individuals and institutions. For more
information, visit www.ucpress.edu.

University of California Press
Berkeley and Los Angeles, California

University of California Press, Ltd.
London, England

© 2008 by The Regents of the University of California

Library of Congress Cataloging-in-Publication Data

Pardes, Ilana.
    Melville's Bibles / Ilana Pardes.
        p.   cm.
    Includes bibliographical references and index.
    ISBN 978-0-520-25454-1 (cloth : alk. paper)
    ISBN 978-0-520-25455-8 (pbk. : alk. paper)
    1. Melville, Herman, 1819–1891. Moby Dick.
2. Melville, Herman, 1819–1891—Religion.
3. Bible—Commentaries.   4. Bible—Hermeneutics.
5. Bible and literature.   6. Religion and culture.
7. Religion and literature—United States—History—
19th century.   8. American fiction—19th century—
History and criticism.   I. Title.

PS2388.B5P37   2008
813'.3—dc22   2007014870

Manufactured in the United States of America

17 16 15 14 13 12 11 10 09 08
10 9 8 7 6 5 4 3 2 1

This book is printed on New Leaf EcoBook 50, a
100% recycled fiber of which 50% is de-inked post-
consumer waste, processed chlorine-free. EcoBook 50
is acid-free and meets the minimum requirements of
ANSI/ASTM D5634–01 (*Permanence of Paper*).

For my mother
and for
Ruth Nevo

Contents

Illustrations

Acknowledgments

I have been fortunate to have had many fellow travelers in the course of this voyage. I will begin with the Melvilleans who have welcomed me into this wild world of whaling. I am indebted to the late Michael Rogin, who encouraged me to embark on the project when I was still far from sure that it was possible. By far my greatest debt is to Samuel Otter, who, with unparalleled generosity, read the entire manuscript and provided invaluable comments and suggestions. Emory Elliott, Viola Sachs, and Bob Wallace also offered comments and help at various points.

On the biblical side, I am deeply grateful to Robert Alter for his unstinting belief in this project and for his remarkably attuned reflections on literary exegesis. I am also indebted to Eitan Bar-Yosef for sharpening my understanding of topics related to the cultural history of the Bible, above all, the circulation of biblical texts in Holy Land travel literature. Jonathan Sheehan read the Job chapter and provided helpful suggestions.

I worked on the final chapters of this book in fall 2005, at the Institute of Advanced Studies at the Hebrew University of Jerusalem, where I took part in a research group on "Ethnography and Literature." It was an exceptionally stimulating and warm intellectual setting where discussions were never confined by normative temporal boundaries. I am particularly indebted to Galit Hasan-Rokem, Carola Hilfrich, Alon Confino, and Amy Schuman for their superb comments on earlier drafts and for their vital companionship. Many thanks go to Eliezer Rabinovici, director of the institute, and Pnina Feldman, associate director.

I have also benefited from the insights of many other friends and colleagues: David Domrosch, Michael Gilmore, Ruth HaCohen, Melila Eshed-Helner, Hannan Hever, Gideon Kunda, Menachem Lurberbaum, Adi Ophir, Michele Rosenthal, and Shira Wolosky.

My students at the Hebrew University were a source of much pleasure and insight. I would like to thank the astute students of two seminars I taught on *Moby-Dick* and the Bible in fall 2002 and spring 2006. Special thanks go to my research assistants, Anat Danziger and Batnadiv HaKarmi-Weinberg, for their help and commitment.

While working on the final touches of this book in fall 2006, I had the privilege of teaching a gifted group of students a graduate seminar on related issues in the Department of Comparative Literature at the University of California, Berkeley. I am grateful to Erich Naiman, chair of the department, for his warm hospitality. I also had the great pleasure of being adopted by the Jewish Studies Program during my stay at Berkeley and am deeply grateful to Chana Kronfeld, Ron Hendel, and Naomi Seidman for their friendship and ongoing support.

For financial support, I am indebted to the Hebrew University Intramural Research Funds and to the Israel Science Foundation. I am also indebted to the Joseph H. and Belle R. Braun Senior Lectureship in Humanities.

I presented different portions of the book at Hebrew University, Ben-Gurion University, the University of California, Berkeley, Stanford University, and Indiana University. I am grateful for the invaluable response of the audiences on these occasions. An earlier version of chapter 2 was published as "Remapping Jonah's Voyage: Melville's *Moby-Dick* and Kitto's *Cyclopedia of Biblical Literature*" in *Comparative Literature* 57, no. 2 (Spring 2005): 135–57.

I owe much to Doron Narkiss, who edited the manuscript with unusual acumen and a Melvillean passion. Special thanks go to Reed Malcolm at the University of California Press for his support and to the entire editorial team—Sheila Berg, Chalon Emmons, and Kalicia Pivirotto—for their meticulous and thoughtful work.

The artist Clifford Ross generously provided me with his beautiful photographs of Melville's bible. His genosity did not end there. He also gave me the unique opportunity to examine this bible, for which I am most grateful.

My family—Itamar, Keren, and Eyal—joined me in every imaginable way. We all spent two memorable summers in New England, wandering in the footsteps of Melville from Nantucket to the Berkshires, not to mention the numerous whaling museums. This book owes much to their precious love and devotion.

This book is dedicated to my mother, Deborah Patinkin, who (as I am writing these pages) is traveling in India doing anthropological fieldwork, at the age of eighty-two. I admire her courage and intellectual passion and can only hope to have such stamina at her age. It is also dedicated to Ruth Nevo, who has been an ever-growing source of inspiration for me during the past three decades. That Shakespeare and the Bible meet in *Moby-Dick* only enriched our ongoing dialogue. I cannot imagine what writing this book would have been like without our conversations and wondrous, unending excursions.

Jerusalem, February 2007

Introduction

"'Tis high time we should have a bible that should be no provincial record, but should open the history of the planet, and bind all tendencies and dwarf all the Epics & philosophies we have," wrote Emerson in his journal.[1] It seems as if every other writer in antebellum America sought to follow Emerson's call and reinvent the Bible. But no one was as insistent as Melville on redefining biblical exegesis while doing so. In *Moby-Dick* he not only ventured to fashion a grand new, inverted Bible, in which biblical rebels and outcasts assume central stage, but also aspired at the same time to comment on every imaginable mode of biblical interpretation, calling for a radical reconsideration of the politics of biblical reception. I would go so far as to suggest that if *Moby-Dick* has acquired the status of a gigantic Bible of sorts in American culture and beyond, it is precisely because Melville opens up the question of what counts as Bible and what counts as interpretation with unparalleled verve. This book carries through *Moby-Dick*'s invitation to rethink these two concepts.

The invitation to plunge into a world of exegetical contemplation is put forth at the very outset. Ishmael, the narrator, whose voice often merges with that of Melville, defines himself in the opening "Extracts" as the commentator on different "whale statements" provided by the "sub-sub librarian"—from biblical verses on whales in Genesis, Job, Jonah, Psalms, and Isaiah to commentaries on whales by great writers and thinkers such as Montaigne, Rabelais, Shakespeare, and Hobbes to encyclopedic considerations of the topic, newspaper accounts, and an anonymous whale song.[2] Ishmael's list is a mock catalogue of extracts that calls into question our capacity to cover any hermeneutic problem whatsoever—be it a theological problem or one that pertains to "gospel cetology." It is, however, at the same time a preliminary expression of Melville's strikingly broad conception of exegesis and insatiable passion to fathom the stubborn vitality of interpretive endeavors.

The same kind of virtuosity and openness, I propose, character-izes Melville's perception of biblical exegesis. For Melville, the Bible is a cultural text whose interpretation is carried out in highly diverse realms. He engages in a dialogue with an impressive array of interpre-tive discourses—from literary renditions of biblical texts to traditional commentaries (among them, Calvin's commentaries and rabbinic lore), Gnostic mythos, popular sermons, political speeches, compara-tive accounts of religions and mythologies, and biblical encyclopedias. Melville does not limit himself to normative mappings of interpretive boundaries. Much like Ishmael, he is willing to consider any "book whatsoever, sacred or profane" (xix), any biblical interpretation what-soever—high or low, ancient or contemporary, of any religious bent or scholarly tradition. He never ceases to be intrigued by the interpretive strategies of every commentary he touches on, always attentive to the ways in which his own exegetical obsessions may intersect with those of other commentators.

Melville's critique of the politics of exegetical mappings is bound up with his challenge to the all too common tendency to mitigate the radi-cality of the biblical text. He foregrounds the anomalies and oddities of the Hebrew canon, countertraditions such as Job, Jonah, and Eccle-siastes that challenge predominant presuppositions of biblical belief. Even when Melville selects stories that are set within major biblical texts (e.g., Genesis or Kings) he reads them against the grain, high-lighting the fragility of concepts such as chosenness and promise. His Bible is not meant for those who would "[dodge] hospitals and jails, and [walk] fast crossing grave-yards, and would rather talk of operas than hell" (424). It strives to lure readers who would be willing to sit down on "tomb-stones, and break the green damp mould with unfath-omably wondrous Solomon," readers who would not hesitate to probe the bleak, unsettling truths of texts such as Ecclesiastes, "the fine ham-mered steel of woe" (424).[3]

Given the Hebraic bent of *Moby-Dick,* I focus on texts pertaining to the Hebrew Bible.[4] I do, however, address pertinent links with the

New Testament. I also take into account the fact that for Melville the question of what counts as Bible is not confined to the canonical Western Bible. He is ready to meditate on all modes of scriptural writing—be they Indian mythologies, Islamic texts, or the sacred traditions and customs of Polynesian communities. Jonah, Vishnu, St. George, and Hercules may be evoked at once as part of the same "member-roll."

In calling my book *Melville's Bibles* I wish not only to position Melville's commentary and metacommentary at the center of attention but also to highlight Melville's own sense of *Moby-Dick* as a book of biblical proportions.[5] The question of how to write a "mighty book" on a "mighty theme" (456) that would recapitulate in new terms the tantalizing experience of reading an all-encompassing book like the Bible is a pivotal aesthetic-hermeneutic question throughout the text. I read Melville's insistence on combining different modes of discourse—poetic, historical, legal, scientific, encyclopedic, political, descriptive—as a homage to the Bible's own attempt to capture every shade of human experience and every imaginable mode of discourse in its incredible mixture of narrative, poetry, history, legal codes, and detailed (notoriously detailed) blueprints of the tabernacle and temple.[6]

Melville's biblicism was never doubted—from the groundbreaking studies of Nathalia Wright (*Melville's Use of the Bible,* 1949) and Lawrence Thompson (*Melville's Quarrel with God,* 1952), the first to excavate Melville's biblical poetics, to the more recent studies of Americanists and postcolonial critics (Sacvan Bercovitch, Michael Rogin, Lawrence Buell, Elisa New, Hilton Obenzinger), whose inquiries added a much-needed historical contextualization of Melville's use of the Bible.[7] But while the former focused on Melville's readings of biblical texts, devoting little attention to the cultural context, the latter did the opposite. That is, they primarily discussed Melville's innovative exegesis in relation to American religious and political thought, dealing only sporadically with the biblical material itself.

I want to argue that these two lines of inquiry need to be combined. To understand Melville's commentary, I believe, means to explore its embeddedness in metacommentary and vice versa. But I do not merely wish to combine these two lines. The chapters that follow call for a consideration of the particular forms and textures of Melville's vast aesthetic-hermeneutic project. Melville knew the Bible so well, writes Nathalia Wright, that "he could smell the burning of Gomorrah and the pit; hear the trumpet in the Valley of Jehoshaphat[,] . . . taste Belshazzar's feast, feel the heat of the fiery furnace."[8] But she does not dive into these biblical scenes with Melville to follow the details of his intimate, sensuous encounter with the ancient verses and the particular features of his biblical aesthetics. Nor does Thompson, who highlights Melville's debt to Job and Jonah in his "quarrel with God," go far enough in probing the rhetoric and cries of the two great questioners of biblical tradition. The same holds for those who have dealt with Melville's exegetical milieu. Such readings provide only panoramic views of Melville's dialogues with other interpretive modes, primarily shedding light on American literature and culture rather than on the history of biblical exegesis.

I wish to contribute not only to the understanding of Melville's exegetical imagination but also to the understanding of the biblical text itself and of biblical reception. Melville's biblical exegesis, it seems to me, deserves the same kind of comprehensive examination one would devote to the writings of Calvin, Herder, or Buber.[9] For Melville, the poetic license of writers does not make their exegetical reflections less "faithful" or earnest. Quite the contrary, literary flights of the imagination may entail interpretive insights available to no other exegetical mode. I am indebted to the work of critics such as Robert Alter, Harold Fisch, and Northrop Frye who have sought to combine literary theory and biblical criticism in their study of the Bible and literature (though none of the above has tackled Melville's work).[10] My book has also been conceived within the framework of current research on the Bible as cultural text by Mieke Bal, Elizabeth Castelli, Stephen Moore, Gary A. Phillip, and Regina Schwartz—with its unique blend of biblical criticism, cultural studies, and postmodern theories—and of recent studies by Paul Gutjahr and Jonathan Sheehan on the Bible's cultural history.[11] In *Moby-Dick*, I believe, Melville brilliantly anticipates some of the postmodern attempts to remap biblical exegesis and redefine the cultural role of the biblical text.

To attempt to address all the (meta)commentaries Melville juggles at once in *Moby-Dick* would be as impossible as the sub-sub librarian's pursuit of whale statements through the "long Vaticans and street-stalls of the earth."[12] I set five principal biblical texts/characters in *Moby-Dick*—Job, Jonah, Ishmael, Ahab, and Rachel—against five modes of biblical exegesis in antebellum America: literary exegesis, biblical encyclopedias, Holy Land travel narratives, political sermons, and women's Bibles. Although Melville was intrigued by all commentaries, he had, I believe, a special fascination with the new exegetical trends of his time and was particularly interested in reflecting on the cultural role of the Bible in antebellum America.

Nineteenth-century America witnessed several influential exegetical shifts. The first shockwaves of the new trends in German biblical criticism were felt in American intellectual circles by the opening decades of the nineteenth century. In a forceful demystification of the origin of Scripture, biblical scholarship shattered the traditional notion of the Bible as the Word of God, a unified text of divine inspiration, and suggested that it be treated as a composite work, a product of human endeavor, whose intricate history of composition may be examined like that of any other ancient text. Determining the historicity of the biblical texts as well as dating the various sources and documents became a major scholarly concern.

As textual critics in antebellum America followed in the footsteps of their German precursors, debating the accuracy of the biblical text itself, other scholars, among them the founder of biblical archaeology/ geography, Edward Robinson, turned from textual analysis to biblical geography, their underlying assumption being that the scientific study of the geographic features of Palestine was indispensable to the assessment of scriptural veracity. Popularized adaptations of the historical-geographic approach were to be found in biblical encyclopedias, in the large, newly designed American family bibles with their topographic maps and historical notes, and in Holy Land travel literature.

The American literary market was in fact flooded in the nineteenth century by numerous narratives and diaries of travelers to the Holy Land. This literature set out to capture the "original" Oriental qualities of the Bible by touring the Holy Land and searching for the biblical traces inscribed in it. Palestine was now construed, to quote William M. Thomson in *The Land and the Book,* as "one vast tablet whereupon God's messages to men have been drawn, and graven deep in living characters by the great Publisher of glad tidings, to be seen and read by all to the end of time."[13] And accordingly, contemporary Easterners were perceived as an ethnographic window into the past, or as a living embodiment of biblical characters and customs.

The most influential shift within literary circles was the aesthetic turn in biblical exegesis. The Bible was not always venerated as an aesthetic touchstone. The literary Bible emerged in the context of English and German Enlightenment as the invention of writers and literati, alongside the new scientific approach of biblical criticism. The prominent advocates of the redefinition of the boundaries between belles lettres and sacred writing in America were Emerson, Whitman, Stowe, Dickinson—and, of course, Melville. All sought, albeit differently, to rekindle the Bible's poetic grandeur in their writings and saw themselves as the ultimate interpreters of biblical vision.

To be sure, these new trends were made possible by a certain erosion of religious dogma. But, as Jonathan Sheehan claims, it would be a mistake to conflate this posttheological project with secularization.[14] What the pursuers of these new approaches—be it the historical, the aesthetic, or the geographic-ethnographic—strived to do, above all, was to rejuvenate the Bible and transform it from a book justified by theology to one justified by culture. Religion did not disappear in the European Enlightenment or in antebellum America; rather, it became part of the very definition of modernity.

Within the political realm, the Bible played a central role in the major debates of the time. One cannot exaggerate the importance of the Bible within the American political tradition. From the very beginning, on board the *Arbella* in 1630, John Winthrop, in his famous sermon "A Model of Christian Charity," designated the new Puritan community as a "city upon a hill," to be observed and admired by "the eyes of all people."[15] Each generation, however, sought to reinterpret America's covenantal mission in light of its own urgent concerns. Whereas for some antebellum politicians the nineteenth-century "city upon a hill" was to expand to the west and to the south as part of America's Manifest Destiny, for others, expansionism, the Mexican War in particular, was a "sin of covetousness" analogous to King Ahab's usurpation of Naboth's vineyard. Exegetical battles took place in other realms as well, primarily in relation to slavery and women's rights. Proslavery advocates quoted the Pauline command in Ephesians 6:5, "Slaves, obey your earthly masters with fear and trembling," against abolitionists who evoked Exodus and Jesus' command to love one's neighbor in Matthew 22:39. Similarly, in the debate over woman's suffrage, each side underscored its own cherished verses. While opponents cited the divine punishment of Eve in Genesis 3—"in sorrow thou shalt bring forth children; and thy desire shall be to thy husband, and he shall rule over thee"—suffragists such as Sarah Grimké regarded Genesis 1:27, with its depiction of the egalitarian creation of man and woman, as a cherished interpretive key.

The entrance of women into the political scene was accompanied by the rise of women's Bibles. The burgeoning of exegetical writings by women, evident in diverse cultural spheres in nineteenth-century America, exhibited a wide range of religious, aesthetic, and political stances. The primary objective of this exegetical corpus was to reinterpret female characters in the Bible, positioning at the center a biblical feminine realm that previous interpreters had regarded as marginal.

These interpretive realms were by no means isolated. The spirit of Manifest Destiny hovered over many Holy Land travel narratives much as the tools and methodologies of biblical scholarship were used in the political sphere to support the antislavery campaign and women's suffrage. Thus Theodore Parker could be at once an advocate of the new findings of German biblical scholarship, the translator of W. M. L. De Wette's *Einleitung,* a fervent abolitionist, an opponent of the Mexican War, and a supporter of the feminization of American religion.

In the following chapters I explore the ways in which Melville's biblical commentaries are inextricably connected with his reflections on these exegetical shifts and battles. Given that Melville is primarily devoted to literary exegesis, I begin with the chapter on Job. Chapter 1, "Playing with Leviathan: Job and the Aesthetic Turn in Biblical Exegesis," considers Melville's reading of Job in light of a whole genealogy of continental scholars and writers (from Lowth and Herder to Goethe and Blake) who regarded the Book of Job as an exemplary code of art within the great code of art. I follow the ways in which Melville's projection of Job onto the world of whaling redefines continental perceptions of Joban sublimity in its tantalizing juggling of physical and metaphysical leviathans. Special attention is given to Melville's translation of Joban impatience into aesthetic terms in his unending probing of the limits of representation, of faith, and of life itself. Here as elsewhere, my choice of matching a given biblical text and a given interpretive trend depends primarily on salience (within a given exegetical milieu and/or in Melville's reflection on it). Job was by no means the only biblical text to be evoked by the advocates of the literary Bible, but it had a central position in this context.

The next two chapters revolve around Melville's response to the interrelated interpretive modes of biblical scholarship and Holy Land travel literature. Chapter 2, "'Jonah Historically Regarded': Improvisations on Kitto's *Cyclopedia of Biblical Literature,*" regards Melville's reading of Jonah as a comment on the reception of German biblical scholarship in America. While exposing the charms and absurdities of the scientific approach to the Bible, Melville does not hesitate to use Kitto's *Cyclopedia* in shaping his own reading of the Book of Jonah as a radical reflection on the paradoxes of prophecy and the arbitrary rule of God. Chapter 3, "'Call Me Ishmael': The Bible and the Orient," regards Melville's positioning of Ishmael in the pivotal role of narrator

and exegetical guide in *Moby-Dick* not only as a token of admiration
for the biblical Ishmael, the quintessential wild outcast, but also as
a reflection on the prevalent tendency in American Holy Land travel
literature to construe the Orient and its inhabitants, the so-called descendants of Ishmael, as indispensable keys to understanding scriptural
truths. I also consider the ways in which Melville's privileging of the
outcast underscores the Bible's own concern with the instability of the
boundaries between the chosen and the nonchosen in the interrelated
tales of Abraham-Isaac and Hagar-Ishmael.

In chapter 4, I move on to the political sphere. "Ahab, Idolatry, and
the Question of Possession: Biblical Politics" spells out Melville's penetrating reading of the critique of royal rule in Samuel and Kings, high-
lighting its relevance to a critique of American expansionism. Captain
Ahab is construed as a response to the numerous references to King
Ahab's usurpation of Naboth's vineyard in the political discourse opposing the Mexican War. The discussion entails a consideration of the
Bible's role in other major political debates—primarily the debate over
slavery—and attempts to consider Melville's debt to and departure
from the political uses of biblical texts. Chapter 5, "Rachel's Inconsolable Cry: The Rise of Women's Bibles," explores Melville's choice
to end *Moby-Dick* with an evocation of Jeremiah's verse on Rachel's
defiant and inconsolable cry on behalf of her exiled children. Melville's
rare allusion to a biblical female figure is set against the background
of the feminization of biblical exegesis. I follow different nineteenth-
century Rachels: from the image of weeping Rachel in Harper's *Illuminated Bible* to Harriet Beecher Stowe's readings of Jeremiah's Rachel in *Uncle Tom's Cabin* and in her less known book, *Woman in
Sacred History*. The epilogue offers a final account of Melville's exegetical project and an overview of the ways in which the reception
of *Moby-Dick* in diverse cultural realms—from children's adaptations
to musical interpretations, literary exegesis, artworks, films, television
productions, and political discourse—repeats the dynamics of biblical reception. Throughout the book I examine the interplay between
the different characters and the different interpretive modes. I consider
Melville's fascination with the poetic dimension of nonliterary modes
of exegesis alongside his insistence on the political potential of literary
exegesis and biblical scholarship.

My contextualization of Melville's reading of biblical texts focuses
on antebellum American culture, but I discuss other interpretive mi-
lieus as well. I share the current concerns of critics such as Lawrence

Buell and Donald Pease who have called attention to the transnational dimension of American literature.[16] Melville never hesitated to underscore the shiftiness and fluidity of all cultural distinctions. While his biblicism strives to be quintessentially American, avoiding all imitation—"we want no American Miltons," he declares in "Hawthorne and his Mosses"[17]—it is at the same time deeply indebted to European exegetical traditions. Similarly, his dark prophecy on the disastrous route of the American ship of state is by no means relevant only to America a decade before the Civil War. Rendering a new poetically inspired Bible for Melville ultimately means to acquire the position of the original Book of Books: to compose a formative text for a particular community in a particular place in time that would nonetheless transcend its national and temporal borders, touching the lives of readers in other cultural contexts as well. I would indeed venture to suggest that if *Moby-Dick* was largely misunderstood or ignored at the time of its publication in 1851 and discovered only in the 1920s, and more substantively in the 1940s, it was, in part, because Melville's exegetical imagination was in many ways ahead of its time.[18]

Although each chapter in the book is devoted to a single biblical character, I should make clear from the outset that Melville rejects all notions of character consistency. Curiously enough, Melville's primary aesthetic-hermeneutic strategy in his readings of the Bible—the splitting or duplication of biblical characters among the different crew members of the *Pequod*—has gone unnoticed in previous studies of *Moby-Dick*. The key to understanding this strategy lies in a passage from *The Confidence-Man:* "Upon the whole, it might rather be thought, that he, who, in view of its inconsistencies, says of human nature the same that, in view of its contrasts, is said of the divine nature, that it is past finding out, thereby evinces a better appreciation of it than he who, by always representing it in a clear light, leaves it to be inferred that he clearly knows all about it."[19]

To represent human character as consistent means to smooth out the incomprehensibility of human nature, the prevalent lack of coherence that characterizes human life. In a playful iconoclastic move, Melville demands that the same attention that is given to divine inconsistencies (all the more so since the rise of biblical scholarship) should be given to human ones.[20] This ars poetic/hermeneutic passage on the mysteries of character sheds light on the numerous splittings or duplications of the confidence man, but is as relevant to the splittings and merging of biblical characters in *Moby-Dick*. In *Moby-Dick*,

however, such inconsistencies are all the more spectacular given that
they are the hallmark of several characters at once.

Exegesis, for Melville, means above all to open up potentialities,
to take typology beyond its limits, to experiment with the possibility
of thinking that Ishmael (or any other crew member for that matter)
could simultaneously be a Jonah, an Ahab, a Job, or a Rachel. That
such a study of biblical texts and characters is always on the verge
of admitting—through its unparalleled exegetical excess—that hermeneutic enigmas are "past finding out" does not make it less alluring.
Somehow it is the impossibility of fathoming divine and human character and the vanity of all knowledge that seems to propel Ishmael/
Melville with an ever-growing drive to continue the search.

The fluidity of Melville's typology reinforces its pronounced democratic bent. Melville—via Ishmael—waggishly insists that his common
heroes are "knights and squires" and that God is nothing but a democratic Author:

> But this august dignity I treat of, is not the dignity of kings and robes,
> but that abounding dignity which has no robed investiture. Thou shalt
> see it shining in the arm that wields a pick or drives a spike; that dem-
> ocratic dignity which, on all hands, radiates without end from God;
> Himself! The great God absolute! The center and circumference of
> all democracy! . . . If, then, to meanest mariners, and renegades and
> castaways, I shall hereafter ascribe high qualities, though dark; weave
> round them tragic graces . . . then against all mortal critics bear me out
> in it, thou just Spirit of Equality, which hast spread one royal mantle
> of humanity over all my kind! Bear me out in it, thou great democratic
> God! (117)

Once God is construed as "the center and circumference of all democracy," common people (be it Andrew Jackson or anyone else) can, or
even must, be elevated to biblical stature. By the same token, literary
typology need not dwell up high: whalers may hold an august biblical dignity no less—and perhaps even more—than those who have
"robed investiture."

Ursala Brumm argues that Melville's typologies are a celebration of
American democracy.[21] She is right only to a point, for Melville is, at
the same time, highly critical of the limited scope of democracy in antebellum America and of the concomitant narrow contours of American typologies.[22] In his radical typological world, even Pip, the black
boy who is deserted in the midst of seas, can be a Jonah, and Fleece,
the black cook who is forced to deliver a sermon to the sharks, can be

a Job. What is more, typology is not confined to the Christians aboard. Queequeg prefigures the *Rachel*'s role as deliverer and Tashtego is one of the *Pequod*'s most prominent Ishmaels. No one is left outside of the exegetical vortex.

In privileging the term *exegesis,* I want to emphasize the extent to which Melville sees himself as part of a long genealogy of exegetes. He may mock the "German exegitist" who regards his reading of Jonah in historical terms as the ultimate reading, much as he can offer amusingly sharp parodies of other exegetical pursuits, but the very radicality of his exegesis depends on, and is inspired by, the cumulative power of layers upon layers of unending attempts to read Scripture anew. *Exegesis* comes from Greek *exēgeisthai,* "to show the way," "to interpret" (*ex-,* "out of" + *hēgeisthai,* "lead" or "guide"). The primary objective of many exegetical traditions from antiquity on has been to draw out of Scripture its presumably deeper and less accessible latent meanings. One possible way to do so—most notably in the Midrash but also in popular sermons of all times (Father Mapple's reading of Jonah is an exquisite case in point)—is to retell the biblical tale. Exegesis, then, not only within the realm of modern literature, often entailed an attempt to find in the Bible the potential for another narrative.[23] My occasional use of the term *hermeneutic* is meant to call attention to the reflective qualities of Melville's exegesis, inseparable as it is from metaexegesis.

Melville's biblical exegesis neither begins in *Moby-Dick* nor ends there. It is an ongoing preoccupation that may be traced throughout his entire career. In *Typee* he renders an earthly Eden; in *Omoo* he follows the circulation of missionary bibles in Tahiti; in *White-Jacket* he offers an often-quoted definition of America's sense of biblical destiny ("And we Americans are the peculiar, chosen people—the Israel of our time; we bear the ark of the liberties of the world"); Bartleby is a Wall Street Job; *The Confidence-Man,* as we have seen, offers its own extravagant experiments with typology; *Clarel* is a momentous pilgrimage-poem that depicts every step in the Holy Land as a step into numerous biblical texts; and *Billy Budd* retells the story of the fall and the crucifixion as it redefines "the mystery of iniquity." I focus on *Moby-Dick* because it is undoubtedly the climactic moment of this project. It is the one book in Melville's oeuvre that aspired to be a grand Bible and has become one.

A few biographical notes about Melville's religious education and background are necessary. Melville's family was steeped in Calvinist

traditions on both sides. His great great grandfather was a Congrega-
tionalist clergyman in Scotland, and his grandfather, Thomas Melvill
(the final *e* was added only in the 1830s), was a divinity student at
Princeton. Influenced by the liberal atmosphere of New England, his
father, Allan Melvill, eventually became a member of the Unitarian
Church, but on marrying Maria Gansevoort he decided to return to
the Calvinist arena and joined Maria's Dutch Reformed Church. It was
from his mother, Andrew Delbanco suggests, "that Herman received
the rudiments of a religious education"; it was she who "brought biblical stories, exempla, and precedents into the lives of all her children,
and for her second son characters from the Bible always remained as
vividly alive as the worthies and villains of his own time."[24] As a child,
Herman Melville went to the "God fearing" Albany Academy, where
Historia Sacra formed part of the curriculum. Later, on his return
from sea, he married Elizabeth Shaw whose upbringing was Unitarian.
He ended up becoming an official member of the All Souls Unitarian
Church of New York in 1884. Melville was never much of a church-
goer—of neither the Dutch Reformed nor the Unitarian Church—but
the great insoluble questions posed by religion, among them "the Calvinistic sense of Innate Depravity and Original Sin, from whose visita-
tions, in some shape or other, no deeply thinking mind is always and
wholly free," never ceased to fire his imagination.[25]

"It is strange," writes Hawthorne of Melville, "how he persists—
and has persisted ever since I knew him, and probably long before—in
wandering to-and-fro over these deserts, as dismal and monotonous as
the sand hills amid which we were sitting. He can neither believe, nor
be comfortable in his unbelief; and he is too honest and courageous
not to try to do one or the other. If he were a religious man, he would
be one of the most truly religious and reverential; he has a very high
and noble nature, and better worth immortality than most of us."[26]
Hawthorne's renowned remark is indispensable to the understanding of Melville's religious imagination. It calls for a consideration of
Melville as a blasphemous believer, as a "pilgrim-infidel" who never
ceases to wander between the two poles.[27] Following Hawthorne,
Jenny Franchot has succinctly suggested that "rather than pondering
whether Melville ultimately found answers to his religious questions
or chose route 'a' or 'b' in response to his spiritual predicament, it is
more fruitful to consider how his narratives and poetry construct this
duality, coupling belief and unbelief, force and exhaustion, the deity's
simultaneous oppression and abandonment of humanity."[28] One of the

most intriguing ways to begin to fathom this duality, it seems to me, is to follow his biblical exegesis. It is not accidental that Hawthorne's metaphor for Melville's spiritual restlessness leads us to the biblical scenes of wandering in the wilderness.

And a few remarks about Melville's actual bibles and use of biblical lexicon. Melville's family owned various bibles. The most important of these, the one of primary use for Melville, was the bible he bought in the initial stages of working on *Moby-Dick,* in which he inscribed "March 23rd 1850 New York."[29] Published by E.H. Butler & Co. (Philadelphia, 1846), it is a large nineteenth-century family bible, with gold embellishments on its red-brown leather cover and an embossed image of the Tablets on its front (fig. 1). It contains the Old and New Testaments together with Apocrypha and a section of family records, where familial births and deaths were written, mostly by Melville himself. One of the intriguing features of this bible is its erased marginalia. Approximately forty-three passages were erased and at points the margins themselves cut off, presumably because of their skeptical theology or impropriety. Scholars differ in their assessment of the likely censors, the general tendency being to regard one of Melville's family members as responsible for the deed.[30] The bulk of scholarly attention, however, has been devoted to the numerous markings in this bible. There are, as Nathalia Wright points out, a few conspicuous discrepancies.[31] Some of the texts that are central to his work bear no markings, whereas others to which he does not allude are profusely marked. But all in all, they bear witness to Melville's immersion in Bible reading and underscore some of his notable preferences.

Melville's bibles, like most of the English bibles in antebellum America, were editions of the King James Version.[32] His elaborate allusions to the King James Version, one should bear in mind, are accompanied by numerous minute echoes of the particular idioms and textures of this canonical translation: "whoso," "forasmuch as," "verily," "thee," and "thou" are but a few of his favorite adverbs and pronouns. In a self-reflexive moment, Ishmael describes the Quakers of Nantucket as "naturally imbibing" from childhood "the stately dramatic thee and thou of the Quaker idiom" (73). At another revealing point, he quotes Bildad's words to Queequeg on hiring him—"Son of darkness . . . if thou still clingest to thy Pagan ways, which I sadly fear, I beseech thee, remain not for aye a Belial bondsman"—and remarks that the ship owner's language was "heterogeneously mixed with Scriptural and domestic phrases" (89).

FIGURE 1. Melville's bible, from the collection of Clifford Ross. Photograph by William Schick. Courtesy of Clifford Ross.

But Melville was not only interested in the resonant language of the King James Version. He was as attuned to the unlexicalized biblical expressions invented in the course of everyday life on whalers. "Bible leaves! Bible leaves!" as Melville explains in "The Cassock," "is the invariable cry from the mates to the mincer. It enjoins him to be careful, and cut his work into as thin slices as possible, inasmuch as by so doing the business of boiling out the oil is much accelerated, and its quantity considerably increased, besides perhaps improving it in quality" (420). Melville's evocation of such whaler lingo offers a mock imitation of the solemn use of biblical terms and leaves within the realm of institutional religion. Here the expression "Bible leaves" depicts the fine ritualistic cutting of blubber by a mincer (Ishmael's "candidate for an archbishoprick") whose cassock is made out of the foreskin of a whale.

Laurie Anderson reminds us that Melville's actual bibles are not merely of limited scholarly concern. In the accompanying notes to her multimedia show *Songs and Stories from Moby-Dick,* in a section titled "Melville's Bible," she recounts the following anecdote:

> When I told a friend I was working on a project based on *Moby-Dick* he just about went crazy. He said, "Moby Dick?! Moby Dick?" He said

he had something for me and a few days later he brought over a big box. Inside was Melville's Bible, which Melville bought just before he began writing *Moby-Dick*. It was filled with pencil notes and markings, many of which his wife had apparently erased (their relationship being far from idyllic). My friend, who had gotten the Bible at Sotheby's, had checked through the Morgan Library and their contacts with the FBI, to see if it would be possible to reconstruct the passages that had been erased. The consensus was that this would have been possible if the marks had been erased thirty years ago, but not a hundred and fifty. So I went combing through the Bible with a magnifying glass, looking for little marks, signs, anything that might have something to do with a whale. And then I found it. Isaiah 27:1. "In that day the Lord with his sore and great and strong sword shall punish leviathan the piercing serpent, even leviathan that crooked serpent; and he shall slay the dragon that is in the sea." Next to this verse was a check mark and a long squiggle. And I thought. That's it! The whale is his snake and the ocean is his garden, the place where he works out good and evil.[33]

This incident could not have happened if *Moby-Dick* were not a cultural icon. I refer not only to Laurie Anderson's choice to compose an artistic homage to *Moby-Dick* but also to the very fact that one could consider approaching the FBI with a request to decipher the erased notes in Melville's bible—as if knowing what was written on the margins of this bible were a national affair of top security. But her anecdote is illuminating in two other ways. It highlights the status of Melville himself as a grand mystery that remains undecipherable. It is also a reminder of the immense exegetical passion *Moby-Dick* generates among readers.

I end my introduction with Maurice Blanchot's "The Song of the Sirens." Melville's compulsion to approach the seductive, deadly "voice of the void," writes Blanchot, is even greater than that of Homer, who leaves Odysseus tied to the ship as he listens to the human, inhuman Song of the Sirens. Melville, like his Ahab, is willing to go so far as to approach the imposing reaches where the portentous Moby Dick roams about and probe, as if unbound, the very limits of the mind, of life, and of space. For Blanchot, the momentous clash between Ahab and Moby Dick, on the verge of the abyss, turns out to be a crucial moment of inspiration, a literary event—not only within the book but also, paradoxically, prior to the writing of the book:

> Of course it is true that only in Melville's book does Ahab meet Moby Dick; yet it is also true that only this encounter allows Melville to write the book, it is such an imposing encounter, so enormous, so special that it goes beyond all the levels on which it takes place, all the moments in

time where we attempt to situate it, and seems to be happening long
before the book begins, but it is of such a nature that it also could not
happen more than once, in the future of the work and in that sea which
is what the work will be, having become an ocean in its own scale.[34]

"The Song of the Sirens" sets out to carve out the unique space
of writing, but in many ways it maps out the unique space of exegesis, all the more so in Melville's work, where the two are inextricably
connected. Retelling scriptural texts or reflecting on other readings of
Scripture, for Melville, is not a detached leisurely activity anchored
within the known boundaries of "slavish shores." It means to embark
on a voyage into an alluring, ungraspable text, where the possibility
of losing one's mind or life lurks between the lines. But it is Ishmael, I
believe, rather than Ahab, who is more relevant to the understanding
of this exegetical writing scene. Though Ishmael comes close to the
abyss with Ahab, he does not sink into the darkness that draws him.
In "The Try-Works" Ishmael depicts a dramatic night scene where the
try-works, with their red fire, make the Pequod look like a savage,
demonic ship on its way to "that blackness of darkness," as if she were
"the material counterpart of her monomaniac commander's soul." Ishmael stands at the helm, silently guiding "the way of this fire-ship on
the sea," when all of a sudden he lapses into a world of alluring dreams
and hallucinations, managing only at the very last moment to "prevent
the vessel from flying up into the wind, and very probably capsizing
her" (424). "Look not too long in the face of the fire," exclaims Ishmael. "Never dream with thy hand on the helm! . . . To-morrow, in
the natural sun, the skies will be bright; those who glared like devils in
the forking flames, the morn will show in far other, at least gentler, relief; the glorious, golden, glad sun, the only true lamp—all others but
liars!" (424). The sun's light, however, does not lead Ishmael to a safe
haven. For it is this "true lamp" of the universe that sheds light on the
darker side of the earth and the darker experiences of humanity and
leads him, via his associative ruminations, to "the truest of all books,"
to Solomon's Ecclesiastes, "the fine hammered steel of woe." Much
like Solomon of Ecclesiastes, Ishmael is ready to plunge into every site
of darkness and woe and to lay bare the vanity of it all, but he also sees
the value of Solomon's statement in Proverbs 21:16, according to which
"the man that wandereth out of the way of understanding shall remain
(i.e. even while living) in the congregation of the dead" (424–25).[35]
"Give not thyself up, then, to fire, lest it invert thee, deaden thee; as for
the time it did me. There is wisdom that is woe; but there is a woe that

is madness" (425). Ishmael is both unbound and bound—there is, as it were, a Catskill eagle in his soul "that can alike dive down into the blackest gorges, and soar out of them again" (425)—and it is precisely this paradoxical position that turns him into the narrator-exegete who survives to retell the tale.

And Moby Dick? Let me venture to heap yet another potential interpretation on the creature and suggest that he is, among many other things, a grand embodiment of the Bible. I would go on to suggest that the momentous encounter with Moby Dick at the end of the voyage can be construed not only as a parable for the moment of literary inspiration, where the boundaries between the imaginary and the real become blurred and Melville emerges as the writer of *Moby-Dick,* but also as a dramatization of an immense exegetical encounter. Bringing Melville and the Bible together into one space generates "the most terrible, and most beautiful of all possible worlds: a book, alas, only a book," but one that ventures to be a Bible in its own scale, or a Commentary of Commentaries, however pointless all commentaries may be.[36]

CHAPTER I

Playing with Leviathan

*Job and the Aesthetic Turn
in Biblical Exegesis*

But if, in the face of all this, you still declare that whaling
has no aesthetically noble associations connected with it,
then am I ready to shiver fifty lances with you there, and un-
horse you with a split helmet every time. The whale has no
famous author, and whaling no famous chronicler, you will
say. *The whale no famous author, and whaling no famous
chronicler?* Who wrote the first account of our Leviathan?
Who but mighty Job!

"The Advocate" (111)

In regarding Job as an admirable founding author whose representation
of Leviathan proves beyond doubt the "aesthetically noble" heritage of
whales, Ishmael not only extols whaling with the passion of a hot-tempered,
stubborn advocate but also endorses the new, ever-growing perception
of the Bible as a whole and the Book of Job in particular as the grand
aesthetic touchstone for all times. Ishmael, indeed, strives throughout the
text to model his obsessive whale meditations on Job's Leviathan. But as
the above passage from "The Advocate" indicates, persuading readers
that the chronicle of whales should be treated with the same kind of
aesthetic veneration one would feel for the book of "mighty Job" is not
a simple task. Rhetoric, as Ishmael playfully suggests, may need to be
supplemented (as it all too often is) by the threat of physical might.

Of the various biblical texts Melville evokes in *Moby-Dick,* Job is
the one text that received considerable attention in the heyday of New
Criticism. Lawrence Thompson chooses to open his classic reading
of *Moby-Dick* in *Melville's Quarrel with God* with Job. In his quest
to liberate himself from the tyrannies of Calvinism and God, writes

Thompson, Melville "turned to the Bible for inspiration, particularly to the book of Job. Without any difficulty he could identify himself with the suffering Job, and could join Job in blaming God for the sorrows, woes, and evils which distressed and perplexed him."[1] Though, he hastens to add, Melville could not take part "in the final tableau of abject submission and acceptance of God's inscrutable ways."[2] Other critics—C. Hugh Holman and Janis Stout—attempted to determine whether the defiant Ahab or the reflective Ishmael who ruminates about the wonders of Leviathan should be regarded as the primary Joban character in the text.[3] What remains beyond the scope of these New Critical studies is the aesthetic-exegetical shift that looms behind Melville's evocation of "mighty Job."

If the New Critics ignored Melville's part in advancing the literary Bible, the Americanists, who did consider his exegetical milieu, ignored Job. Speaking of "literary scripturism" as the hallmark of New England's culture, Lawrence Buell regards Melville, along with Emerson, Dickinson, Stowe, Whitman, and Thoreau, as a primary advocate of the new redefinition of boundaries between sacred writing and belles lettres in antebellum America.[4] And yet his influential discussion of the ways in which antebellum writers construe Scripture as "a form of poesis" and see themselves as the ultimate interpreters of such an inspired vision remains panoramic. Job is not mentioned at all.

To begin to fathom Melville's grand homage to Job in *Moby-Dick*, I want to argue, requires a consideration of Melville's response to the aesthetic turn in biblical exegesis. More specifically, I read Melville's Job in relation to a whole genealogy of continental scholars and writers who regarded the Book of Job as an exemplary code of art within the great work of art. Melville is as committed as his New England contemporaries to fashioning a new, quintessentially American, literary Bible that would rekindle the poetic power of the ancient text in unknown ways. But his commitment to such "literary independence" does not preclude the passion with which he aligns himself with continental genealogies.[5] Melville oscillates between European and American traditions, deeply committed to both, shunning any mode of parochialism.[6] Melville's Job, accordingly, is a work of translation that hovers between the two continents as it introduces the European preoccupation with Job's aesthetic heritage—above all, with Joban perceptions of sublimity—into American landscapes and inscapes.

But my goal is not merely to show that Melville's commentary and metacommentary are embedded in each other. I spell out Melville's

unparalleled exegetical imagination as it is revealed in the details of
his aesthetic-hermeneutic project. I explore Melville's all-encompassing response to the textures, rhetoric, cries, and metaphors of the Book
of Job alongside his obsessive juggling of previous literary readings of
Job. To understand why the encounter with Melville's Job changes our
perception of the biblical Job as it changes our perception of the aesthetic, requires, I believe, plunging precisely into such details.

THE LITERARY JOB AND THE SUBLIME

The Bible, Jonathan Sheehan reminds us, was not always venerated as
a founding text of Western literature.[7] The literary Bible emerges in the
eighteenth century both in England and in Germany as the invention
of scholars and literati who tried to rejuvenate the Bible by transform-
ing it from a book justified by theology into one justified by culture.
The aim of this posttheological project was not quite to secularize the
Bible—though it was now construed as the product of human imagination—but rather to reconstitute its authority in aesthetic terms. The
Book of Job had a vital role in enhancing this transformation. Sheehan
goes so far as to trace what he calls a "Job revival" in the context of the
English and German Enlightenment, a revival that included numerous
new translations and scholarly studies of the text. Among the leading
scholars of this trend was Robert Lowth, a prominent forerunner of the
literary approach to the Bible, whose book on biblical poetry, *De Poesi
Sacrae Hebraeorum* (1753)—known primarily for its groundbreaking
study of biblical parallelism—includes a substantive comparison of the
poetic form of Job with that of Greek tragedy.[8] Indeed, the Book of
Job acquired so prominent a position as an aesthetic touchstone that
it was evoked in Edmund Burke's *Philosophical Enquiry into the Sublime and the Beautiful* (1757) as an exemplary text for the exploration
of the sublime experience in its relation to power and terror.[9]

   But the aesthetic revival of Job continues beyond the age of Enlightenment. It becomes even more prominent in Romantic thought and
literature, though its poetic grandeur is now colored by Romantic aesthetic ideals. J. G. Herder, another important forerunner of the literary
approach to the Bible, devotes an entire section of his renowned *Spirit
of Hebrew Poetry* (1782–83, translated into English by 1833) to Job.
Setting his work against the dry technical study of Lowth, he transfers
Job into the realms of the heart, vision, and vivid Oriental imagination.[10] God's whirlwind poem is the poetic epitome of Job, for like the

Oriental descriptions of nature "it awakens a love, an interest, and a sympathy for all that lives":

> What wretch, in the greatest tumult of his passions, in walking under a starry heaven, would not experience imperceptibly and even against his will a soothing influence from the elevating contemplation of its silent, unchangeable, and everlasting splendors. Suppose at such a moment there occurs to his thoughts the simple language of God, "Canst thou bind together the bands of the Pleiades," etc.—is it not as if God Himself addressed the words to him from the starry firmament? Such an effect has the true poetry of nature, the fair interpreter of the nature of God. A hint, a single word, in the spirit of such poetry often suggests to the mind extended scenes; nor does it merely bring their quiet pictures before the eye in their outward lineaments, but brings them home to the sympathies of the heart.[11]

For Herder, God's rhetorical questions, the aesthetic hallmark of the divine response from the whirlwind—"Canst thou bind together the bands of the Pleiades?" (Job 38:31)—hold the power of an irresistible address that no one can ignore. He marvels at the sublimity of God's depiction of nature, at the power of the "simple language of God," with its minute hints, to interpret the starry firmament so that it becomes tangible to the observing eye. The experience of this vision is even richer: the external natural sights do not remain animate only "in their outward lineaments," but rather seep inward, bringing heavenly scenes into the inmost spheres, to the "sympathies of the heart." "It is as *effect,* then, that theodicy is redeemed. Not through knowledge of, nor through insight into, the workings of God, but rather in the *power* that these workings exert over our imaginations."[12]

The impact of Herder's reading is evident in Thomas Carlyle's evocation of the Oriental sublimity of Job's visionary rendition of natural sights in his discussion of Islamic culture in *On Heroes, Hero-Worship, and the Heroic in History* (1840). Carlyle may not have been a prominent advocate of the literary Bible, but his brief comment on the Book of Job (he too focuses on the divine rhetorical questions) succinctly captures the Romantic adoration for the text as one of exceptional literary merit whose nature descriptions have an unparalleled impact on the eye and the heart. Job, he declares, is

> A noble Book ... our first oldest statement of the never-ending Problem,—man's Destiny, and God's ways with him here in this earth. And all with such free flowing outlines; grand in its sincerity, in its simplicity; in its epic melody, and repose of reconcilement. There is the seeing eye, the mildly understanding heart. So *true* everyway; true eyesight

and vision for all things; material things no less than spiritual: the Horse,—'hast thou clothed his neck with *thunder?*'—he 'laughs at the shaking of the spear!' Such living likenesses were never since drawn. Sublime sorrow, sublime reconciliation; oldest choral melody as of the heart of mankind;—so soft, and great; as the summer midnight, as the world with its seas and stars! There is nothing written I think, in the Bible or out of it, of equal literary merit.[13]

English and German Romantic literary and artistic exegesis followed suit. Blake and Goethe carved out their respective Jobs—Blake in his *Illustrations of the Book of Job* (1825) and Goethe in *Faust* (1832)—but in contradistinction to the scholarly studies of Lowth, Burke, and Herder, they defined the book's sublimity as inseparable from its predominant antitheodician character. To modern readers, Job's acute protest against the arbitrariness of divine conduct is the thrust of the book, but until the Romantic period the prevailing interpretive tendency was to read the Book of Job as theodicy and to prefer the patient pious Job of the folkloric Prologue to the rebellious Job of the poetic Dialogues.[14] Romantic writers and artists were, in fact, the first to put forth the radical possibility of reading both God and Job as imperfect.[15] Instead of seeing the book as a confirmation of normative faith, they treated it as an inspiring point of departure for a critique of institutional modes of religion.

In Blake's *Illustrations* the patient Job of the Prologue lives in a mode of error under the auspices of institutional churches. His erroneous mode of being is poignantly conveyed by the first illustration, in which musical instruments hang, unused, on the tree under which Job sits, all too drowsy, with his family. It takes a crisis to free him from clinging to the false God of conventional faith and find the way to the true God of imagination, the mirror image of his poetic self. In shaping the contours of the spiritual transformation Job undergoes, Blake relies on Burke, but his notion of "fearful symmetry" modifies the latter's definition of sublime experience by combining horror with wonder, mystery, and the infinite power of imagination.[16]

Goethe, who was the first to superimpose a Joban dimension upon the drama of Faust, offers yet another version of an imperfect Job and an imperfect God.[17] Faust is not a righteous Job who knows no evil. He roams about with Mephistopheles, taking advantage of the latter's devilish powers. Similarly, the Lord's ways are rather dubious. The wager between God and the Adversary in the Prologue is turned into a parody of divine vigilance in *Faust*. Indifferent to the potential

suffering that may be inflicted upon Faust, the Lord readily ε
Mephistopheles (a court jester of sorts) to lure the doctor witho
stricting his moves.

In contradistinction to the central position of Job in European κo-
manticism, it had but little resonance in the American Romantic milieu. Job did not lend itself to the optimism of leading literary figures
such as Emerson or Whitman. But even Hawthorne and Dickinson—
whose biblical poetics were of a darker hue—offered only dim echoes
of Job rather than elaborate interpretations of the text. Melville filled
this lacuna in American literary biblicism with a splash. While joining
the above distinguished genealogy of continental advocates of Job he
carved out a Job no European could have imagined.

If Melville were asked to single out the most sublime moment in
Job he undoubtedly would have pointed to the whirlwind poem, as
do Herder and Carlyle. Neither the starry sky nor the wild horse,
however, would have led him to do so. The ultimate source of inspiration for Melville is located in the climactic closing lines of the poem,
where Leviathan is presented as the inscrutable, ungraspable epitome
of creation:

> Canst thou draw out leviathan with an hook?
> Or his tongue with a cord which thou lettest down?
> Canst thou put an hook into his nose?
> Or bore his jaw through with a thorn?
> Will he make many supplications unto thee?
> Will he speak soft words unto thee?
> Will he make a covenant with thee?
> Wilt thou take him for a servant for ever?
> Wilt thou play with him as with a bird? . . .
> Canst thou fill his skin with barbed irons?
> Or his head with fish spears? . . .
> Behold, the hope of him is in vain. . . .
> Who can open the doors of his face?
> His teeth are terrible round about.
> His scales are his pride, shut up together as with a close seal. . . .
> By his neesings a light doth shine,
> And his eyes are like the eyelids of the morning.
> Out of his mouth go burning lamps,
> And sparks of fire leap out.
> Out of his nostrils goeth smoke,
> As out of a seething pot or caldron. . . .
> He maketh the deep to boil like a pot:
> He maketh the sea like a pot of ointment.
> He maketh a path to shine after him;

One would think the deep to be hoary,
Upon earth there is not his like,
Who is made without fear.
He beholdeth all high things:
He is a king over all the children of pride

                    (Job 41:1–34)

Nothing is more exhilaratingly sublime within the framework of Melvillean aesthetics than exploring the seething path of the wondrous monster who can make the deep boil. Nor is it accidental that this path is evoked already in the opening "Extracts." But Melville's distinct exegetical brilliance does not lie in foregrounding Leviathan's sublimity (a distinct poetic feat in itself) but in the unexpected projection of this poem onto the world of American whaling. Leviathan in *Moby-Dick* is at once an imaginary demonic-divine phantom—"the overwhelming idea of the great whale"—and a concrete marine mammal, caught, dissected, and sold as a commodity in one of America's largest industries. With unique Romantic irony and humor (rather dark at times), Melville situates Joban sublimity between the metaphysical and the physical in ways that offer a decisive departure from his continental precursors. If the Bible can count as "aesthetically noble" (to return to "The Advocate"), so can the supposedly "unpoetic" business of whaling, with its infamous butchering. The refreshing redefinition of the boundaries between sacred writing and belles lettres that the aesthetic turn in biblical exegesis brought about should, Melville proposes, lead to an even more radical opening of concepts such as aesthetic and sublime.

I see this aesthetic sacrilegious position as indebted to Job's insistence on taking no acceptable belief for granted. Job, for Melville, is a work whose power lies in its unparalleled capacity to probe the limits of the imagination, of faith, justice, power, sanity, nature, and life itself. No Romantic was as eager as Melville to try out Joban impatience in every imaginable realm.

The blasphemous bent of this quest, however, does not preclude a desperate craving for the divine. In Job, more than in any other biblical character, Melville finds an admirable model for his own tantalizingly paradoxical position as a blasphemous believer. Thompson's focus on the defiant skeptical aspects of *Moby-Dick* does not do justice to what Jenny Franchot has defined as the "recurrent movement between belief and unbelief" in Melville's restless spiritual world.[18]

Hermeneutic projects become vast in Melville's hands. His attempt to redefine the aesthetic heritage of Job is no exception. There are many Jobs aboard the *Pequod* (there is no need to limit the scope to Ahab and Ishmael). They seem, indeed, to proliferate at the rate of the different leviathans that crop up in the text. The splitting of Job among the various crew members allows Melville to explore the different genres that intersect in Job—theophany (the whirlwind poem), dialogues, tragedy, folkloric tales, and sermons. Indeed, the multiplicity of genres in Job (and by extension, in the Bible as a whole) never ceases to compel Melville as a liberating aesthetic possibility.[19]

I devote the bulk of the following discussion to Ishmael, whose ongoing meditations on Leviathan as a "whale author" underscore the aesthetic questions at stake. But I also take into account the ways in which Ahab captures the tragic antitheodician line in Job, Stubb and Flask act out a parody of the folkloric Prologue, and Fleece—with his sermon to the sharks—highlights Job's scathing depiction of the thriving of the wicked.

ISHMAEL'S RESPONSE TO GOD'S RHETORICAL QUESTIONS

That Ishmael is a Job underscores the predominant Romantic identification of Job as an Oriental, evident in the readings of Herder and Carlyle.[20] In the age of Romanticism the Bible as a whole was considered the product of Oriental imagination, but the Book of Job was regarded as exemplary of this given that Job allegedly lived in the land of Uz, which according to biblical geography was located in the arid land of Idumea. Travelers to the Holy Land in the nineteenth century often found traces of Joban verses in this zone. On seeing a sheik on an admirable horse in the desert of Idumea, John Lloyd Stephens comments, "I could almost imagine I saw the ancient warhorse of Idumea, so finely described by Job—'His neck clothed with thunder. Canst thou make him afraid as a grasshopper?'"[21]

But what kind of guidance does Ishmael provide to those who seek to fathom Joban aesthetics? Does he too perceive God's whirlwind poem as animating the heart and the eye, evoking what Herder calls "sympathy"? Leviathan, the "portentous and mysterious" monster who rolls his "island bulk," never remains solely in his outward lineaments. As Ishmael embarks on his voyage, opening the "flood-gates" of the "wonder-world," "endless processions of whales" float two by

two into his "inmost soul . . . and, midmost of them all, one grand
hooded phantom, like a snow hill in the air" (7). The movement of
sublime Joban sights inward, toward the heart or the inmost soul, is
dramatized as an actual event, happening in real time and space.

To follow Leviathan in distant or internal seas is not something
everyone would venture to do. The "undeliverable, nameless perils of
the whale" are likely to appall most travelers. But for Ishmael, who
is willing to "be social" with horror, the inscrutable monster is the
chief reason for going to sea. Like Blake, Ishmael combines horror,
wonder, and imagination in his definition of Joban sublimity, though
he adds a peculiar touch of solemn humor to the picture. Horror does
not prevent him from "being on friendly terms," he claims, even with
such "inmates" (7).

Most of Ishmael's reflections on Leviathan revolve around the divine rhetorical questions that open the depiction of the creature in Job
41. He first evokes these questions in "Cetology" on setting out to map
the anatomies of whales:

> To grope down into the bottom of the sea after them; to have one's
> hands among the unspeakable foundations, ribs, and very pelvis of the
> world; this is a fearful thing. What am I that I should essay to hook the
> nose of this leviathan! The awful tauntings in Job might well appal me.
> "Will he (the leviathan) make a covenant with thee? Behold the hope
> of him is vain!" But I have swam through libraries and sailed through
> oceans; I have had to do with whales with these visible hands; I am in
> earnest; and I will try. (136)

God's rhetorical questions are "awful tauntings" rather than an address. Or if they are a heavenly address their impact is not a soothing
one. In their poignant ridicule of human abilities they are as violent
as the rhetoric that is mocked in "The Advocate." But Ishmael does
not hesitate to pick up the gauntlet. To God's "Canst thou draw out
leviathan with an hook? . . . Canst thou put an hook into his nose?"
Ishmael seems to respond: Watch me! Instead of being paralyzed by
God's bullying, he regards the divine questions as if they were literal
and sets out to capture Leviathan with his pen and "visible hands."
As a whaler-author, he holds all the gifts that are necessary for this
hunt. He can swim through oceans and libraries, between the concrete
bodies of whales and an unending sea of texts, in a defiant quest of the
fearful creature.

If Job becomes reticent on hearing God's Voice from the whirlwind,
Ishmael continues the momentous, mythical quarrel of the biblical rebel

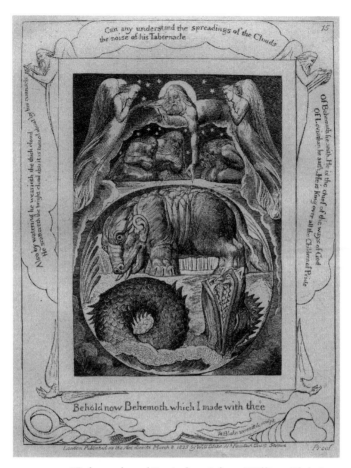

FIGURE 2. "Behemoth and Leviathan," from William Blake's
Illustrations of the Book of Job. Print 1868–8-22–3962,
© The British Museum.

with God where it ended. Questioning the divine questions, he refuses
to accept the Voice as the final note.[22] Reading against the grain, with
remarkable attention to the underlying seduction at stake, he construes
the whirlwind poem as an alluring invitation to engage in a daring
imitatio dei. God may underscore the evasiveness of Leviathan, but
while doing so, he provides (wittingly or unwittingly) a detailed representation of the creature. For Ishmael, this unexpected partial unveil-
ing of divine secrets, this teasing gift of vision, is an intimate call to
explore further the sublimity of Leviathan, using the divine account
as a point of departure.[23] With the obsessive fervor of a lover, Ishmael

depicts each and every body part of Leviathan In "Cetology" he does
so by means of a parody of scientific discourse, but *Moby-Dick* as
a whole offers unending poetic commentaries on every aspect of the
creature's anatomy.[24] Sure enough, the features God chose to render do
not suffice. Ishmael probes the limits of human imagination in peeking
at what was declared beyond human sight altogether. "Who can open
the door of his face?" God asks. But given that Ishmael is a whaler, he
spends many hours precisely behind such doors, eagerly exploring the
forbidden sights that lie in the heads and bellies of whales.

To God's "Wilt thou play with him as with a bird?" Ishmael would
reply that the creature is by no means God's pet alone.[25] Playing with
Leviathan is the ever-alluring, risky, sublime game one needs to pursue
in order to write.

Like other Romantic poets, Melville/Ishmael assumes a heavenly
posture in regarding his art as approaching the divine. But there is
a good deal of irony in his approach. Whereas Blake's Job ultimately
merges with the image of the true sublime god of imagination and
Blake's tiger (another Leviathan of sorts) remains in the invincible
hands of the poet, Ishmael is well aware of the limits of his poetic
game. The great Leviathan, he claims in "Of the Monstrous Pictures
of Whales," "is that one creature in the world which must remain un-
painted to the last. True, one portrait may hit the mark much nearer
than another, but none can hit it with any very considerable degree of
exactness" (264). Melville's aesthetic-hermeneutic position is ultimately
a paradoxical one: he both challenges the divine rhetorical questions
and admits the validity of the divine portrait of Leviathan as ungraspable. He is both an omnipotent "whale author" and a perplexed author
for whom Leviathan is synonymous with the fracturing of authorship;
it is, in Eyal Peretz's terms, "that which is associated in the novel with
the crisis of authority; it is that which interrupts, which calls into question, any stabilizing attempt of authoritative mastery."[26]

Ishmael's double reading of God's rhetorical questions becomes
more apparent in his depiction of the literal task of catching whales.
Observing the suspended body of a huge sperm whale in "The Pequod
Meets the Virgin," he asks:

> Suspended? and to what? To three bits of board. Is this the creature
> of whom it was once so triumphantly said—"Canst thou fill his skin
> with barbed irons? or his head with fish-spears?. . . . the arrow cannot
> make him flee; darts are counted as stubble; he laugheth at the shaking
> of a spear!" This the creature? this he? Oh! that unfulfilments should

follow the prophets. For with the strength of a thousand thighs in his tail, Leviathan had run his head under the mountains of the sea, to hide him from the Pequod's fish-spears! (356)

The renowned creature is suspended by three mundane bits of board to the *Pequod,* making the divine rendition of its invincibility seem ridiculous. Ishmael adds his own rhetorical questions—"Suspended?" "This he?"—to mock the "unfulfilments" of divine discourse. Despite Leviathan's legendary bodily strength, the monstrous creature cannot but hide from the *Pequod*'s spears. But then the victory over Leviathan is short-lived. Sinking with its gigantic weight, the dead whale ultimately forces the crew to slash the fluke-chains and release the ties to avoid sinking with it to the bottom of the sea. "'Hold on, hold on, won't ye?' cried Stubb to the body, 'don't be in such a devil of a hurry to sink!'" (359). His cry was of no avail.

The most elusive of all whales, the closest to the divine Leviathan, is Moby Dick. "Though groves of spears should be planted in his flanks, he would still swim away unharmed." Ubiquitous in space and in time, Moby Dick can appear at all sites, defying all spears, springing unexpectedly back to life. No one can stop the creature from "gliding at high noon through a dark blue sea, leaving a milky-way wake of creamy foam, all spangled with golden gleamings" (183). The memorable path Job's Leviathan leaves behind becomes a take-off lane leading to a remarkable alliterative blend of sounds and sights, textures and tastes: "milky-way wake," "gliding . . . golden gleamings." Ishmael imagines Leviathan as carrying the vast expanses of the sea in his wake up to the sky, or rather as transferring the galaxy of the Milky Way to the dark blue sea with a sweep that turns the deep into a gleaming heaven. No one, it seems, can stop Ishmael from pursuing the creature's grand dreamy creamy wake. "Hoary" and shiny, it lures him to dare approach the exuberant monsters of the deep time and again, however impossible such a game may be.

VISIONS OF THE NIGHT

While he explores Leviathan's natural sublimity, Ishmael is no less concerned with its position as commodity. In a mock-Romantic gesture, he offers meticulous accounts not only of the ways in which the wondrous epitome of Creation is caught but also of the methods by which it is thoroughly dissected and processed on whaling ships. If Carlyle

marvels at the equal attention given to the spiritual and material aspects of nature in the whirlwind poem, Melville ventures to extend the
material pole so that it includes industrial materiality.

The juxtaposition of Leviathan's transcendence and industrial use is
especially amusing in "The Squeeze of the Hand," in which the crew
engages in a prolonged squeezing of spermaceti. Every bodily element
of the whale is processed, even its spermaceti—related in appearance
and through a mistaken etymology to "sperm" (as Ishmael explains
in "Cetology"). Although others would consider this transformation
of spermaceti into a marketable cultural artifact as the very antithesis
of the sublime, Ishmael is unwilling to curb the contours of sublimity.
True vision may lie not only in the renowned natural features of Leviathan but also in its human consumption:

> Would that I could keep squeezing that sperm for ever! For now, since
> by many prolonged, repeated experiences, I have perceived that in all
> cases man must eventually lower, or at least shift, his conceit of attain-
> able felicity; not placing it anywhere in the intellect or the fancy; but
> in the wife, the heart, the bed, the table, the saddle, the fire-side, the
> country; now that I have perceived all this, I am ready to squeeze case
> eternally. In thoughts of the visions of the night, I saw long rows of an-
> gels in paradise, each with his hands in a jar of spermaceti. (416)

It is the earthly, even pragmatic aspects of objects—be they spermaceti, tables, beds, or countries—Ishmael asserts, that may (far more
than the intellect or the fancy) end up leading to heavenly sights and
insights. He goes so far as to envision paradise as a place where rows
of angels happily place their hands in jars of spermaceti, imitating the
nocturnal pleasures of mere whalers. The row of asterisks that follows
his description adds a visual correlate of angelic stars while hinting at
what remains inexplicable in the "inexpressible sperm." Commodities
no less than natural objects are cryptic texts that demand interpretation. What is more, the demarcation between the two is never clear-
cut. Something about the sensuous mystical immersion in spermaceti
in the course of commodity creation seems to bring the crew closer to
Leviathan's primary natural core.

The paradisiacal "visions of the night" lead us to the Dialogues.
"Visions of the night" is an expression used by Eliphaz, one of Job's
comforters, in his account of God's horrifying oneiric interventions: "In
thoughts from the visions of the night, when deep sleep falleth on men/
Fear came upon me, and trembling, which made all my bones to shake.
Then a spirit passed before my face; the hair of my flesh stood up/It

stood still, but I could not discern the form thereof" (Job 4:13–16). Edmund Burke quotes this passage as an exemplary sublime moment. "We are first prepared with the outmost solemnity for the vision," he writes, "we are . . . terrified, before we are let even into the obscure cause of our emotion; but when this grand cause of terror makes its appearance, what is it? Is it not, wrapt up in the shades of its own incomprehensible darkness, more awful, more striking, more terrible, than the liveliest description, than the clearest painting could possibly represent it?"[27]

Melville scoffs at Burke in inverting the nightmarish quality of the nocturnal visions into a pleasurable erotic fraternal squeezing of spermaceti on board a whaler. He certainly introduces modes of sublimity unaccounted for in Burke's *Enquiry into the Sublime and the Beautiful*.

But the primary target of Ishmael's critical reading is the normative religion of Job's friends. The quest for sublimity is inextricably connected with an exploration of the radical social critique of the Book of Job. Ishmael would have agreed with René Girard that Job's so-called friends are not merely erroneous in their mode of faith. Rather, they are violent persecutors who are infuriated by Job's refusal to admit his guilt. Their piety serves, more than anything else, as a way to sanctify their violence and to cover up their indifference to the suffering of innocents.[28]

Eliphaz's visions serve as a prelude to a speech about the ways of God. The terrifying divine spirit that passed before his face had a revelatory quality. It made him realize that no mortal can be more just than God and that even if humanity was "born unto trouble" (5:7), one must accept the human condition with equanimity. Job, in response, mocks Eliphaz's self-righteous speech, claiming that when God appoints him "wearisome nights" it is only to increase his torments. He likens his life (and that of humanity as a whole) to the agonizing life of a hireling or a slave who "desireth the shadow" (7:2–3) to rest from taxing work, but can find no rest. "When I say, My bed shall comfort me, my couch shall ease my complaint; Then thou scarest me with dreams, and terrifiest me through visions" (7:13–14). Only one who is blind, Job asserts, would yield to such a merciless deity and regard him as just.

Joining Job's audacious struggle against the oppressively conforming views of the friends, Ishmael ridicules Eliphaz's manipulative use of divine terror. Instead of fear and trembling, he puts forth a very different concept of divine vision that is based on a more fluid and playful crossing between the heavenly and earthly spheres. His angels do not scare mortals but rather, like them, place their hands in jars of spermaceti.

Behind the mirthful nocturnal visions of Ishmael, however, lies a darker Joban cry on behalf of human misery. The crew's squeezing of spermaceti at night attests to the dire working conditions aboard the "sweatshops of the Pacific," to use Charles Olson's definition for whalers, to the endless work demanded day and night from the hirelings of the whaling industry. Leviathan has an ominous dimension not only as untamed Nature but also as a commodity in an untamed American industry, the nineteenth-century precursor of the globalized industries of today.

It comes as no surprise that the owner of the *Pequod,* who under the guise of piety exploits his crew with no qualms, is named after another of Job's comforters, Bildad. Earning close to nothing, "his crew, upon arriving home, were mostly all carried ashore to the hospital, sore exhausted and worn out" (74). Normative religion, Melville seems to suggest, terrorizes innocent sufferers in the name of God. It may speak of divine visions but offers none.

"AND I ONLY AM ESCAPED ALONE TO TELL THEE"

Melville cannot accept the legendary Epilogue of the Book of Job, according to which Job's ending was more prosperous than his beginning (42:12). Such a happy ending would be false in its implicit affirmation that the righteous are ultimately rewarded—the mistaken agenda of Job's friends (though one should bear in mind that even in the Epilogue the comforters' approach is condemned: "And my servant Job shall pray for you: for him will I accept: lest I deal with you after your folly, in that ye have not spoken of me the thing which is right, like my servant Job"; 42:8). Inventing another conclusion to the tale, closer to the disturbing truths that Job of the Dialogues ventures to unveil, Melville has all the *Pequod* Jobs drown, with one exception: Ishmael.

The happiest ending Melville could fashion for Ishmael is that of assuming the role of Job's messenger, escaping from the site of catastrophe to tell the tale. The verse which serves as epigraph to Ishmael's "Epilogue"—"And I only am escaped alone to tell thee"—appears four times in Job 1 as the somber concluding remark of each one of the four harbingers of evil tidings. In Job the messengers' verse is part of the Prologue, the opening note of the catastrophe. In *Moby-Dick* it is at once an ending and a beginning. This is where the "drama ends," but it is also a poetic point of departure, the point at which Ishmael assumes the position of narrator.

Job's messenger—a marginal figure most readers of the text over-look—thus becomes in *Moby-Dick* a pivotal poetic model inseparable from that of Job. The messengers in Job are brief: they come in rapid succession, one after another, announcing the various disasters in few words, bearing witness to the sudden overwhelming collapse of Job's world—from the demolition of his flocks to the death of his children, struck during a feast by a mighty wind. In Ishmael's tale testifying cannot be brief. To begin to respond to anything as unassimilable and ineffable as a disaster demands a certain excess. The final fall of the *Pequod* opens up in retrospect a whole chain of earlier disasters that need to be recorded: from the "hypos" that drives Ishmael to go to sea and seek Leviathan to Ahab's wound, the one inflicted upon him by Moby Dick, and the daily agonies of the hirelings of the whaling industry. In turning Ishmael into a witness, Melville underscores the change Job undergoes in the course of the Dialogues. If at first Job is wholly concerned with his own agony, he gradually realizes, as Gustavo Gutiérrez points out, that innocent suffering is all too pervasive.[29] His cry accordingly becomes more than a solitary cry over a particular pain: it strives to bear witness to the unjust wounds of many other innocent sufferers whose voices remain unheard.

Ishmael's aesthetics, then, rely on two inextricably connected notions of Joban sublimity: the first revolves around an experience of transcendence, entailing a momentous, exuberant game with the ungraspable Leviathan, the monstrous and wondrous epitome of creation whose shiny wake is unending; the second revolves around catastrophic events, around the fissures of pain and melancholy, in which the unspeakable becomes dark, maddening, and deadly.[30] The latter mode prevails in Ishmael's account of Ahab's wounds and cries.

TRAGIC AHAB: "CHASING WITH CURSES A JOB'S WHALE ROUND THE WORLD"

Robert Lowth compared the Book of Job with the tragedies of Sophocles, reaching the conclusion that despite certain similarities, the former did not rely on the kind of plot that would make it tragic. The definition of the Book of Job as tragedy was, however, common in nineteenth-century biblical criticism. Thus De Wette, whose *Einleitung* was translated into English by Theodore Parker in 1843, regarded the Book of Job as a "Hebrew tragedy," which unlike Greek tragedy represents "the tragic idea by words and thoughts, rather than by action."[31]

Neither Lowth nor De Wette linked the tragic in Job to the question of impatience. Only in twentieth-century criticism does one find a consideration of Job as an impious tragic figure, most notably in Richard B. Sewall's reading of Job in *The Vision of Tragedy,* a reading that, interestingly, relies on Melville's Ahab.[32]

Ahab is indeed Melville's tragic Job, the one whaler through whom he extensively explores the potential of the biblical rebel to serve as an exemplary tragic hero. While maintaining language as a primary medium for expressing Ahab's tragic vision, Melville adds a Greek touch to the scene by allowing the *Pequod*'s captain to spell out his hubris by means of action as well. Melville's tragic Job does not sit by an ash heap but rather rushes through oceanic space, fervently "chasing with curses a Job's whale round the world" (186). Unlike Starbuck, who regards the hunt for the "dumb brute" as a blasphemous "ill voyage," Ahab ventures to cross all boundaries and chase the monster, with Satanic maddened fervor, "round the world," "round perdition's flames," seeking vengeance upon his "dismemberer" to death.

"Am I a sea, or a whale?" (7:12) asks Job (Job too is a master of rhetorical questions), crying against God's ongoing persecution of him. Ahab's chase changes the tenor of the metaphor. God here is the one who is regarded as a mythological primordial sea monster, a titanic rival that needs to be pursued at all costs, at all times. With unabashed hubris, "the grand, ungodly, god-like" Ahab aspires to crush Moby Dick much as the Creator crushed the monstrous sea rebels in primeval times.[33] He craves to reverse the chase, to hunt his hunter rather than be chased by him. He is willing to go so low as to approach the flames of hell in his pursuit of Moby Dick, as he is willing to ascend to the heavenly sphere and "strike the sun" that insulted him.

But as Melville adds Greek qualities to his Joban tragedy, he also savors the ways in which the Bible can offer vital departures from Aristotelian principles, above all, the Aristotelian supposition that nobility is a necessary tragic trait. Job was neither a king nor a noble but simply a "man" who lived in the land of Uz. Through Job, Melville can thus change not only the definition of which topics count as "aesthetically noble" but also the definition of who counts as a suitable character for "noble tragedies." In accordance with the democratic spirit of his biblical typologies, Melville's Jobs are mean mariners and outcasts endowed with "tragic graces," bearing quintessential tragic attributes: a "ponderous heart," a "globular brain," and "nervous lofty language."

Ahab, however, towers above all the other *Pequod* mariners in his
tragic Joban grandeur. Job's wounds are spelled out large in the captain's body and soul. It is in his blasphemous and scarred language
that Job's cry breaks forth with unique force. Roaming, unbound, at
the limits of the mind and space, Ahab dramatizes those sections in
Job where darkness, pain, and sorrow reign, where cursing is the only
mode of speech conceivable, the only mode of speech with which one
can respond to an overwhelming inexplicable catastrophe. In cursing
while chasing Leviathan, he sets in motion one of the most exquisite
poems in the Book of Job, the opening note of the Dialogues, where
Job, no longer willing to bear his pain with equanimity, "opens his
mouth" and curses:[34]

> Let the day perish wherein I was born,
> And the night in which it was said,
> There is a man child conceived.
> Let that day be darkness;
> Let not God regard it from above,
> Neither let the light shine upon it;
> Let darkness and the shadow of death stain it;
> Let a cloud dwell upon it;
> Let the blackness of the day terrify it. . . .
> Lo, let that night be solitary,
> Let no joyful voice come therein.
> Let them curse it that curse the day. . . .
> Let the stars of the twilight thereof be dark;
> Let it look for light but have none;
> Neither let it see the dawning of the day:
> Because it shut not up the doors of my mother's womb,
> Nor hid sorrow from mine eyes.
> Why died I not from the womb?
> Why did I not give up the ghost when I came out of the belly? . . .
> For now should I have lain still and been quiet,
> I should have slept:
> Then had I been at rest,
> With kings and counsellors of the earth. . . .
> Why is light given to a man whose way is hid,
> And whom God hath hedged in?
> For my sighing cometh before I eat,
> And my roarings are poured out like the waters.

> (3:3–24)

Job does not actually curse God, as the Adversary had predicted
he would, but comes close to doing so in cursing the day of his birth,

the divinely ordained gift of life. He summons up darkness, blackness, and clouds to hide the light of that cursed day, even its first twilight stars, and wishes that his cursing be reinforced by expert cursers, who have the power to blot out days from the calendar.[35] His cursing is a powerful cry of anguish and rage. If only the womb were a tomb, if only no breasts had welcomed him into the world. Death, the ultimate rest, is preferable. He abhors the thought of living in a world in which sorrows, sighs, and catastrophes pile up ceaselessly, in a world whose Creator provides light and life only to "hedge in" mortals.

The punishment for cursing God, according to biblical law, is death.[36] Approaching such a speech act thus means coming close to the brink of the abyss. But it is precisely this desperate defiant move that is the prerequisite for Job's poetry. As long as Job insists on blessing God despite the calamities that befall him—"the Lord gave, and the Lord hath taken away; blessed be the name of the Lord" (1:21)— his agony and despair remain untold, but once he ventures to deliver a flow of curses, he can finally suspend belief and call divine justice into question in long, painful responses to the conforming position of his friends.

Strictly speaking, Job does not proceed in a rhetoric of cursing beyond chapter 3, but there is an ongoing blasphemous, or semiblasphemous, line in his poetic discourse that is a direct continuation of the opening curses. "God," he ventures to assert, "destroyeth the perfect and the wicked. If the scourge slay suddenly, he will laugh at the trial of the innocent. The earth is given into the hand of the wicked: he covereth the faces of the judges thereof; if not, where, and who is he?" (9:22–24).

The power and beauty of Job's initial outburst did not escape Blake. In his illustration of the opening curse of chapter 3, "Let the day perish wherein I was born," he renders a scene of spiritual awakening. Job no longer sits beneath the stone cross of institutional religion, as he did initially. He raises his arms toward a cloudy dark sky, with an agonized face and open mouth, allowing his wrath to break forth, making the first step in his search for a truer God. Only his friends remain by the conforming cross in a state of error.[37]

Goethe was equally attuned to the importance of Job's cursing. Faust curses every basic aspect of human existence, from love, family, and labor to the primary Christian virtues of faith, hope, and patience *(spes, fides, patientia),* in his initial dialogue with Mephistopheles: "Cursed be the balsam of the grape!/Cursed, highest prize of lovers' thrall!/A curse on faith! A curse on hope!/A curse on patience, above all!"[38] It is indeed the doctor's cursing that summons up devilry, paving the road to the following wager and setting the drama in motion.

The maddened Ahab, a Yankee Faust of sorts, in F. O. Matthiessen's words, magnifies Job's blasphemous wrath.[39] Never ceasing to curse, he rages restlessly, in a continual storm, as he wages war against the White Whale that inflicted unforgivable pain on him. In a famous monologue in "The Quarter-Deck" he pours out his grievances against his "accursed" opponent:

> Aye, aye! it was that accursed white whale that razeed me; made a poor pegging lubber of me for ever and a day!. . . . Aye, aye! and I'll chase him round Good Hope, and round the Horn . . . and round perdition's flames before I give him up. . . . All visible objects, man, are but as pasteboard masks. But in each event—in the living act, the undoubted deed—there, some unknown but still reasoning thing puts forth the mouldings of its features from behind the unreasoning mask. If man will strike, strike through the mask! How can the prisoner reach outside except by thrusting through the wall? To me, the white whale is that wall, shoved near to me. . . . He tasks me; he heaps me; I see in him outrageous strength, with an inscrutable malice sinewing it. (163–64)

Setting out to "strike through the mask," Ahab seeks to lay bare the arbitrary malevolence that lies behind the impenetrable overbearing wall of the deity—be it Moby Dick or God. Blasphemy does not scare him. Quite the contrary, it is closer to the bleak Truth ("Truth has no confines") and serves as a means to unmask divine injustice. It is an indispensable weapon in the struggle against the walls that make mortals prisoners. The theodocian problematic was succinctly formulated by Epicurus:

> God either wishes to take away evils, and is unable; or He is able and is unwilling; or He is neither willing nor able, or He is both willing and able. If he is willing and is unable, He is feeble, which is not in accordance with the character of God; if He is able and unwilling, He is envious, which is equally at variance with God; if He is neither willing nor able, He is both envious and feeble, and therefore not God; if He is both willing and able, which alone is suitable to God, from what source then are evils? or why does He not remove them?[40]

Ahab is determined to leave these questions bluntly open. More precisely, he sees God as the source of all evils but finds no justification for God's unwillingness to remove them. "Inscrutable malice" is at the very core of divine rule, which means that any attempt to deny divine evil or to see it as deserved or redemptive is nothing but a refusal to speak "the sane madness of vital truth."[41]

And yet there is something about Ahab's obsessive, blasphemous chase of the White Whale that seems to disclose, beneath the intense hate, the same kind of metaphysical passion evident in Job. Job aspires against all odds to approach God, to converse with him, to make him listen, to summon him to a trial, to appeal to his Persecutor against his Persecutor. He knows only too well that no one in his right mind would dare seek an impossibly terrifying encounter with an opponent who has trampled many a sea monster, not to mention mere mortals. But he insists on trying, even if God would only "multiply" his wounds and sorrows in response to this demand (Job 9:13–19). "Though he slay me," Job declares, "yet will I trust in him: but I will maintain mine own ways before him" (13:15).[42]

"I now know that thy right worship is defiance" (507), exclaims Ahab on watching the strange white fire that lights up the *Pequod* one stormy night.[43] His quest for Moby Dick is likewise a defiant mode of worship, an uncompromising passionate monomaniacal attempt to grasp the inscrutable grand white whale/deity/demon, "to lay the world's grievances before the bar," to find some kind of answer to the question of evil. With a "torn body" and a "gashed soul" bleeding "into one another" (185), he never ceases to seek the ever-alluring, omnipresent, demonic creature that embodies all his desires, longings, hatred, and rage, "all that most maddens and torments; all that stirs up the lees of things" (184).

However different, Melville's antitheodician stance intersects at points with the Kantian perception of Job's "authentic theodicy." For Kant, Job is a text that endorses a system of "unconditional divine decision," according to which confession of ignorance is unmistakably preferable to any pretense of knowledge. In the end "sincerity of heart[;] . . . honesty in openly admitting one's doubts; repugnance to pretending conviction where one feels none, especially before God[,] . . . these are the attributes which . . . have decided the preeminence of the honest man over the religious flatterer."[44]

That Ahab's chase ends with a momentous encounter with the one whale that injured him is as unimaginable as God's sudden revelation at the end of the Book of Job. But whereas God's whirlwind speech ultimately leads Job back to life, Moby Dick offers Ahab no relief or consolation. Like Faust, Ahab is doomed to face the limits and fragility of human aspirations. Unlike Faust, he dies unredeemed.

LEVIATHAN'S JAWS

When Moby Dick appears one day, out of the blue, Ahab is granted a
vision of the creature he has so desperately longed to see. The vision
is a close-up of the tremendous horrors that lie within the creature's
gigantic, predatory jaws.

> But suddenly as he peered down and down into its depths, he pro-
> foundly saw a white living spot no bigger than a white weasel, with
> wonderful celerity uprising, and magnifying as it rose, till it turned,
> and then there were plainly revealed two long crooked rows of white,
> glistening teeth, floating up from the undiscoverable bottom. It was
> Moby Dick's open mouth and scrolled jaw; his vast, shadowed bulk
> still half blending with the blue of the sea. The glittering mouth
> yawned beneath the boat like an open-doored marble tomb; and giving
> one sidelong sweep with his steering oar, Ahab whirled the craft aside
> from this tremendous apparition. (549)

The "glittering mouth" of Moby Dick, with its "crooked rows of
white, glistening teeth"—Melville's vivid variation on Leviathan's "terrible teeth" (Job 41:14)—yawning beneath the ship, seems to promise
only death, bestowing nothing but the light of an "open-doored marble
tomb." The apparition does not lack sublimity in its exceptional celer-
ity and magnified power. Ultimately it cannot but seduce Ahab to join
the underworld from which it momentarily emerged.

In *The Art of Biblical Poetry,* Robert Alter, a prominent twentieth-
century advocate of the literary approach to the Bible, suggests that
God's whirlwind poem offers a superb poetic response to the themes
and images with which Job unfolds his agonies in the course of the
Dialogues. It provides, above all, an affirmation of life against Job's
recurrent yearning for death and darkness. "The remarkable and celebrated phrase 'eyelids of dawn' which Job in Chapter 3 wanted never
to be seen again," writes Alter, recurs in the divine poem to depict the
dazzling vital light flashing from Leviathan's eyes.[45]

Ahab is a Job who is unwilling to see light and life in divine revelation
or to move beyond disaster. He is a Job whose worse fantasies and night-
mares come true. Much as the defiant Bartleby ends up "sleeping" in the
"Tombs" "with kings and counsellors," calling to mind Job's death wish
in chapter 3:14, so Ahab finds a tomb in the mouth of Moby Dick whose
door—unlike the uterine doors of Job's mother—remains shut.[46]

In his tragic, lonely grandeur, Ahab defies death until the very end,
cursing and chasing the White Whale with his very last breath: "Oh,

lonely death on lonely life! Oh, now I feel my topmost greatness lies in my topmost grief. . . . Towards thee I roll, thou all-destroying but unconquering whale; to the last I grapple with thee; from hell's heart I stab at thee; for hate's sake I spit my last breath at thee. Sink all coffins and all hearses to one common pool! and since neither can be mine, let me then tow to pieces, while still chasing thee, though tied to thee, thou damned whale! *Thus*, I give up the spear!" (571–72). His spear-hurling at Moby Dick on the brink of the abyss may be futile—the "damned whale" seems to "[laugh] at the shaking of a spear" (Job 41:29)—but the relentless heretical drive to proceed in the struggle against the "unconquering whale" serves as his ultimate source of inspiration, even in the face of failure and death.[47] Ahab ends up realizing the blasphemous, desperate proposal of Job's Wife. He curses God and dies.

THE FOLKLORIC VERSION:
THE GOVERNOR AND THE DEVIL

Although Melville rejects the patient Job of the Prologue, other aspects of this section—primarily the lively folkloric tale about the wager between God and Satan (the Adversary)—compel Melville toward yet another aesthetic route. For Herder, among others, the Bible's poetic grandeur was in fact indebted to its folkloric origin. Melville underscores the folkloric qualities of the wager scene by inserting it, in modified form, as a spicy tale told by Stubb to Flask in the course of their conversation about the dubious bond between Ahab and Fedallah:

> "Why, do ye see, the old man is hard bent after that White Whale, and the devil there is trying to come round him, and get him to swap away his silver watch, or his soul, or something of that sort, and then he'll surrender Moby Dick."
> "Pooh! Stubb, you are skylarking; how can Fedallah do that?"
> "I don't know, Flask, but the devil is a curious chap, and a wicked one, I tell ye. Why, they say as how he went a sauntering into the old flag-ship once, switching his tail about devilish easy and gentlemanlike, and inquiring if the old governor was at home. Well, he was at home, and asked the devil what he wanted. The devil, switching his hoofs, up and says, 'I want John.' 'What for?' says the old governor. 'What business is that of yours,' says the devil, getting mad,—'I want to use him.' 'Take him,' says the governor—and by the Lord, Flask, if the devil didn't give John the Asiatic cholera before he got through with him, I'll eat this whale in one mouthful." (325–26)

Stubb does not refer to Job explicitly, but the tale about the governor and the devil is an unmistakable travesty of the wager in Job 1.[48] Fedallah, the *Pequod*'s devil in disguise, is eager to draw a pact with Ahab, whether it entails swapping away the latter's soul or watch (the spiritual and the material are jovially interchangeable in a parodic metacommentary on the wager in *Faust*).[49] The tale seems to suggest that the God who does not rescue Job or Ahab is as indifferent as the old governor who yields to the devil's request and allows him to "take" "John" (note the phonetic affinity with "Job") without asking too many questions.

The folkloric tale, Melville realizes, is not as naive as many readers assume. It has the potential to serve as a sharp critique of the concept of divine justice and vigilance. Martin Buber's reading of Job 1 goes so far as to suggest that "here God's acts are questioned more critically than in any of Job's accusations, because here we are informed of the true motive, which is one not befitting a deity."[50] The story of the Adversary's enticing of God to test Job "gratuitously" poses a challenge to any attempt to read Job as theodicy.

The critique of divine rule is forever intertwined with a critique of human rule in *Moby-Dick*. The governor is also analogous to the *Pequod*'s captain. Ahab, Stubb intimates, is no innocent suffering in the devil's hands. Obsessively immersed in his own wound and vengeance, he turns a deaf ear to the reservations and suffering of his crew and would send them off with the devil if asked to. He may assume the role of one who suffers and rages on behalf of "his whole race from Adam down" (160), but in many ways he is incapable of hearing any cry but his own.

Ahab is not quite the governor Hobbes had in mind in *Leviathan*. "Hitherto," writes Hobbes,

> I have set forth the nature of man, whose pride and other passions have compelled him to submit himself to government: together with the great power of his governor, whom I compared to *Leviathan*, taking that comparison out of the two last verses of the one-and-fortieth of Job; where God having set forth the great power of *Leviathan*, calleth him King of the Proud. There is nothing, saith he, on earth, to be compared with him. He is made so as not to be afraid. He seeth every high thing below him; and is king of all the children of pride.[51]

Hobbes's governor, whose force is comparable to that of Leviathan, rises to power by the people's consent in an attempt to promise the commonwealth's peace. That is, he is the sovereign to whom the people

submit themselves in order to set limits to their natural brutish state
and to tame the potential for war embedded in their pride. Ahab too
holds tremendous power, but nothing is farther from his thoughts than
peace. He unites his crew under one keel for the purpose of revenge.
And although initially he manages to acquire the consent of his crew
("The Quarter-Deck" scene), his chase after Moby Dick does not depend on it. He is determined to proceed with Fedallah even when the
resentment of the crew grows. Mitigating the pride of those below him,
he never limits his own grand hubris. As Starbuck puts it, "Horrible
old man! Who's over him he cries—ay, he would be a democrat to all
above; look how he lords it over all below!" Ahab may be the product of a nation that prides itself on being the epitome of democratic
rule, but his rule is as arbitrary and tyrannical as the overlords of the
past—or, for that matter, of God.

Stubb and Flask play with the idea of resisting Ahab's abuse of
power by ducking the devilish Fedallah:

> "But see here, Stubb, I thought you a little boasted just now, that you
> meant to give Fedallah a sea-toss, if you got a good chance. Now, if he's
> so old as all those hoops of yours come to, and if he is going to live for
> ever, what good will it do to pitch him overboard—tell me that?"
> "Give him a good ducking, anyhow."
> "But he'd crawl back."
> "Duck him again; and keep ducking him."
> "Suppose he should take it into his head to duck you, though—yes,
> and drown you—what then?"
> "I should like to see him try it; I'd give him such a pair of black eyes
> that he wouldn't dare to show his face in the admiral's cabin again for
> a long while. . . . Damn the devil, Flask; do you suppose I'm afraid of
> the devil? Who's afraid of him, except the old governor who daresn't
> catch him and put him in double-darbies, as he deserves, but lets him
> go about kidnapping people; aye, and signed a bond with him, that all
> the people the devil kidnapped, he'd roast for him? There's a governor!"
> (326–27)

Stubb's Job is a Job from the bottom up. He imagines himself toss-
ing off the devil, acting out the role God or Ahab would have assumed
in a more just world. He assures Flask that unlike the governor he is
by no means afraid of the devil, nor would he hesitate to give him a
"pair of black eyes." Governors—whether divine or human—tend to
"roast" victims with the devil rather than protect them. It is left to
the common people to question devils, governors, and captains if they
wish to avoid the brink.[52]

But neither the jovial Stubb and Flask nor the earnest Starbuck can stop Ahab from following his dark cravings. Nor do they venture to leave the ship. Ahab's charismatic dark charm lures them inexplicably, much as Fedallah lures Ahab. No one is as perfect as the legendary patient Job was said to be.

FLEECE'S SERMON

Being something of a victim of Ahab's mad chase does not stop Stubb from humiliating those who are lower in rank than he is. He too is a democrat only to "those above." In "Stubb's Supper" he summons Fleece, the old black cook, and orders him to deliver a sermon to the sharks. The great noise the sharks make while devouring the body of the whale that is moored to the ship, the very same whale Stubb is busy eating, disturbs him. "Fellow-critters," says Fleece, "I'se ordered here to say dat you must stop that damn noise dare. You hear? Stop dat dam smackin' ob de lip! Massa Stubb say dat you can fill your dam bellies up to de hatchings, but by Gor! you must stop dat dam racket!" (294). Stubb's cruel pranks do not end here. He insists that Fleece avoid swearing and deliver the kind of sermon that would "convert sinners" by coaxing them. Fleece is thus forced to deliver an anti-Joban sermon or a mock-Hobbesian one in which evil and brutishness are presented as "governable." "Your woraciousness, fellow-critters, I don't blame ye so much for; dat is natur, and can't be helped; but to gobern dat wicked natur, dat is de pint. You is sharks, sartin; but if you gobern de shark in you, why den you be angel; for all angel is not'ing more dan de shark well goberned. Now, look here, bred'ren, just try wonst to be cibil, a helping yourselbs from dat whale. Don't be tearin' de blubber out your neighbor's mout, I say" (295).

But soon Fleece gives up the possibility of educating sharks to govern themselves and curses them instead: "Cussed fellow-critters! Kick up de damndest row as ever you can; fill your dam' bellies 'till dey bust—and den die" (295). Ultimately, on leaving, he will curse Stubb too: "Wish, by gor! whale eat him, 'stead of him eat whale. I'm bressed if he ain't more of shark dan Massa Shark hisself" (297). The literal sharks pale in comparison to their metaphorical human counterparts, who know no limits in tormenting their "fellow creatures." Like Job, Fleece finds cursing closer to the bleak truth. Like Job, he regards the world as devoid of divine vigilance, where predators prevail and the privileged only augment the agony of the poor and the oppressed. A speech Fleece would have wholeheartedly delivered is Job's scathing account of the ways by which the wicked thrive on harassing the outcasts of society: "They drive away the ass of the fatherless, they take the widow's ox for a pledge. . . . They cause the naked to lodge without clothing. . . . Men groan from out of the city, and the soul of the wounded crieth out: yet God layeth not folly to them" (24:3–12).[53]

KAFKA'S PRECURSORS

In my reading of the various *Pequod* Jobs, I focused on Melville's response to a whole lineage of eighteenth- and nineteenth-century continental advocates of the Book of Job as an exemplary code of art. But Melville's Jobs, it seems to me, also pave the road for the subsequent genealogy of modern and postmodern Jobs. The Book of Job, interestingly enough, has maintained its primary role as an aesthetic touchstone in modern and postmodern literature as well. Indeed, it has been used as a key text by means of which to define the sublime melancholies of modern times by writers as different as Kafka, Paul Celan, and Hanoch Levine.

I see *Moby-Dick* and "Bartleby" primarily as precursors of Kafka's reading of Job in *The Trial*.[54] To begin with, Melville anticipates Kafka's transfer of the drama of Job into a modern work setting. *Moby-Dick*'s whale-ship and Bartleby's Wall Street office lead to the entangled world of K. within the halls of legal bureaucracy. Thomas Mann's comment on *The Trial* is relevant in this connection. He characterizes Kafka as a religious humorist who depicts the transcendent world "as an Austrian 'department'; as a magnification of a petty, obstinate, inaccessible, unaccountable bureaucracy; a mammoth establishment of documents and procedures, headed by some darkly responsible official hierarchy."[55] In *Moby-Dick,* as in *The Trial,* the shift to the modern work setting is accompanied by a greater concern with the social critique of Job and the dynamics of human persecution and oppression. But perhaps, above all, Melville anticipates Kafka in foregrounding hermeneutic questions in the course of redefining Joban sublimity. Derrida's renowned essay, "Devant la Loi," positions the parable in the Cathedral as an exemplary text in its insistence on the impossibility of interpretation.[56] What emerges from the discussion between Joseph K. and the priest on the meaning of the parable is that all readings are necessarily misreadings. We shall never comprehend with certainty what lies behind the succession of guarded doors that divide us from the "Law." Following Derrida, Harold Fisch wonders whether the parable in the Cathedral is specifically meant to question the very possibility of interpreting the Book of Job, with its inexplicable trial.

Melville, I believe, is not concerned with misreadings. The profusion of potential readings, as far as he is concerned, does not mean that there are necessarily erroneous readings. But *Moby-Dick* does point to a certain sublime explosion of meaning, an inaccessibility of interpretation that only accentuates the infinitude of Job's dialogue with a God whose answer is a series of taunting questions. There always seems to crop up another Job chasing another potential Leviathan chasing another potential Job chasing another potential Leviathan to the very end of space.

CHAPTER 2

"Jonah Historically Regarded"

Improvisations on Kitto's Cyclopedia of Biblical Literature

Just before the *Pequod* sets sail, Father Mapple delivers a memorable sermon on the Book of Jonah from his shiplike pulpit at the Whaleman's Chapel in New Bedford, adding "sea-taste" to the well-known tale about the stubborn, disobedient prophet who escaped to the sea. The sermon opens with an alluring invitation to dive into the Book of Jonah. "Shipmates," Mapple declares as he turns over the leaves of the Bible, "this book, containing only four chapters—four yarns—is one of the smallest strands in the mighty cable of the Scriptures. Yet what depths of the soul does Jonah's deep sea-line sound! What a pregnant lesson to us is this prophet! What a noble thing is that canticle in the fish's belly! How billow-like and boisterously grand! We feel the floods surging over us; we sound with him to the kelpy bottom of the waters; sea-weed and all the slime of the sea is about us!" (42). Mapple seeks to take his listeners on an exegetical voyage. He captures their ears through a flow of sonorous alliterations—"soul" / "sea-line" / "sound"; "belly" / "billow" / "boisterously"; "seaweed" / "slime" / "sea"—that echo Jonah's canticle in the belly of the fish— "The waters compassed me about, even to the soul: the depth closed me round about, the weeds were wrapped about my head" (Jon. 2:5)—and urges them to cling to Jonah's sea-line, to follow him way down to "the kelpy bottom of the waters," beneath the surging floods, to the seductively dangerous, unknown, dark, slimy geography of the deep.

Mapple's sermon, however, is but an opening interpretive note. *Moby-Dick* as a whole is a "billow-like" and "boisterously grand" interpretation of the Book of Jonah. It offers a virtuoso projection of the terse text of Jonah on a gigantic canvas: the long epic story of the *Pequod*'s search after the inscrutable White Whale. What would happen, Melville ventures to ask, if we were to transfer Jonah from biblical times into the nineteenth century and split his figure between the outcasts and renegades of an American whaling ship? What new interpretations would emerge once Jonah is set in a context where intimate encounters with the bodies of great fish are a daily experience? Each crew member of the *Pequod* strives—wittingly or unwittingly—to map out Jonah's route. Ishmael, who slips into the mouth of a right whale, playfully exclaiming, "Good Lord! is this the road that Jonah went?" (334), and Ahab, who leans over his wrinkled sea charts relentlessly searching after the route of the inscrutable White Whale, are but two notable examples. Queequeg, Tashtego, and even the maddened Pip are also Jonahs of sorts, each highlighting a different course in the travel narrative of the biblical prophet, all reaching realms unheard of within Mapple's Calvinist framework.[1]

In rendering his Jonahs, Melville responds to a dizzyingly diverse array of other readings of the Book of Jonah. Calvin's commentaries on Jonah, popular sermons of a Calvinistic bent (Mapple's sermon is modeled on this genre), Defoe's *Robinson Crusoe* (Crusoe is regarded as a sinful Jonah in one of the opening episodes), Pierre Bayle's account in *Dictionnaire historique et critique,* and John Kitto's *Cyclopedia of Biblical Literature* are but a few of the prominent ones. Other, less traceable Jonahs peep out at different junctures. Ishmael's ruminations about the possibility of painting Jonah's eye looking through the "bow-window" (262) eye of the whale in Captain Colnett's picture may be an allusion to the famous midrash on Jonah's sight-seeing through the windowlike eyes of the big fish while traveling in the deep.[2] And one could conjecture, in light of Sterling Stuckey's studies on Melville's exposure to African American culture, that Melville was not unaware of Jonah's major role in African American spirituals in his shaping of Pip as Jonah.[3]

Given my focus on the new exegetical trends prevalent in nineteenth-century America, I single out Melville's response to Kitto's *Cyclopedia,* one of the first British encyclopedias to endorse the findings of German biblical criticism. Soon after its publication in 1845, it became, as Howard P. Vincent put it, "a standard decoration for

English and American parlor tables."[4] It had the advantage of providing a popularized scholarly introduction to the historical-geographic research of the Bible in an accessible format, "illustrated by numerous engravings" (as the title page promises; fig. 3). Kitto's successful reception in America was part of a broader process of cultural translation through which the continental scientific approach to the Bible became part and parcel of the American exegetical scene.

Melville devotes an entire chapter—"Jonah Historically Regarded"— to John Eadie's entry on Jonah in Kitto's *Cyclopedia*. In this chapter Ishmael engages in a mock debate with the scholars whose readings are surveyed by Eadie, calling into question their scientific presuppositions, among them the assumption that "history" is a traceable, concrete concept. Though this chapter serves as the core of Melville's reflections on the exegetical innovations of biblical criticism, his dialogue with Kitto, as I show, reverberates through the entire novel, serving as a vital springboard for Melville's own reading of Jonah as a text whose historical significance cannot be detached from its implications within contemporary cultural settings, above all, antebellum America.

That Melville had Kitto's *Cyclopedia* by his side while writing *Moby-Dick* was noted already in Wright's *Melville's Use of the Bible* (1949) and in Vincent's *The Trying Out of Moby-Dick* (1949). But it is only in Elisa New's "Bible Leaves! Bible Leaves!" that Melville's subtler hermeneutic exchange with Kitto is first examined (beyond source criticism). New draws attention to Kitto in her attempt to define Melville's "Hebraic historicism." Melville, she argues, follows Kitto's lead in showing that "the proper aim of hermeneutics is not the discovery of an allegorical Word" but rather the fashioning of a historical view of the text that would be attuned to the ways in which every culture constructs its own worldview, its own distinct "clothing" of truth.[5]

And yet Melville's endorsement of the historicism of biblical scholarship, I believe, is far from uncritical. What is more, Melville is equally intrigued by the exegetical potential of allegorical readings. He plays historical and allegorical readings of the Bible against each other— Kitto and Mapple in Jonah's case—never hesitating to thrive on both while uncovering their respective limitations. But, above all, New does not go far enough in exploring the vast aesthetic-hermeneutic project of *Moby-Dick*. Melville does not merely allude to other commentaries in passing. His metacommentary on Eadie's entry offers an extensive consideration of the actual reading strategies of biblical scholarship as it dwells on the most minute details in the Book of Jonah.

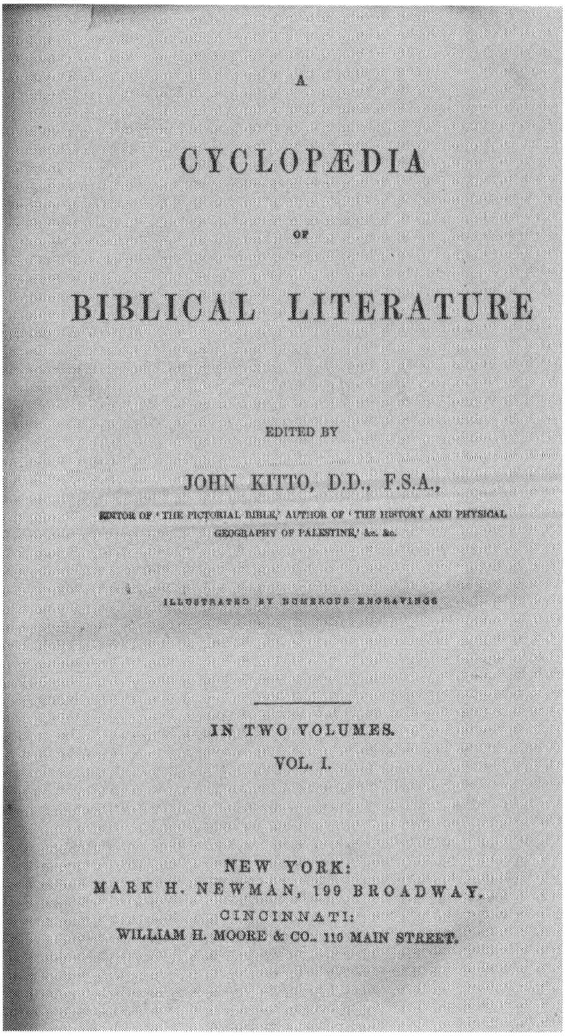

A

CYCLOPÆDIA

OF

BIBLICAL LITERATURE

EDITED BY

JOHN KITTO, D.D., F.S.A.,

EDITOR OF ' THE PICTORIAL BIBLE,' AUTHOR OF ' THE HISTORY AND PHYSICAL
GEOGRAPHY OF PALESTINE,' &c. &c.

ILLUSTRATED BY NUMEROUS ENGRAVINGS

IN TWO VOLUMES.

VOL. I.

NEW YORK:
MARK H. NEWMAN, 199 BROADWAY.
CINCINNATI:
WILLIAM H. MOORE & CO. 110 MAIN STREET.

FIGURE 3. Title page of John Kitto's *A Cyclopedia of Biblical Literature*, 1845. Courtesy of the University of Iowa Libraries, Iowa City, Iowa.

Melville's interest in biblical scholarship, I should add, is compatible with his preoccupation with scientific discourses altogether. In *Melville's Anatomies*, Samuel Otter offers a remarkable reading of Melville's detailed explorations of the discursive world of nineteenth-century studies of craniology, cetology, and ethnology in his major

works. Otter challenges both the traditional critical view of Melville
as an "isolato," "striving for expression against the constraints of conventional antebellum America," and the newer "historical" view of
Melville as "the product of circumstance."[6] He argues "for a Melville
fascinated with the rhetorical structures and ideological functions of
antebellum discourse," whose critique is voiced both from an outsid-
er's position and from within the discursive contours of the period.
Melville, according to Otter, does not reject the scientific methods he
chooses to explore. Rather, he savors their pleasures, tests their limits,
and makes palpable their dangers. Otter's observations are relevant to
Melville's response to the new scientific approach to the Bible as well.
While distancing himself from biblical scholarship and exposing its
absurdities through one parody after another, Melville is nonetheless
intrigued by its charms, always attentive to the ways in which his own
interpretive passions may intersect with those of other readers.

THE RECEPTION OF BIBLICAL CRITICISM IN AMERICA

The long history of biblical exegesis is punctuated by numerous revolutionary shifts, but the application of scientific methods to Scripture
is undoubtedly one of the most prominent. The beginnings of this interpretive line may be traced to seventeenth-century Europe, in particular, to Spinoza's call in *Tractatus theologico-politicus* (1670) for
a critical examination of Scripture that would not be subservient to
dogmatic conceptions of biblical authorship or shy away from dealing
with textual inconsistencies. Other forerunners include Jean Astruc
(1684–1776), founder of the renowned documentary hypothesis, who
used Spinoza's observations regarding conflicting elements in the Bible
as a point of departure for tracing different sources in Genesis, each
distinguished by a different divine name and presumably composed in
a different period.

It is only in the late eighteenth and early nineteenth century, however, that biblical criticism became an academic field, primarily in
German universities. J.G. Eichhorn, W.M.L. De Wette, and J.S.
Vater, among others, set out to develop and sharpen the documentary hypothesis, grounding it in a more extensive historical-philological framework. In a forceful demystification of the origin of Scripture,
they shattered the traditional notion of the Bible as the Word of God, a
unified text of divine inspiration, and suggested that it be treated as a
composite work, a product of human endeavor whose intricate history

of composition may be examined like that of any other ancient text. Determining the historicity of the biblical texts as well as the dating of the various sources and documents became a major scholarly concern. Although the opponents of biblical scholarship challenged the piety of its followers, this turn toward history was motivated, more often than not, by an interest in critical scientific analysis rather than secularism.

Within the realm of New Testament scholarship, one of the most influential thinkers was David Friedrich Strauss whose *Life of Jesus,* published in 1835, generated a heated controversy. Applying historical and critical methods to the Gospels, he concluded that they did not contain much historical fact about Jesus. While denying the historicity of the bulk of the text, he called for a consideration of its mythical qualities. Identified with the "Mythical" school, he did not construe such myths as lies but rather as sensuous, rich accounts shaped against the background of their specific cultural and religious context.[7]

The first shock waves of the new trends in German biblical criticism were felt in American intellectual circles by the opening decades of the nineteenth century. New England liberals, as Jerry Wayne Brown points out, "attempted to use the new biblical studies as a destructive weapon against orthodox Calvinism."[8] First and foremost among them was Theodore Parker. He called into question the predominant tendency to idolize the biblical text as the emblem of divine inspiration and instead accentuated its human origin. "Modern criticism," he argues, "is fast breaking to pieces this idol which men have made out of the scriptures. It has shown that here are the most different works thrown together; that their authors, wise as they sometimes were, pious as we feel often their spirit to have been, had only that inspiration which is common to other men equally pious and wise; that they were by no means infallible, but were mistaken in facts or in reasoning[,] . . . men who in some measure partook of the darkness and limited notions of their age, and were not always above its mistakes or its corruptions."[9] In a sharp anti-Calvinist gesture, Parker claimed that the biblical notions of hell, election, and damnation made it difficult to speak of God's universal love, for the biblical God seemed more often than not a capricious deity who "loved only a few, and them not overmuch."[10]

The task, declares Parker in *A Discourse Pertaining to Religious Matters,* was to read the Bible selectively, to "divide the word rightly; separate mythology from history, fact from fiction, what is religious and of God from what is earthly and not of God; to take the Bible for what it is worth."[11] Such critical consideration would make adherence to the Bible as an ultimate unquestionable authority impossible. "Pausanias," he writes, "says he saw a dolphin carry a boy on his back as a recompense for being healed of a wound by the boy! Lib. III. C. 25. A man who should believe such a story on such evidence would be thought of . . . credulous by the men who declare it dangerous to doubt the stories in Jonah and Daniel" (*Discourse* 224). Defiant as he was, Parker's goal was not to reject the Bible altogether but rather to make it a "servant" of "Common Sense and Reason" (*Discourse* 243), to distinguish between the "chaff and the husks" in quest of the Bible's transcendent eternal truths (*Discourse* 246). The dramatic ending of the essay encapsulates his position: "Let its errors and absurdities no longer be forced on the pious mind, but perish for ever; let the Word of God come through Conscience, Reason, and holy Feeling, as light through the windows of morning. Worship with no master but God, no creed but Truth, no service but Love, and we have nothing to fear" (*Discourse* 250). To enhance the revolutionary impact of German scholarship in New England, Parker translated into English De Wette's groundbreaking work, *Einleitung,* supplementing the original with notes and clarifications. The translation, titled *A Critical and Historical Introduction to the Canonical Scriptures of the Old Testament,* was first published in 1843 (fig. 4).

Parker's scholarship was inextricably connected with his political activities. The selective reading of Scripture was an indispensable reading strategy in his abolitionist writings as well. In "A Sermon of Slavery," delivered on January 31, 1841, he harshly criticizes supporters of slavery in the South for their use of the Bible to consecrate their sins. "Has He sanctioned slavery? 'Oh yes,' say some, and cite Old Testament and New Testament in proof thereof. . . . We need not settle that question now, but it is certain that men can quote it to support despotism when that is the order of the day—or freedom when that is the 'law of the land.'"[12] Even if the Bible may be quoted to support slavery, such an interpretive move is unacceptable. Slavery remains a sin even if Jesus did not condemn it explicitly. And for those who strive to find scriptural Truth, Parker provides numerous biblical passages that would confirm the abolitionist cause in spirit.

Biblical criticism was not the domain of liberals alone. In response to the threat posed by the questioning of scriptural authority, conservatives sought to defend the Bible's canonical status by using the methods of biblical scholarship within the framework of Calvinism. Whereas Harvard became the center for liberal, mostly Unitarian,

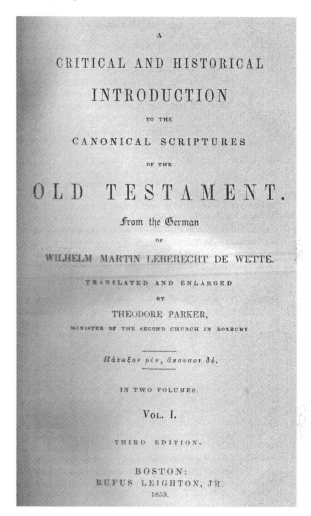

FIGURE 4. Title page of De Wette's *A Critical and Historical Introduction to the Canonical Scriptures of the Old Testament,* translated by Theodore Parker, 1843. Courtesy of the University of Iowa Libraries, Iowa City, Iowa.

biblical studies, led by scholars such as Edward Everett and George Bancroft, Andover seminary (whose prominent figures were Moses Stuart and Josiah Willard Gibbs) served as the conservative stronghold of biblical research in its ardent defense of biblical inspiration and its concomitant defense of slavery.[13]

As textual critics debated the accuracy of the biblical text itself, certain American scholars turned from textual analysis to biblical geography, their underlying assumption being that the scientific study of the Holy Land was indispensable to the assessment of scriptural veracity. A leading scholar of biblical geography, Edward Robinson, postponed taking up a position as biblical scholar at the Union Theological Seminary in order to travel to Palestine and investigate the physical and historical geography of the Holy Land. He discovered previously unknown biblical sites through meticulous topographic research, relying, among other things, on Arabic place-names. The account of his travels and explorations appeared in the three-volume *Biblical Researches in Palestine, Mount Sinai and Arabia Petraea* in 1841 and won him an international reputation and the gold medal of the Royal Geographical Society of London. He was praised on his death as one "who did not read between the lines" of Scripture but rather "read the lines themselves."[14]

Popularized adaptations of the new historical-geographic research appeared in various forms in antebellum America, from Holy Land travel literature to illustrated bibles with topographic maps and historical notes. The Brattleboro Bible, for example, marketed from the 1830s on, had an appendix titled "A New Geographical and Historical Index," which included numerous landscape pictures of the Holy Land as well as drawings of historical artifacts and scenes.[15]

John Kitto was familiar with the American scene of biblical criticism. Indeed, among the contributors to his encyclopedia were American scholars. What is more, having a special passion for biblical geography—Kitto wrote several books on the topic, among them, *Palestine: The Physical Geography and Natural History of the Holy Land* (1841)—he was an admirer of Edward Robinson, with whom he corresponded on various occasions. In a letter of October 19, 1840, to Robinson, Kitto recalls his previous anxieties regarding disputed points on the geography and topography of Palestine. Robinson's work, he claimed, changed his life, as it was the first to provide reliable scientific mapping of biblical geography. "Palestine lay before you as a book," Kitto writes, "with whose language you had, by long study, made yourself well acquainted, and which you could, therefore, read with ease; where as to *all* your predecessors . . . the book was sealed."[16]

When Kitto's *Cyclopedia of Biblical Literature* appeared in 1845 it was hailed in the *New Englander* for its invaluable introduction to the new scientific research on the Bible. "No clergyman," the reviewer wrote, "and particularly no young clergyman, can afford" to do without it. "Unless we greatly mistake the signs of the times, theological science is changing its phase. . . . The great commotion which began in Germany a half century since, and has come to its climax in Strauss, has not been for nothing; and its results will not be without significance to the cause of truth and of Christ."[17] But not only clergymen used Kitto's *Cyclopedia*. It soon became one of the most popular biblical encyclopedias in America (several American editions were published from 1845 on, including an abridged version in 1852), finding its way not only to parlor tables in New England but also onto writing desks.[18]

HISTORICIZING THE VOYAGE IN THE BELLY OF THE FISH

Melville relies on Kitto in many of his biblical readings, but the one entry through which he sets out to explore the new hermeneutic possibilities of reading the Bible as a historical text is John Eadie's entry on Jonah. Eadie, a professor of biblical literature at the United Presbyterian Church of Scotland, was one of the more conservative contributors to the encyclopedia.[19] His piece on Jonah contains a curiously ambivalent presentation of new research on the topic, unimaginable in twentieth-century biblical encyclopedias. In an attempt to defend the traditional Calvinistic conception of miracles as literal events, Eadie questions the very readings he surveys. "The history of Jonah," he writes in one of the opening paragraphs, "is certainly striking and extraordinary. Its characteristic prodigy does not resemble the other miraculous phenomena recorded in Scripture; yet we must believe in its literal occurrence, as the Bible affords no indication of being a mythus, allegory, or parable. . . . It requires less faith to credit this simple excerpt from Jonah's biography, than to believe in the numerous hypotheses that have been invented to deprive it of its supernatural character, the great majority of them being clumsy and far-fetched."[20] Despite his reservations, Eadie goes on to consider such "hypotheses" and provides a detailed account of the new scholarly perspectives on Jonah.

The central interpretive problem that biblical scholarship tackles in its investigation of the Book of Jonah, as Eadie points out, is the significance of the marvelous scene of the prophet in the belly of the fish. Nowhere else in the Bible does a fish swallow a human being only to vomit him out safe and sound after three days. The question of how to read this scene has troubled commentators from time immemorial. In the context of biblical scholarship it becomes a question of genre.

Eadie's account moves from those who refute the historicity of the scene and regard it as an allegory (Bertholdt, Rosenmuller, and Gesenius), a dream (Grimm), or a myth (Huet, Bryant, Faber, and Taylor) to various attempts to rationalize the prophet's mysterious voyage and defend its historical character.

Most of the entry is devoted to such rationalizations. Eadie mentions different accounts that set out to identify, with the help of zoological research, the species of fish (the biblical text remains reticent in this connection) whose anatomy would have been such that it could carry Jonah intact.[21] Thus Bochart classifies Jonah's "big fish" as pertaining to "the shark species, *Lamia canis carcharias*," while Jebb maintains that it was indeed a whale (in accordance with traditional classification), though Jonah was entombed in its mouth rather than in its belly. Eadie is highly critical of both, but all the more so of Jebb's speculations: "There is little ground for the supposition of Bishop Jebb, that the asylum of Jonah was not in the stomach of a whale, but in the cavity of its throat, which, according to naturalists, is a very capacious receptacle, sufficiently large . . . to contain a merchant ship's jolly-boat full of men."[22]

Other pertinent lines of historicization, which Eadie surveys, smooth out the hermeneutic difficulty by replacing the fish with alternative carriers: "imagining that Jonah, when thrown into the sea, was taken up by a ship having a large fish for a figure-head," or that he was rescued by a life preserver, given that *dag* (supposedly on philological grounds) may signify not merely "fish" but also "life-preserver" (Taylor). The hypothesis that Jonah "took refuge in the interior of a dead whale, floating near the spot where he was cast overboard" (Rosen), is but a variation on this theme.[23]

In "Jonah Historically Regarded," Melville follows Eadie's critical line, not in the name of a more pious traditional reading of the biblical text, but rather in an amusing consideration of the pitfalls of the different types of biblical literalism, biblical criticism being one of them, however different its quest for the historical veracity of Scripture may be. The parody provided in this chapter entails a juxtaposition of Sag Harbor's exegetical questions concerning scriptural veracity with the scholarly accounts of Bishop Jebb and unidentified "continental exegetists." Ishmael cites the opinions of the scholars in a playful attempt to address Sag Harbor's concern about the discrepancy between his experience as seaman and the picture of a whale in his old-fashioned "unscientific" Bible—the very antithesis of the new antebellum illustrated bibles containing historical-geographic notes and scientific maps:

> One old Sag-Harbor whaleman's chief reason for questioning the He-
> brew story was this:—He had one of those quaint old-fashioned Bibles,
> embellished with curious, unscientific plates; one of which represented
> Jonah's whale with two spouts in his head—a peculiarity only true
> with respect to a species of the Leviathan (the Right Whale, and the
> varieties of that order), concerning which the fishermen have this say-
> ing, "A penny roll would choke him;" his swallow is so very small.
> But, to this, Bishop Jebb's anticipative answer is ready. It is not neces-
> sary, hints the Bishop, that we consider Jonah as tombed in the whale's
> belly, but as temporarily lodged in some part of his mouth. . . . For
> truly, the Right Whale's mouth would accommodate a couple of whist-
> tables, and comfortably seat all the players. Possibly, too, Jonah might
> have ensconced himself in a hollow tooth; but, on second thoughts, the
> Right Whale is toothless.
>   Another reason which Sag-Harbor (he went by that name) urged for
> his want of faith in this matter of the prophet, was something obscurely
> in reference to his incarcerated body and the whale's gastric juices. But
> this objection likewise falls to the ground, because a German exege-
> tist supposes that Jonah must have taken refuge in the floating body
> of a *dead* whale. . . . Besides, it has been divined by other continental
> commentators, that when Jonah was thrown overboard from the Joppa
> ship, he straightway effected his escape to another vessel near by, some
> vessel with a whale for a figure-head; and, I would add, possibly called
> "The Whale," as some craft are nowadays christened the "Shark," the
> "Gull," the "Eagle." Nor have there been wanting learned exegetists
> who have opined that the whale mentioned in the book of Jonah merely
> meant a life-preserver—an inflated bag of wind—which the endangered
> prophet swam to, and so was saved from a watery doom. (364–65)

Biblical exegesis has had its full share of oddities, but biblical scholarship has surely contributed some of the most fanciful ones. Ishmael
highlights the imaginative speculations of biblical scholars, playing
them against each other, exploring their poetic potential while adding
his own contribution. The zoological discussion in Kitto concerning
the definition of the marine species is taken ad absurdum in the attempts of Sag Harbor and Ishmael (following suit) to assess whether
or not the right whale may be construed as the "right" classification
for Jonah's fish. And Jebb's speculative suggestion that a cavity in the
whale's throat "is a very capacious receptacle, sufficiently large . . . to
contain a merchant ship's jolly-boat full of men," is embellished with
additional (more dubious) details. The whale's mouth, Ishmael waggishly assures us, is large enough to accommodate several "whist-tables"

and "comfortably seat all the players" (364). Similarly, Ishmael savors
the details of the reading of the fish as a figurehead of a vessel and adds
his own exegetical improvisation in conjecturing that the biblical text
may be referring to the name of the vessel (rather than to an actual
fish)—be it "Whale" or "Shark."

From the enigma of the fish, Ishmael moves on to tackle Sag Harbor's doubts with respect to the identification of the coast on which
Jonah had landed. If Jonah was swallowed by a whale in the Mediterranean Sea, Sag Harbor ponders, "and after three days he was vom-
ited up somewhere within three days' journey of Nineveh, a city on the
Tigris, very much more than three days' journey across from the near-
est point of the Mediterranean coast. How is that?" (365). The whale,
he goes on to speculate, "might have carried him round by the way of
the Cape of Good Hope" up the Persian Gulf to the site of Nineveh,
the only drawback of this hypothesis being that it requires a circum-
navigation "of all Africa in three days," not to mention the fact that
the waters of the Tigris are "too shallow for any whale to swim in"
(365). Sag Harbor's doubts point to the absurdity of the geographic
dimension of biblical scholarship. The scholarly maps that accompany
Kitto's *Cyclopedia* and the detailed depictions of biblical sites in separate entries ("Nineveh" is one such entry) do not seem to guarantee ac-
cess to historical truth.[24] Melville may be alluding not only to scholars
such as Kitto and Robinson, who explored the physical geography of
Palestine, but also to the archaeological sensation of the discovery of
Nineveh. A.H. Layard's *Nineveh and Its Remains* appeared in 1849
and was received with much enthusiasm by American reviewers.[25] Layard, in keeping with the practices of biblical geography, relies on figures provided in the Book of Jonah to calculate the size of the ancient
city of Nineveh.[26]

Distinctions between history and myth, fact and fiction, which biblical criticism treats as clearly delineated, are called into question time
and again. Jonah, we discover, may be regarded as both history and
myth, for the two are embedded in each other to the extent of being
inseparable. "Now some Nantucketers rather distrust this historical
story of Jonah and the whale," claims Ishmael. "But then there were
some sceptical Greeks and Romans, who, standing out from the orthodox pagans of their times, equally doubted the story of Hercules
and the whale, and Arion and the Dolphin; and their doubting those
traditions did not make those traditions one whit the less facts, for all
that" (364).

JONAH AS MYTH

The blurring of history and myth is reinforced by the precedin
ter, "The Honor and Glory of Whaling," in which Jonah is pla
among historical figures but rather among mythical heroes, demigods,
and gods. "With careful disorderliness," Ishmael traces a mythical genealogy of whalemen who had "the heart in them to march boldly up
to a whale," beginning with Perseus, who slew the monster while res-
cuing Andromeda, and continuing with St. George, Hercules, Jonah,
and Vishnu (362–63).

The target of Melville's parody in this case is not only the scholarly obsession with questions of historicity but also the concomitant
interpretive practice: the pursuit of mythical parallels. Although the
most extensive consideration of ancient myths was carried out within
another burgeoning field—comparative mythology—the topic was of
much interest to biblical scholars as well.

Eadie considers such research in the context of Jonah with characteristic ambivalence: "Though we cannot accede to the system of Gale,
Huet, Bryant, Faber, and Taylor in tracing all pagan fiction, legend and
mythology to scripture facts and events, yet we are inclined to believe
that in the miraculous incident of the Book of Jonah is to be found
the origin of the various fables of Arion and the Dolphin (Herodot. I.
24), and the wild adventure of Hercules which is referred to in Lyco-
phron (*Cassandra*, v. 33)."[27] For Eadie, as for many others, the very
possibility of setting biblical traditions on an equal footing with pagan myths, not to mention the discovery of Christlike saviors in India,
Egypt, Peru, and Polynesia, was deeply unsettling for, as Bruce Franklin notes, it "turned much of Western Scripture from historical fact
into metaphorical or psychological fact—or, perhaps, mere fancy."[28]
Eadie's response, then, is typically conservative: he not only criticizes
the conflation of Scripture and myth but also attempts to mitigate the
unorthodox aspects of this comparative practice by insisting on the
primacy of the biblical text and positioning it as the decisive origin of
the classical myths.

Ishmael offers a mock response: "But, by the best contradictory au-
thorities, this Grecian story of Hercules and the whale is considered to
be derived from the still more ancient Hebrew story of Jonah and the
whale; and vice versa; certainly they are very similar" (363). Eadie's
insistence on the Bible's primacy and superiority is ridiculed in light of
the interchangeability of source and derivation. What is more, the very

notion that the similarity between the tales is sufficient to determine direct literary influence in any direction whatsoever is challenged as well. The affinity between the two heroes seems to be as loose as that among St. George, Vishnu, and all the other distinguished figures in Ishmael's "member-roll" of whalemen.

But Melville is not only interested in mocking such comparative practices. Biblical scholarship and comparative religion/mythology carve out new possibilities for thinking about the biblical text and its hidden mythological layers. Whereas in traditional Christian exegesis comparisons were usually typological in character, taking into account affinities between Old Testament and New Testament figures, these new approaches allowed for a marvelous broadening of horizons. Jonah's entombment in the fish's belly for three days could now be seen not only as a prefiguration of Christ's death and resurrection (in light of Matt. 12:40) but also as analogous to numerous other mythological tales about heroes who ventured to struggle with monsters. However groundless some of these discoveries tended to be, the quest for mythical parallels was alluring on a symbolic-literary level. It offered a path through which to explore the symbolic configurations of diverse cultures beyond the traditional dissociation—which begins in the Bible itself—of monotheistic traditions from pagan myths. Melville, as Buell points out, "is forever engaged in the acts of reading and writing, in establishing and dismantling his myths," approaching "biblical (and non-Christian) myth, at least to a point[,] as a vehicle of symbolic expression."[29]

JONAH GOES WHALING:
VIEWING THE WHALE FROM WITHIN

Melville's transfer of Jonah to the nineteenth century is a bold countertypology—a provocative elevation of contemporary outcasts and renegades to the position of exemplary biblical figures—but it also serves as a comment on the impossibility of maintaining the objectivity biblical scholarship aspires to preserve in its search for the historically valid biblical past. The stamp of the present, for Melville, is necessarily evident in pursuits of the past and is precisely that which endows them with a sense of urgency and power. Accordingly, to regard Jonah historically not only means to view the Book of Jonah in its original historical setting but also to imagine its relevance in the context of antebellum America. Melville's critique is akin to the critique leveled at the historical-philological approach to the Bible in the introduction to *The Postmodern Bible*. Against the tendency of historical criticism to "bracket out" the "contemporary milieu and exclude any examination of the ongoing formative effects of the Bible," the editors of this volume problematize the positivist emphasis on the "objective text" and call for a consideration of the cultural conditions that produce, sustain, and validate any given interpretation.[30]

Before going on to explore the ways in which Melville shapes his multiple nineteenth-century Jonahs through and against Eadie's account, let me emphasize once again that the very strategy of splitting or duplicating biblical characters—the hallmark of Melvillean aesthetics/ hermeneutics—is indebted to the premises of biblical scholarship. Biblical scholarship's concern with the inconsistencies of the divine character, or rather the contrasting configurations (and names) of God in the different sources, allows Melville to discard the quest for consistency and coherence in the representation of human character as well. To render Jonah—or any other biblical character—within the domain of one character and a single name means, as far as Melville is concerned, to do little justice to the unfathomable dimensions of human nature.

I begin with Ishmael. Here as elsewhere, Ishmael is the one to provide the most distinct line of metacommentary. It is fascinating to see how different elements from "Jonah Historically Regarded" reverberate in Ishmael's recurrent reflections on the Book of Jonah in his Jonah-like excursions within the bodies and skeletons of different whales. In "The Right Whale's Head-Contrasted View," Ishmael inspects the fissured lip of a right whale and slides over the lip, "as over a slippery threshold," into the mouth, defining himself as one who is following "Jonah's road" (334). His ensuing description of the interior of the whale's mouth calls to mind the mock scholarly debate on the anatomy of Jonah's fish and the hosting potential of its "cavity":

> The roof is about twelve feet high, and runs to a pretty sharp angle, as if there were a regular ridge-pole there; while these ribbed, arched, hairy sides, present us with those wondrous, half vertical, scimetar-shaped slats of whalebone, say three hundred on a side, which depending from the upper part of the head or crown bone, form those Venetian blinds. . . . But now forget all about blinds and whiskers for a moment, and, standing in the Right Whale's mouth, look around you afresh. Seeing all these colonnades of bone so methodically ranged about, would you not think you were inside of the great Haarlem organ, and gazing upon its thousand pipes? For a carpet to the organ we have a rug of the softest Turkey—the tongue, which is glued, as it were, to the floor of the mouth. (334–35)

Samuel Otter sees this passage as an example of Melville's obsessive desire in *Moby-Dick* to "get inside heads," a desire he shares with scholars of craniology and cetology.[31] But this passage is no less relevant to Melville's interpretive passions and ongoing dialogue with biblical scholarship. Ishmael, much like the "continental exegetists" in Eadie's account, strives to retrieve the unknown facets of Jonah's voyage by examining the so-called literal living conditions within a whale's body. In "Jonah Historically Regarded," Ishmael adds "whist-tables" to Jebb's "jolly-boat full of men." Here, in his more extended ruminations on the interiors of the whale's body, he not only considers the question theoretically, but follows, as if literally, in Jonah's footsteps. Ishmael is supposedly capable of corroborating the scholarly rationalizations regarding Jonah's lodging in practice, proving that the concrete body of the whale—particularly a dead whale—may indeed entertain visitors, given that it contains all the necessary furniture: blinds, carpets, and spacious halls.

The realm of the literal by no means suffices for Ishmael. While providing numerous anatomical details in his meticulous cetological depictions, he is no less eager to reflect on the whale as the domain of imagination, metaphor, and myth. He tries to fathom the mysteries of Jonah's head within the enigmatic head of the whale, to capture the experience of being swallowed up by a gigantic marine creature and entrapped in its inner spaces. He imagines Jonah's road as a road that leads to a wonder world where art and philosophy may prevail. The hosting right whale is seen as representative of the Stoic tradition in "his enormous practical resolution in facing death" (335), and its mouth is likened to a musical organ with numerous pipes.

Melville may be far from biblical scholarship at this point, but he is attuned to the biblical text itself. The belly of the fish is, after all, the very place where the reticent prophet, who refused to be prophet, finally discovers his voice and delivers a beautiful psalm:

> I cried by reason of mine affliction unto the Lord,
> And he heard me;
> Out of the belly of hell cried I,
> And thou heardest my voice.
> For thou hadst cast me into the deep,
> In the midst of the seas;
> And the floods compassed me about:
> All thy billows and thy waves passed over me.
> Then I said, I am cast out of thy sight;
> Yet I will look again toward thy holy temple.

The waters compassed me about, even to the soul:
The depth closed me round about,
The weeds were wrapped about my head.
I went down to the bottoms of the mountains;
The earth with her bars was about me for ever:
Yet hast thou brought up my life from corruption, O Lord my God.
When my soul fainted within me I remembered the Lord:
And my prayer came unto thee, into thine holy temple.

(2:2–7)

It is at this liminal site, between life and death, in the solitary, silent, seductive womb-tomb of the deep, that Jonah discovers his prophetic-poetic potential and grasps the liberating power of words. The psalm offers a strikingly tangible representation of drowning in the deep, with nuanced images of entrapment by waters, weeds, and the bars of the earth below. But, unexpectedly, these dark, suffocating seascapes do not block his vision. Quite the contrary, he now has the power to envision something he could not envision before: his grand ascent to God's "holy temple," where his sense of being "cast out" of "God's sight" will be replaced by a sense of intimacy and gratitude. Jonah's poem of the deep allows him, in a sense, to rise up from the underworld even before the big fish vomits him out.[32]

It is no coincidence that Melville chooses to construe the "grand canticle" as Father Mapple's point of departure (rather than have the sermon open with the first episodes in Jonah 1). In doing so, he calls attention, from the very outset, to the scene of inspiration in Jonah's tale, the moment at which the possibility of poetry-prophecy emerges. Interestingly, the aesthetic dimension of prophecy was a central concern for the advocates of the literary Bible. Robert Lowth defines poetry and prophecy in the Bible as identical, with "one common name, one common origin, one common author, the Holy Spirit."[33] Melville would not have endorsed the "Holy Spirit" as the joint author of poetry and prophecy, but he is as eager as Lowth to capture the affinity between the two modes, to meditate on the ways in which prophetic inspiration depends on poetry and vice versa.

In "A Bower in the Arsacides," Ishmael assumes Jonah's mantle once again, promising an even more penetrating representation of the "interior structural features" of the whale: "A veritable witness have you hitherto been, Ishmael; but have a care how you seize the privilege of Jonah alone; the privilege of discoursing upon the joists and beams; the rafters, ridge-pole, sleepers, and underpinnings, making up the

frame-work of leviathan. . . . I confess, that since Jonah, few whalemen have penetrated very far beneath the skin of the adult whale; nev-
ertheless, I have been blessed with an opportunity to dissect him in
miniature" (448–49).

His intimate Jonah-like knowledge of the creature, whom he sensu-
ously "unbuckles" from within, is traced back to an excursion to the
Arsacides, where he wandered in a labyrinthine pagan temple, constructed around the skeleton of a great sperm whale. If Jonah only
imagines visiting the temple as he prays in the belly of the big fish,
Ishmael has the pleasure of scrutinizing a whale whose interiors are
actually turned into a shrine and whose bones serve as the joists and
beams of a peculiar site of worship.

Here too, as in "The Right Whale's Head-Contrasted View," Melville literalizes the interpretive strategies of biblical criticism. Investi-
gating Jonah's psalm and its hidden mythical layers is not an abstract
scientific endeavor but something that Ishmael can supposedly carry
out literally as he explores the ins and outs of the Arsacidean temple. The sacred vertebrae of the Arsacidean whale, he discovers, are
not as lifeless as one would assume, for they are covered by luscious
green boughs and fresh verdure, "woven" by the invisible hand of nature. It is a scene of mysterious, mythical regeneration, in which the
sacred marriage of the "grim god" of Death and "youthful Life" be-
gets "curly-headed glories" among the bones of the worshiped skeleton
(450). Christ's resurrection is not the only episode comparable to Jonah's ascent from the deep. There is an array of pagan myths, Melville
intimates, in the bowers of the Arsacides and beyond, whose notions
of regeneration are far more relevant to understanding the enigma of
Jonah given that they position the whale at their center and are located
in the wild, uncivilized zones of nature.

Comparative religion, for Melville, not only reveals an affinity
between the fundamental questions that preoccupy all cultures—
whether monotheistic or polytheistic—but also uncovers their common flaws. Much like its Western counterparts, Arsacidean religion
is led by manipulative institutional agents who are blind to the depth
of their traditions. Natural sublimity does not seem to suffice for the
Arsacidean priests. They insist on adding special effects to nature's invisible hand. Artificial smoke—which they claim is genuine—ascends
"from where the real jet had issued" to reinforce the impact of the
awesome skeleton of the whale on the devotees. The priests' desire
for control becomes all the more absurd when they attempt to prevent

Ishmael from measuring the whale's skeleton with a green measuring rod: "'How now'! they shouted, 'Dar'st thou measure this our god! That's for us!'" (450).

Not only institutional religion is mocked here. The priests are a parodic parallel of biblical scholars as well. The latter, like the former, assume that the ultimate key to scriptural truths is in their hands. But biblical scholarship, like any mode of interpretation, has its limits. No one can exhaust the potential meanings of Jonah or any other biblical text for that matter. Even in an age in which great fish may be inspected from within and measured meticulously—whether by whalers or scholars—their inscrutability does not diminish.

Throughout this book I focus on Melville's juggling of biblical characters, but one should bear in mind that he is deeply indebted to other poetic aspects of the biblical text, among them catalogues and blueprints. The detailed measuring of the whale skeleton in "A Bower in the Arsacides" (which Ishmael elaborates in the next chapter "Measurement of the Whale's Skeleton") leads us through Jonah to the detailed representations of the Tabernacle and the Temple. These are not minor sections in the Bible. Many chapters in Exodus (25–31, 35–40) and in Kings (5–6) are devoted to the minute features of such sacred structures. "And the house, that is, the temple before it, was forty cubits long. . . . And the oracle he prepared in the house within, to set there the ark of the covenant of the Lord. And the oracle in the forepart was twenty cubits in length, and twenty cubits in breadth, and twenty cubits in the height thereof" (1 Kings 6:17–20). Every cubit of the Tabernacle and the Temple needs to be measured with utmost care. Their very sacredness depends on an aesthetics of precision, wherein measured materiality paradoxically bears witness to the deity who transcends it.

Melville's fascination with biblical catalogues may have been enhanced by the mystical embellishment of this genre. Thus, *Shi'ur Koma* (Measure of the Body), one of the earliest texts of Jewish mysticism that had a great deal of impact on Gnostic writers as well, sets out to measure the body of God.[34] It enumerates the fantastic measurements of his body parts: head, limbs, fingers, and toes, as well as esoteric parts such as the black of his right eye. The basic measurement on which all calculations is based is $236 \times 10,000$ leagues (terrestrial leagues rather than celestial ones). Despite its provocative anthropomorphism, the theory, as Gershom Scholem claims, "does not imply that God in Himself possesses a physical form, but only that a form of this kind may be ascribed to 'the Glory,' which in some passages is called *guf ha-Shekhina* ('the body of the Divine Presence')."[35] The primary source for the catalogues of *Shi'ur Koma* is the description of the beloved in the Song of Songs (5:10–16), but the detailed lists of measurements resemble the meticulous descriptions of the Tabernacle and the Temple.

Ishmael copies the dimensions of the Arsacidean sacred skeleton "verbatim" from his right arm, where he had them tattooed, finding "no other secure way of preserving such valuable statistics" (451). He admits having left other parts of his body as a blank page for a poem he was then composing. Ishmael does not merely imitate Jonah; he becomes a Jonah whose body merges with the body of the monstrous-divine whale and whose poem is, as it were, modeled on the measurements of the inscrutable creature. Gilles Deleuze suggests that "Melville invents a foreign language that runs beneath English and carries it off: it is the OUTLANDISH or Deterritorialized, the language of the Whale." His whale language seeks "to set free at least a skeleton of the inhuman or superhuman originary language[,] . . . to sweep up language in its entirety, sending it into flight, pushing it to its very limit in order to discover its Outside, silence or music."[36] Ishmael, I would suggest, attempts to invent the primary inhuman-superhuman "foreign language" of the whale with Jonah, regarding the prophet's psalm in the silent belly of the deep as a primary, albeit immeasurable, "skeleton" of this language.

Through his obsessive meditations on Jonah, Ishmael highlights the ways in which other crew members of the *Pequod* take part in exploring the scholarly questions regarding life in the interiors of the great fish in a curiously literal fashion. Tashtego, who is buried alive in the head of a whale, as well as Queequeg, who dives in to rescue him from drowning within the creature, are two additional Jonah-like characters. Tashtego and Queequeg are not preoccupied with the history of a prophet who is unknown within the contours of their respective religions, but they too, as whalers, end up following the hazardous and alluring road Jonah took.

Ahab provides yet another curious enactment of the reading strategies of biblical scholars, specifically, of biblical geographers. In "The Chart" he leans over yellowish wrinkled sea charts intently studying "the various lines and shadings which there met his eye," tracing "additional courses over spaces that before were blank" (198). Unlike scholarly exegetes, however, Ahab is intent on actually sailing through the courses he marks in his maps and goes so far as to circumvent the Cape of Good Hope in his search for the course of Moby Dick. The "lines and course" that mark "the chart of his forehead" as the pewter lamp rocks with the motion of the ship remind us that any cartographic pursuit is ignited, above all, by the ever-changing inscapes of the mind.

PIP: DEFIANCE IN THE MIDST OF SEAS

One of Melville's sharpest swerves from Kitto's *Cyclopedia* lies in his rendition of Jonah's rebellion against God. His are unrepentant Jonahs who sail in "forbidden seas" with no intention to return to "slavish shores." Eadie's position is undoubtedly different. Like Father Mapple, he endorses the traditional Calvinist condemnation of Jonah's rebellion. But whereas the old preacher deals with the prophet's "sins" in theological terms, Eadie bases his reservations in medical-psychiatric discourse.

Jonah's attempt "to flee from the presence of the Lord," Eadie writes, "must have sprung from a partial insanity, produced by the excitement of distracting motives in an irascible and melancholy heart. The temerity and folly of the fugitive could scarcely be credited, if they had not been equalled by future outbreaks of a similar peevish and morbid infatuation. The mind of Jonah was dark and moody, not unlike a lake which mirrors in the waters the gloomy thunderclouds which overshadow it, and flash over its sullen waves a momentary gleam."[37] In this case study of Jonah, the prophet's dubious conduct discloses a sick mind—"partially insane," "melancholy," and inclined to recurrent "outbreaks" (a euphemism for Jonah's recurrent death wishes)—for which the ever-changing reflection of "gloomy thunderclouds" (a rare poetic digression in Eadie's text) serves as a metaphor.

Yet there is a remedy for the prophet's disease, as Eadie indicates at a later point: "Under the shadow of a gourd prepared by God he reclined, while Jehovah taught him by the growth and speedy death of this plant, and his attachment to it, a sublime lesson of patient and giving generosity."[38] Eadie sees no value in, or justification for, Jonah's rebellion. It is the product of a mental weakness that is ultimately cured by the all-merciful God, who treats his patient with utmost benevolence and generosity. The underlying plot, then, is one of mad rebellion, forgiveness, and repentance.

Melville's reading of Jonah offers a critique of this plot. The *Pequod* Jonahs may be partially insane and melancholy—and Melville, like Eadie, is fascinated by the psychological dimension of the text—but there is a system in their madness: the God with whom they quarrel is anything but benevolent and merciful. The monomaniacal Ahab, who chases the whale that devoured his leg in *nomine diaboli,* is the most defiant Jonah aboard the *Pequod,* but Pip's history is even more pertinent to the understanding of Melville's radical reading of the mad-melancholy aspect in Jonah.[39]

Pip, the "castaway," is the Jonah of the abyss, the one who best captures the wounds that mark the prophet's history.[40] He is a black boy who has one of the lowliest positions aboard the *Pequod;* indeed, during a whale chase, the crew deserts him in the vast expanses of the sea when he fails to cling to the boat. "Stick to the boat," says Stubb to Pip. "We can't afford to lose whales by the like of you; a whale would sell for thirty times what you would, Pip, in Alabama" (413).

When Pip is finally picked up by the crew after being left for many hours on his own, he is no longer the lively, brilliant Pip who danced with a tambourine in the forecastle scene but rather "an idiot, such at least, they say he was":

> The sea had jeeringly kept his finite body up, but drowned the infinite of his soul. Not drowned entirely, though. Rather carried down alive to wondrous depths, where strange shapes of the unwarped primal world glided to and fro before his passive eyes; and the miser-merman, Wisdom, revealed his hoarded heaps; and among the joyous, heartless, ever-juvenile eternities, Pip saw the multitudinous, God-omnipresent, coral insects, that out of the firmament of waters heaved the colossal orbs. He saw God's foot upon the treadle of the loom, and spoke to it; and therefore his shipmates called him mad. So man's insanity is heaven's sense. (414)

For Melville, a black Jonah is the ultimate victim of God's harsh hand, much as he is the ultimate scapegoat of his shipmates.[41] He is a Jonah whose sufferings are so acute that he never recovers after being cast into the surging sea. "Jonah from de belly ob de whale/And de Hebrew children from de fiery furnace/And why not every man?" asks an African American spiritual.[42] Whether or not Melville was familiar with such spirituals, his black Jonah is one who seeks deliverance in vain.

Pip's affinity with the biblical prophet is evident not only in his being cast away but also in the prophetic powers he acquires after witnessing and speaking to God's indifferent foot in the deep. In surviving, he becomes an agonized seer who can envision the return of the abyss in grand scale when the ship as a whole will be lost in the depths. Pip tries to convey his prophetic vision in his interpretation

of the doubloon. His "crazy-witty" discourse may be as "undecipherable as the doubloon," claims Carolyn Karcher, "but it heralds the
Pequod's watery end" and foretells the revenge of the White Whale.[43]
Nailed to the mast, the much-desired doubloon, says Pip in his mad
split oracular vision ("I look, you look, he looks," 434), is a sign of the
forthcoming "nailing" of the ship by the White Whale. The deification of the white in America at the expense of blacks will ultimately
lead the ship of state to the brink.

Pip rages against heaven. How can one trust a God who "goes 'mong
the worlds blackberrying," picking blacks as "berries" to be "cooked"
mercilessly (435)? How can one be a seer of a God who holds no clear
line of retribution? How can one be a prophet in a world where the
wicked all too often are spared, making the messengers of God seem
like rumbling fools?

Melville's highlighting of the unsettling questions raised by the
Book of Jonah has no echo in the biblical scholarship of his time, but,
interestingly, it does anticipate a central interpretive line in late-twen-
tieth-century biblical criticism, where the Book of Jonah is associated
for the first time with genres such as satire, farce, parody, irony, and
even the absurd. Thus James Ackerman regards it as a satiric reading
of prophecy, E. M. Good as a drama about divine absurdity, and Terry
Eagleton as a surrealist farce.[44] Eagleton's essay is particularly relevant
in this regard. Eagleton begins by defining the paradoxes of prophetic
discourse. "The only successful prophet," he argues, "is an ineffectual
one, one whose warnings fail to materialize. All good prophets are
false prophets, undoing their own utterances in the very act of produc-
ing them."[45] Living with such paradoxes makes the life of the prophet
one of unending torment. Jonah is furious "because he feels he has
been shamelessly used as a pawn in God's self-mystifying game; and
it is this which plunges him into the existential *angst* and nausea we
find overwhelming him at the end of the narrative. . . . If disobedience
on the scale of Nineveh goes cavalierly unpunished, then the idea of
obedience also ceases to have meaning. God's mercy simply makes a
mockery of human effort, which is why Jonah ends up in the grip of
Thanatos or the death drive."[46]

The focal point of Eagleton's essay is the final tense exchange between Jonah and God in Jonah 4. Jonah's psalm in the belly of the fish
was the opening note of his dialogue with God, but this dialogue does
not remain harmonious for long. Seeing his prophecy crumbling down
instead of the city, Jonah protests with despair and anger:

But it displeased Jonah exceedingly, and he was very angry. And he prayed unto the Lord, and said, I pray thee, O Lord, was not this my saying, when I was yet in my country? Therefore I fled before unto Tarshish: for I knew that thou art a gracious God, and merciful, slow to anger, and of great kindness, and repentest thee of the evil. Therefore now, O Lord, take, I beseech thee, my life from me; for it is better for me to die than to live. Then said the Lord, Doest thou well to be angry? So Jonah went out of the city, and sat on the east side of the city, and there made him a booth, and sat under it in the shadow, till he might see what would become of the city. And the Lord God prepared a gourd, and made it to come up over Jonah, that it might be a shadow over his head, to deliver him from his grief. So Jonah was exceeding glad of the gourd. But God prepared a worm when the morning rose the next day, and it smote the gourd that it withered. And it came to pass, when the sun did arise, that God prepared a vehement east wind; and the sun beat upon the head of Jonah, that he fainted, and wished in himself to die, and said, It is better for me to die than to live. And God said to Jonah, Doest thou well to be angry for the gourd? And he said, I do well to be angry, even unto death. Then said the Lord, Thou hast had pity on the gourd, for the which thou hast not laboured, neither madest it grow; which came up in a night, and perished in a night: And should not I spare Nineveh, that great city, wherein are more than sixscore thousand persons that cannot discern between their right hand and their left hand; and also much cattle? (Jon. 4)

Eagleton reads the gourd scene as "a grisly parody of Jonah's black despair" in which God capriciously alternates between being merciful and cruel—providing shade only to snatch it away. This tantalizingly "gratuitous" game, however, does have therapeutic value. "It's in that sheer unfounded gratuitousness of meaning, that abyss of all signification, that God, brutally, therapeutically, rubs Jonah's nose."[47] Eagleton's notion of God's therapeutic methods is the very antithesis of Eadie's reading of the gourd scene. If Eadie insists on the restoration of meaning by means of God's "sublime lesson of patient and giving generosity," Eagleton treats the "abyss of all signification" as the only pedagogical message of divine therapy.

Pip is not only a castaway Jonah. He is also a Job of sorts, an innocent sufferer who is unwilling to accept the blows that have been inflicted upon him with no apparent justification. Melville, in fact, anticipates another predominant twentieth-century interpretive line in combining the impatience of Jonah with that of Job. Jonah and Job, whom no nineteenth-century biblical encyclopedia would regard as impatient (Kitto is but one prominent example) or place together, become in contemporary criticism the two great questioners of biblical tradition.[48] Jonah questions divine mercy while Job questions divine judgment; both, however, are preoccupied with the same fundamental problem: the discrepancy between the law of retribution and reality.

Melville is ahead of his times in reading Jonah as a text that questions the arbitrariness of divine rule, but he is by no means detached from the political exegetical battles of antebellum America. In using scriptural texts to highlight the agonies of blacks, he joins forces with Theodore Parker. "It is known to you all," writes Parker in his "Sermon of Slavery," "that there are some millions of these forlorn children of Adam[,] . . . men whom the Bible names 'of the same blood' with the prophets and apostles" who "are held in this condition and made to feel the full burden of a corrupt society, and doomed from their birth to degradation and infamy . . . for the general and natural effect of slavery is to lessen the qualities of a man in the slave."[49] Pip is, at it were, of "the same blood" with Jonah, but he has been made to feel "the full burden of a corrupt society" that has turned a deaf ear to the miseries of its forlorn black shipmates.

MEDITATING ON A BUOYANT COFFIN

Moby-Dick ends with Ishmael's reflections on a buoyant coffin in the midst of the sea. He is the only Jonah who survives to deliver a prophetic warning to antebellum America-Nineveh of the terrible disaster that lies ahead. Melville may have been skeptical as to his capacity to deliver a prophecy that would have the power of Jonah's (the immediate acceptance of Jonah's warning by Nineveh is surely the most miraculous moment in the text), but he strives against all odds to "sound those unwelcome truths. . . . To preach the Truth to the face of Falsehood!" (47–48), as Mapple puts it in the final pitch of his sermon.[50]

Ishmael's mode of deliverance leads us back to Kitto. He floats on the buoyant coffin Queequeg had made for him until the ship *Rachel* picks him up. These means of rescue are curious allusions to the hypotheses on the fish as synonymous with an "inflated bag" or a "vessel" in Eadie's entry on Jonah. The buoyant coffin and the ship supposedly serve as more realistic modes of deliverance than the wondrous great fish, but Melville does not refrain from adding a miraculous-mythical quality to this final scene, challenging yet again biblical scholars' insistence on setting clear boundaries between history and myth, between monotheistic traditions and polytheistic ones. To begin with, the coffin is covered with hieroglyphic marks of a "departed prophet" and seer of Queequeg's island, whose heathen "mystical treatise on the art of attaining truth" (480) seems to merge here with Jonah's prophecy. But there is more. No predator—no terrifying marine creature with tremendous jaws—haunts him. The sharks that glide past him are "unharming," "as if with padlocks on their mouths," and "the savage sea-hawks sailed with sheathed beaks" (573). The identity of the magical hand that blocks these mouths and beaks remains obscure, but it is inexplicably there, allowing Ishmael to deliver his words.

Here as elsewhere, Melville reflects on Kitto while reflecting on Jonah. Commentary and metacommentary seem to be something of a "life-preserver" one cannot do without, an indispensable source for hope and regeneration in the lonely, vast, merciless expanses of the sea.

CHAPTER 3

"Call Me Ishmael"

The Bible and the Orient

Wandering in the wilderness, after having escaped her mistress, the Egyptian bondwoman Hagar encounters an angel: "And the angel of the Lord said unto her, Behold, thou art with child, and shalt bear a son, and shalt call his name Ishmael; because the Lord hath heard thy affliction. And he will be a wild man; his hand will be against every man, and every man's hand against him" (Gen. 16:11–12). Ishmael's fate is sealed from conception. He will become a wanderer, living the wild, precarious life of an outcast in the desert, following in his mother's footsteps. But the outskirts of civilization are by no means devoid of divine presence and vigilance. The very name "Ishmael," meaning "God hears," as the angel's naming-speech attests, defines God as one who hearkens to the plight of the wandering outcast.[1] Hagar, in a naming-speech of her own, names the fountain where the angel appeared to her after the "seeing" God whom she saw, Beerlahairoi (16:13–14), marking the map of the wilderness with signs of divine revelation.

"Call me Ishmael," the famous opening words of "Loomings," the first chapter of *Moby-Dick,* call us, out of nowhere, to consider the story of Ishmael, the quintessential biblical outcast. The narrator, who was not named in the preliminary "Extracts" on whales, now erupts unexpectedly with a name and asks to be heard. There may not be a God to hearken to his plight, but we are required to listen, to listen and respond to his address, to call him, as if one could cross the boundaries between the real and the fictional and enter the space of

literature from where his call is delivered, or as if he could find a way
to enter our world and make us hear his voice as a real voice calling
in the wilderness.[2] No angel asks that he be called "Ishmael." It is he
who chooses to assume this name as a point of departure for his tale.
Whatever his given name may be, it is not a fixed name that marks his
life from the outset. Likewise, his typological pen name is anything
but fixed. In saying "Call me Ishmael" rather than "I am Ishmael,"
the narrator implies that he could be called Jonah or Job or any other
biblical name, under other circumstances, in other tales. And in the
course of the voyage he does indeed merge with other biblical outcasts, though his primary identification remains Ishmael.

Ishmael serves as a key model for the adventurous wandering outcast in many of Melville's books—from *Redburn* and *Mardi* to *Pierre,
Israel Potter,* and *Clarel*—but only in *Moby-Dick* does one find a full-
fledged reading of the biblical Ishmael delivered by a narrator-commentator named "Ishmael," whose very definition of narrative is inspired by his chosen biblical namesake.[3] What does it mean to be a
"wild man" whose hand—both the literal and the literary—is against
all? This question preoccupies Ishmael from the very outset:

> Call me Ishmael. Some years ago—never mind how long precisely—
> having little or no money in my purse, and nothing particular to interest
> me on shore, I thought I would sail about a little and see the watery part
> of the world. It is a way I have of driving off the spleen, and regulating
> the circulation. Whenever I find myself growing grim about the mouth;
> whenever it is a damp, drizzly November in my soul; whenever I find
> myself involuntarily pausing before coffin warehouses, and bringing up
> the rear of every funeral I meet; and especially whenever my hypos get
> such an upper hand of me, that it requires a strong moral principle to
> prevent me from deliberately stepping into the street, and methodically
> knocking people's hats off—then, I account it high time to get to sea
> as soon as I can. This is my substitute for pistol and ball. With a philo-
> sophical flourish Cato throws himself upon his sword; I quietly take to
> the ship. There is nothing surprising in this. If they but knew it, almost
> all men in their degree, some time or other, cherish very nearly the same
> feelings towards the ocean with me. (3)

Breaking with normative narrative exposition, Ishmael discloses no
biographical background and no date. The usual calendar, with its set
order of months, is of no interest to him. He goes to sea whenever there
is a "damp, drizzly November in his soul," whenever his inner climate
demands that he leave the melancholy suffocating city streets where

one cannot but succumb to the spleen, ending up at the rear of funerals, behind coffins, or on one's sword, like Cato.[4] Ishmael's wild hand and wild imagination—craving to "knock people's hats off," to use "pistol and ball"—require the open vast horizons of the wilderness. His wilderness, however, is not an arid one, like that of the biblical Ishmael, but rather a watery wilderness, where the ocean determines the beat of life and words—be it "growing grim" or "damp drizzly"—however somber, are set free to become sounds.

I read Melville's positioning of Ishmael as narrator and exegetical guide in *Moby-Dick* not only as a token of his admiration for the biblical Ishmael but also as a comment on the ever-growing perception in nineteenth-century America of the Bible as the product of Oriental imagination and the concomitant construction of the Orient and its inhabitants, the so-called descendants of Ishmael, as indispensable keys to understanding scriptural truths. Emerson ended his "Divinity School Address" in July 1838 with a passionate anticipation "for the hour when that supreme Beauty, which ravished the souls of those Eastern men, and chiefly of those Hebrews, and through their lips spoke oracles to all time, shall speak in the West also."[5] Emerson called for a rekindling of the West by the original Oriental beauty of Scripture, not necessarily suggesting that travel to the East was a prerequisite for such a shift. But for many Americans in the nineteenth century the only way to capture the "true" Oriental significance of biblical figures and biblical scenes was to tour the Holy Land and observe the customs of the contemporary Easterners. Numerous Holy Land travel narratives flooded the American literary market, becoming one of the most popular exegetical genres of nineteenth-century America. It is this genre in particular, I suggest, that is vital to the understanding of Melville's reading of Ishmael in *Moby-Dick*.

Melville's fascination with Holy Land travel narratives is already apparent in his early novels, most notably in a memorable moment in *Redburn* (1849), where Wellingborough Redburn, the Ishmael-like protagonist of the novel, recalls a childhood encounter with an Eastern traveler as he dreams of his own travels to distant lands:[6]

> I very well remembered staring at a man myself, who was pointed out to me by my aunt one Sunday in Church, as the person who had been in Stony Arabia, and passed through strange adventures there, all of which with my own eyes I had read in the book which he wrote, an arid-looking book in a pale yellow cover.

'See what big eyes he has,' whispered my aunt, 'they got so big, because when he was almost dead with famishing in the desert, he all at
once caught sight of a date tree, with the ripe fruit hanging on it.'

Upon this, I stared at him till I thought his eyes were really of an
uncommon size, and stuck out from his head like those of a lobster. I
am sure my own eyes must have magnified as I stared. When church was
out, I wanted my aunt to take me along and follow the traveler home.
But she said the constables would take us up, if we did; and so I never
saw this wonderful Arabian traveler again. But he long haunted me; and
several times I dreamt of him, and thought his great eyes were grown
still larger and rounder; and once I had a vision of the date tree.[7]

The "wonderful Arabian traveler" whom Redburn dreams of is presumably John Lloyd Stephens, whose widely acclaimed *Incidents of
Travel in Egypt, Arabia Petraea and the Holy Land,* published in 1837,
raised the popular level of interest in Bible lands in America (it sold
twenty-one thousand copies within two years).[8] Redburn is charmed,
almost hypnotized, by the eyes of the traveler, struck by the sensation
that to travel through the deserts of Arabia means to become "Arabian," bewitched and bewitching, bearing insights that the conventional church of his aunt could never accept.

In *Redburn* the Orient remains a dream and the topic of "arid-
looking books" (Redburn never actually reaches the Orient), but in
Clarel: A Poem and Pilgrimage in the Holy Land (1876) Melville offers
his own, notoriously difficult Holy Land travel narrative, based on his
experience as traveler in Palestine during a three-week visit in 1857.

Hilton Obenzinger's *American Palestine* offers a groundbreaking
reading of Melville's *Clarel* and Mark Twain's *The Innocents Abroad:
or, The New Pilgrim's Progress* (1869) in the context of Holy Land
travel literature, part of what he calls a "Holy Land mania," a nineteenth-century American obsessive preoccupation with Palestine.
"Travel to Palestine," writes Obenzinger, "allowed Americans to 'read
sacred geography,' to experience an exegetical landscape at the mythic
core of Anglo-America's understanding of its own covenantal mission
as a New Israel."[9] If the Puritans in the seventeenth century projected
biblical landscapes onto American landscapes, in the nineteenth century the opposite possibility arose: to redefine America's biblical heritage through the landscapes of Palestine. Melville's "dark pilgrimage,"
with its voyage into the heart of failure and desolation in the Holy
Land, and Twain's satiric travelogue, with its mockery of American
naïveté, provide narratives that are "among the *least* representative"
insofar as they run counter to the dominant typologies,[10] undermining

the all too prevalent assumptions of American exceptionalism in Holy Land travel narratives.

While *Clarel* has received much attention in recent years in studies of nineteenth-century American travel to Palestine, *Moby-Dick*'s relevance to this field has gone unnoticed.[11] At first sight, *Moby-Dick* seems indeed to have nothing in common with Holy Land travel literature, given that it is located in the midst of seas, far from any land, sacred or profane. But Melville invites us from the very opening pages of *Moby-Dick* to open up our notion of "sacred geography" and to replace the Holy Land with the Holy Sea. "Why did the old Persians hold the sea holy? Why did the Greeks give it a separate deity, and make him the own brother of Jove?" (5) are among Ishmael's primary questions. Although the sea is a foreign zone within normative biblical geography—the desert and the mountains are the privileged sites of revelation—it has the potential of becoming a sacred realm, as indeed other non-Christian cultures, be they the old Persians or the Greeks, did not fail to acknowledge.

Moby-Dick, I want to argue, is a counterpilgrimage that calls for a voyage whose purpose is not to visit the well-known sacred sites of Palestine, Sinai, and Arabia Petra but to seek revelation in what remains uncharted in Holy Land travel narratives: the "wild and distant seas," where the "portentous and mysterious" (7) White Whale roams about. Instead of following in the footsteps of Abraham or Jesus in Jerusalem or the Galilee, Melville's counterpilgrimage calls for a whaling voyage, which begins with the dramatic opening of the "great flood-gates of the wonder-world" and sets out to follow "endless processions of the whale, and, midmost of them all, one grand hooded phantom, like a snow hill in the air" (7). The pursuit of the "grand hooded phantom" of an inscrutable White Whale, though analogous to a wild goose chase, seems to be the ultimate way to approach the inner voyage all pilgrims attempt to realize, albeit in different ways. As Ishmael opens the great floodgates to the sea, he at the same time opens up the gates to an internal wonder world, allowing endless processions of whales to float two by two into his "inmost soul." Ishmael's soul is a gigantic boundless Noah's ark, or a vast inner sea, or perhaps something of Milton's Leviathan: "Hugest of living creatures, on the deep/Stretched like a promontory sleeps or swims,/And seems a moving land; and at his gills/Draws in, and at his trunk spouts out a sea" (xxii). These are "wild conceits," Ishmael admits, but they are the kind of wild imaginings that make Ishmael worthy of his pen name and of his role as guide to the deep.

In *Moby-Dick* the Holy Sea rather than the Holy Land becomes an exegetical screen through which to reflect on the biblical heritage of America, though it is always a transnational America whose history is interrelated with other histories and other cultures.[12] The *Pequod* is an American whaling ship, whose captain and officers are New Englanders (the number of mariners is thirty—the number of states in mid-nineteenth-century America), but its crew, as C.L.R. James has pointed out, are renegades and castaways who come from all over the world, each "living on a separate continent of his own."[13] The *Pequod*'s pilgrimage is accordingly a pilgrimage in which the critique of America's history and destiny is accompanied by moments in which all national affiliations dissolve alongside "the miserable warping memories of traditions and of towns" (190).

I focus on the ways in which Melville's rendition of Ishmael in *Moby-Dick* responds in particular to the representations of Ishmael in the biblical ethnographies of American Holy Land literature. Although Obenzinger has shed much light on Melville's dialogue with Holy Land travel literature, he seldom discusses the specificity of Melville's exegetical choices. Thus, Melville's ongoing fascination with Ishmael—evident in *Clarel* as well—and its relevance to his perception of the Orient receive but little attention.[14] More recently, Timothy Marr, in *The Cultural Roots of American Islamicism,* has devoted an entire chapter to Melville's imaginings of Ishmael, regarding them as an attempt to revise prevalent images of Islam (primarily in millennial discourse).[15] But in the end both Obenzinger and Marr treat literature as a resource for the study of culture. The distinct aesthetic and hermeneutic qualities of Melville's work are relegated to the margins. Neither one of these studies realizes that Melville aspires no less than to redefine what counts as Bible and what counts as interpretation, nor do they acknowledge Melville's profound debt to the questioning of concepts such as chosenness and promise in the biblical text itself—in the story of Ishmael and beyond. My goal, of course, is not to relinquish cultural questions but rather to argue for a reading of *Moby-Dick* that would be attuned to the ways in which literature may respond to cultural phenomena and hermeneutic endeavors.[16]

BIBLICAL ETHNOGRAPHIES: ORIENTAL GUIDES

References to Arabs as the descendants of Ishmael, stamped by their ancestor's character, were common in Holy Land travel narratives. In

Incidents of Travel in Egypt, Arabia Petraea and the Holy Land, Stephens reflects on the Bedouins whom he had encountered at the foothills of Mount Sinai and refers to them as the "sons of Ishmael":

> The sons of Ishmael have ever been the same, inhabitants of the desert, despising the dwellers under a roof, wanderers and wild men from their birth, with their hands against every man, and every man's hand against them. . . . These principal and distinguishing traits of Bedouin character have long been known; but as I had now been with them ten days, and expected to be with them a month longer. . . . I was curious to know something of the lighter shades, the details of their lives and habits; and I listened with exceeding interest while the young Bedouin, with his eyes constantly fixed upon it, told me that for more than four hundred years the tent of his fathers had been in that mountain. Wild and unsettled, robbers and plunderers as they are, they have laws which are as sacred as our own; and the tent, and the garden, and the little pasture-ground are transmitted from father to son for centuries.[17]

Stephens's ethnography, like the ethnographies of many nineteenth-century American travelers to the Holy Land, is based on the biblical text.[18] He reads the customs of the Bedouins in light of the biblical verses on Ishmael, with the assumption that ethnic character, regardless of the chasms of time, remains the same: the sons of Ishmael, like their ancestor, are wanderers and wild men who cannot but despise "dwellers under roof."

The most influential advocate of such biblical ethnography, one with whom Stephens maintained an intricate dialogue, was the Scottish divine, Alexander Keith, whose book *The Evidence of Prophecy* set out to map the literal fulfillment of biblical prophecies in the Holy Land. Among the bearers of such prophecies, according to Keith, were the Arabs, the living embodiment of what "was prophesied concerning Ishmael:—'He will be a wild man; his hand will be against every man; and every man's hand will be against him.'"[19] Keith relies on several accounts in defining the character of "The Arabs" (as the chapter is titled), among them, the account of a "recent traveler" and "eye-witness," R. K. Porter, whose premises confirm his own: "And that an acute and active people, surrounded for ages by polished and luxurious nations, should, from their earliest to their latest times, be still found a wild people, dwelling in the presence of all their brethren, (as we may call these nations,) unsubdued and unchangeable, is indeed a standing miracle,—one of those mysterious facts which establish the truth of prophecy."[20]

The miracle of unchanging ethnic character is all the more remarkable for Keith given that the Arabs are unwitting bearers of such prophecies. On describing at an earlier point in the book a particularly violent Arab tribe that dwells on the border of the land of Edom (which was cursed in the Bible and whose unending desolation and inaccessibility to travelers is regarded by Keith as further evidence of prophetic truth), Keith comments, "And hence, while they used unconsciously the very words of one prophecy, their universal character, as well as their conduct, bear witness to another, 'It shall be called the border of wickedness.'"[21] In its attacks on all those who venture to set foot in the land of Edom, this tribe "unconsciously" fulfills both the "universal character" of Ishmael and the prophecies of doom concerning Edom (primarily Isa. 34:5, 10–17; Ezek. 35:7).

For Stephens, however, Keith's literal exegesis holds only up to a point. Stephens's insistence on traveling through the land of Edom to Petra, dressed in Oriental clothes and disguised as a merchant from Cairo, is undoubtedly his most provocative challenge to Keith, but his critique is also evident in his reflections on the sons of Ishmael, where, careful not to undermine the validity of the biblical prophecy concerning Ishmael, he suggests that in addition to the well-known traits of this people, there are unknown ones that need to be explored. The sons of Ishmael may be wild robbers, but they have sets of laws and customs that are no less respectable than those known within the so-called civilized world.

An adventurous traveler inspired by American frontier literature, Stephens was also seeking something other than evidence of fulfilled biblical prophecies. He was eager to engage in long conversations with the Bedouins of Sinai, to learn about the "lighter shades" of their habits of life. Sisters, he learns, remain with their brothers until they are married. And "if the brothers did not choose to keep a sister with them, what became of her?" asks Stephens, only to find that his question is absolutely incomprehensible within the moral framework of that tribe. "It is impossible—she is his own blood," the young Bedouin claimed repeatedly. Even plunder has its rules. To the question if they paid tribute to the pasha (given that they regard God alone as their governor), the Bedouin answered, "No, we take tribute from him. . . . We plunder his caravans."[22]

The attempt to reinterpret Ishmael's role is carried on in later American travel narratives such as William C. Prime's renowned *Tent Life in the Holy Land* (1857). "I have traveled seven months among Mussulman people of every name and shade," writes Prime. "I had carried large sums of money, some of the time in open baskets [and] . . . had left my boat or my tents often without other guard than my Arab servants[,] . . . and have never lost a farthing by the dishonesty of a follower of Mohammed. . . . An Arab, finding you traveling through his country as a stranger, without having applied to his tribe for permission and protection, regards you as an enemy, open to plunder. Such is the law of his fathers, even to Ishmael. But once having placed yourself under his protection, or confided in his honor, you are safer than in your own house in New York."[23] Here too the biblical assertion regarding Ishmael is not refuted, though the experience of traveling in Palestine generates new possibilities of defining the conditions under which Genesis is valid, especially for those who are capable of drawing fresh analogies between tent life in Palestine and everyday life in New York.

The preoccupation with Ishmael was part of a broader framework of biblical ethnographies in Holy Land travel narratives. Travelers often regarded the contemporary inhabitants of Palestine as unwitting witnesses not only of the outcasts but also of the chosen ones. The study of Arab customs and practices, or even appearance, was perceived as a window to understanding major scenes in the lives of the patriarchs, of the wandering Israelites, or of Jesus and his followers. Seeing an Arab sitting on a rock, Stephens observes, "Like almost every old man one meets in the East, he looked exactly the patriarch of the imagination, and precisely as we would paint Abraham, Isaac, or Jacob."[24] Similarly, Sarah Haight, the "Lady of New York" who sent letters from the "Old World," likens her "treading in the soil of Palestine" to stepping into a "theatre of so many mighty events," where one can fancy seeing in "every face a patriarch, and in every warrior chieftain an apostle."[25] Traveling in the Holy Land was synonymous with walking between the lines of an illuminated Bible, where the locals reenact through their daily practices the text and accompanying images.

In *Innocents Abroad,* Twain records such exegetical scenes with characteristic humor. Watching two men kissing in an Arab village in the Galilee, he claims to have gained new insight into what had always seemed to him "a far-fetched Oriental figure of speech," namely, "the circumstance of Christ's rebuking a Pharisee or some such character, and reminding him that from him he had received no 'kiss of welcome.'" "It did not seem reasonable to me," writes Twain, "that men should kiss each other, but I am aware now that they did. There was reason in it, too. The custom was natural and proper; because people must kiss, and a man would not be likely to kiss one of the women of this country of his own free will and accord. One must travel and learn.

Every day now old Scriptural phrases that never possessed any significance for me before take to themselves a meaning."[26] Even Twain, who
thrives on laying bare the absurdity of the quest for biblical truths
in Palestine, is moved by the possibility of finding new significance
in scriptural phrases through ethnographic observation. Kissing men,
he discovers, may have a different significance in an Oriental context,
where the kissing of women is strictly forbidden. And kissing, Twain
observes, is something people (i.e., men) "must" do.

The inhabitants of Palestine held a privileged position in scientific
studies as well. In *Biblical Researches in Palestine, Mount Sinai and
Arabia Petraea* (1841), a curious cross between biblical scholarship
and travel literature, Edward Robinson remapped biblical sites by examining biblical residues in Arabic place-names. E. Smith, his fellow
traveler, meticulously wrote down some of the undocumented Arab
place-names, attempting to record the exact pronunciation of his Arab
interviewees.[27] For Robinson, "common people" (rather than monks)
were the most reliable source of information, the only ones to have
truly preserved the ancient names of biblical times:

> This is a truly national and native tradition, not derived in any degree
> from the influence of foreign convents or masters, but drawn in by the
> peasant with his mother's milk, and deeply seated in the genius of the
> Semitic languages. The Hebrew names of places continued current in
> their Aramaean form long after the times of the New Testament; and
> maintained themselves in the mouths of the common people.... Af-
> ter the Muhammedan conquest, when the Aramaean language gradu-
> ally gave place to the kindred Arabic the proper names of places, which
> the Greeks could never bend to their orthography, found here a ready
> entrance; and have thus lived on upon the lips of the Arabs, whether
> Christian or Muslim, townsmen or Bedawin, even unto our own day,
> almost in the same form in which they have also been transmitted to us
> in the Hebrew Scriptures.[28]

Robinson depicts a genealogy of "common people"—from the peasants who spoke Aramean in the times of the New Testament to contemporary Arabs whose language is akin to Aramaic—who in their innocent, childlike manner maintained the living truth "upon their lips"
with their "mother's milk."

In addition to their exegetical role, Arabs were often guides in the
literal sense of the word. Pilgrims rarely traveled on their own. Dragomans in Oriental costume, turbans, and rifles led the way from Jaffa to
Jerusalem, the Dead Sea, and other popular pilgrimage sites. At times
the dragomans themselves were perceived as taking part in the sacred

theater of the Holy Land. Prime's dragoman, who falls ill by the side of the road, reminds him of a picture of the Good Samaritan. Stephens goes so far as to rely on his Bedouin guide, Toualeb, in his attempt to find the authentic site of the crossing of the Red Sea. Toualeb, he recounts with some amusement, was as sure of his identification of the site as if he were there when it happened and could see, until this very day, on still nights, the "ghost of Pharaoh himself, with the crown upon his head, flying with his chariot and horses over the face of the deep."[29]

DISLOCATING ISHMAEL

Combining the two grand passions of his life—travel and exegesis—Melville could not but welcome Holy Land travel literature. Like Stephens, Haight, and Prime, he never ceases to be compelled by the unique pleasures of traveling in an exegetical landscape. What could be more intriguing than to explore hermeneutic problems through travel? What could be more excitingly intense (especially for a writer) than to travel in a Book whose characters unfold before the eyes of the voyagers as they, in their turn, become characters in it?

Yet his admiration is not uncritical. Melville probably would have endorsed Edward Said's critique of Western pilgrimages for overlooking the contemporary Orient in their quest for the ancient layers of biblical realities. "All pilgrimages to the Orient," writes Said, "passed through, or had to pass through, the Biblical lands; most of them in fact were attempts either to relive or to liberate from the large, incredibly fecund Orient some portion of Judeo-Christian" actuality.[30] Melville complicates the matter, however, by suggesting that such blindness often prevails in a culture's interpretation of itself as well. By juxtaposing the exegetical practices of Holy Land travel literature to those of traditional American typology, he seems to intimate that both the projection of biblical dramas on Arab peasants in Palestine and the glorification of figures in American history through their identification with cherished biblical characters (never with biblical sinners or outcasts) are equally detached from reality.

In a move that questions both these modes of exegetical projection, with their respective constructions of biblical lineage (one based on ethnic continuity and the other on spiritual parallels), *Moby-Dick*'s Ishmael is not an Oriental who wanders about in the plains of the East but rather a white American whaler. As the name of a biblical outcast and one that became part and parcel of the definition of the Islamic Orient,

FIGURE 5. Thomas Hicks's portrait of Bayard Taylor, 1855. National Portrait Gallery, Smithsonian Institution/Art Resource, NY.

"Ishmael" could not be used—as "Abraham" and "Moses" could—to corroborate the image of America as a New Israel. Wearing Oriental costumes, as American travelers to the Holy Land often did (Bayard Taylor, author of *The Land of the Saracen,* went so far as to give lectures on his return from the Holy Land in full Arab dress; fig. 5), was a daring yet acceptable cross-dressing, but bearing the name "Ishmael" would have been perceived as endangering the very core of American identity (there is no instance of the name in the *Nantucket Vital Records*).[31] For Melville, however, who believes in no consistency whatsoever in individual character let alone in collective character, "Ishmael" is a vital name and a text that needs to be regarded differently both in the context of American typology and in that of Holy Land travel literature.

Melville attempts to go further than Stephens in correcting the all too common unfavorable readings of Ishmael in Holy Land travel literature and beyond.[32] He does not merely provide a respectful account of the untamed customs of Ishmael's sons but rather calls upon us to see wild life on the outskirts of civilization as superior to any settled mode of living. Melville's Ishmael in *Moby-Dick* is by no means an unconscious bearer of biblical prophecies or an unwitting exegetical guide but a narrator-commentator who adopts "Ishmael" as namesake in an attempt to explicate life in the oceanic wilderness. "But as in landlessness alone," claims Ishmael, "resides the highest truth, shoreless, indefinite as God—so, better is it to perish in that howling infinite, than be ingloriously dashed upon the lee, even if that were safety!"(107). To wander in the "howling infinite" of the ocean—a play on the definition of the wilderness in Deuteronomy 32:10 as a "howling wilderness"—means to be closer to the "shoreless" truth of divine infinity precisely because of the indefinite, ever-changing nature of seascapes. Death is preferable to the illusory safety of the civilized lee shore.

THE EVERYDAY LIFE OF WHALERS

With a keen ethnographic eye, Ishmael is eager to consider what being a "wild man" may mean through ongoing meditations on his fellow wandering whalers. To explore Ishmael's character, we discover, one need not necessarily travel to the Orient to study the customs of Bedouins or Arab peasants. Ishmaels of diverse ethnic backgrounds and religious persuasions may be found on whalers in the oceans of the world. The wonder at the base of Ishmael's biblical ethnography is not the "miracle" of unchanged ethnic character but rather the ever-surprising possibilities of tracing biblical dramas in the daily lives of whalers of every imaginable origin—be they American, Polynesian, Chinese, or European.[33]

Let me add that Melville's critique in this case is directed not only at the biblical ethnographies of Holy Land travel narratives but also against the thriving school of American ethnology, aligned, at the time, with the justification for American slavery and Native American dispossession. By the 1850s, as Otter suggests, "the claim that American racial groups were inherently unequal, the result of separate and hierarchical divine creations, was approaching the status of 'fact.'"[34]

As an observer-participant, Ishmael sets out to interpret both the Ishmael-like inclinations of others and his own. His biblical ethnography, in other words, has a pronounced autoethnographic, self-reflexive dimension. Consider Ishmael's first impressions of the Polynesian Queequeg: "No more my splintered heart and maddened hand were turned against the wolfish world. This soothing savage had redeemed it. There he sat, his very indifference speaking a nature in which there lurked no civilized hypocrisies and bland deceits. Wild he was; a very sight of sights to see; yet I began to feel myself mysteriously drawn towards him. And those same things that would have repelled most others, they were the very magnets that thus drew me. I'll try a pagan friend, thought I, since Christian kindness has proved but hollow courtesy" (51).

Something in the palpably wild appearance and conduct of Queequeg frees Ishmael from his tendency to turn his "maddened hand" against the "wolfish" world, a melancholy variation on "his hand will be against every man and every man's hand against him." Sitting calmly, "a sight of sights," Queequeg reveals a different mode of becoming an Ishmael. He opens up the possibility of opposing "civilized hypocrisies" without a "splintered heart" and without relinquishing the gift of friendship, especially the kind of unconventional friendship that would be an ongoing celebration of the wild side of life.[35]

Or consider Tashtego, the "wild Indian" harpooner from Gay Head, the heir of "proud warrior hunters" who had scoured, "bow in hand, the aboriginal forests of the main." In shaping Tashtego as an Ishmael, Melville may be alluding in particular to the common conflation of Arabs and Indians in Holy Land travel literature—"The Bedouin roams over [the desert of Idumea] like the Indian on our native prairies," writes Stephens—as well as to the common identification of Native Americans as the descendants of the lost tribes of Israel.[36] But, above all, Tashtego is another distinct embodiment of a "wild man." No longer "snuffing in the trail of the wild beasts of the woodland, Tashtego now hunted in the wake of the great whales of the sea; the unerring harpoon of the son fitly replacing the infallible arrow of the sires" (120). Moving from land to sea, from bow to harpoon, Tashtego underscores the lure of the ocean for those whose hunt of beasts is as wild as their target. Always attuned to the aesthetic potential of being wild, Ishmael is drawn to the musicality of Tashtego's hunt, to his capacity to turn the conventional whaler alert on spying whales—"There she blows"—into a wild rhythmic cry—"There she blows! there! there! there! she blows! she blows!" (215).

Everyday life on a whaling ship seems particularly relevant to an understanding of Ishmael given that the biblical Ishmael is not only an untamed wanderer but also a hunter. He becomes a hunter in commemoration of another story of plight in the wilderness. In Genesis 21,

Hagar and Ishmael, then but a child, are forced to leave Abraham's household. Wandering in the wilderness of Beersheba, left with no water, the desperate Hagar "cast the child under one of the shrubs" and sat "over against him a good way off, as it were a bowshot: for she said, Let me not see the death of the child. And she sat over against him, and lift up her voice, and wept. And God heard the voice of the lad; and the angel of God called to Hagar out of heaven, and said unto her, What aileth thee, Hagar? fear not; for God hath heard the voice of the lad where he is. Arise, lift up the lad, and hold him in thine hand; for I will make him a great nation. . . . And God was with the lad; and he grew, and dwelt in the wilderness, and became an archer" (15–20).

Ishmael's vocation as archer captures his misery as a castaway whose weeping mother sat a "bowshot" away, unwilling to witness his death, yet unable to leave. It entails a continuation of the death risk of the plight in the wilderness. But his bow also serves as a mark of divine protection, an endowment of power, indicating that although God has assigned Isaac the privileged position of the chosen son of Abraham, Ishmael too is destined to become a great resilient nation.

Whereas the Bible provides no account of Ishmael's adventures as archer, *Moby-Dick* abounds in detailed depictions of the sorrows and pleasures of the minutest moments in the life of a whale hunter. To come close to losing one's life, to approach "the jaws of death," is a daily experience in the whaling world, where whales are chased in the midst of squalls and whalers are left soaking wet in their small leaking boats, never certain that they will be able to find their way back to the ship or that their fellow mariners will make an effort to rescue them. Illuminating Genesis via the *Pequod*'s whalers is but one of Melville's goals. He strives to do the reverse as well: to fathom the untold realities of mere mariners with the help of scriptural texts.

The *Pequod*'s whalers are wild hunters and adamant pilgrims at once. By undermining the customary demarcation in Holy Land travel literature between pilgrims and indigenous populations, Melville fashions an exegetical voyage in which the ordinary hunting practices of his Ishmael-like whalers are part and parcel of a metaphysical search for the inscrutable White Whale, Moby Dick. In thinking of ways to ensure his crew's ongoing commitment to the chase of the White Whale, Ahab realizes (or so Ishmael surmises) that even "the high lifted and chivalric Crusaders of old times were not content to traverse two thousands miles of land to fight for their holy sepulcher, without committing burglaries, picking pockets, and gaining other pious perquisites by

the way" (212). Ahab's equivalent for the Crusaders' "pious" burglaries is the normative chase of whales as commodities, which he maintains at least in the initial stages of the voyage. But the crew's double
quest—whale hunt and pilgrimage—is not only a result of Ahab's ma-
nipulations and obsessions. Haunted by obsessions of their own, the
daily lives of the *Pequod*'s whalers continuously oscillate between the
two quests. Any lowering of the boats can potentially lead not only to
more blubber but also to the sought for White Whale, whose lure, it
seems, is far greater than that of the Holy Sepulcher in Jerusalem.

FOLLOWING THE TURBANED FEDALLAH:
"THE SPIRIT-SPOUT"

The Orient does have one representative aboard the *Pequod,* Fedallah
the Parsee. Ascending at night to the top of the masthead (the oceanic
equivalent of the camel), the turbaned Fedallah becomes, in the course
of the journey, the *Pequod*'s Oriental guide to the celestial traces of
spirit spouts in the sea:

> It was while gliding through these latter waters that one serene and
> moonlight night, when all the waves rolled by like scrolls of silver; and,
> by their soft, suffusing seethings, made what seemed a silvery silence,
> not a solitude: on such a silent night a silvery jet was seen far in advance
> of the white bubbles at the bow. Lit up by the moon, it seemed celestial;
> seemed some plumed and glittering god uprising from the sea. Fedallah
> first descried this jet. For of these moonlight nights, it was his wont to
> mount to the main-mast head, and stand a look-out there, with the same
> precision as if it had been day. And yet, though herds of whales were
> seen by night, not one whaleman in a hundred would venture a lowering
> for them. You may think with what emotions, then, the seamen beheld
> this old Oriental perched aloft at such unusual hours; his turban and the
> moon, companions in one sky. But when, after spending his uniform in-
> terval there for several successive nights without uttering a single sound;
> when, after all this silence, his unearthly voice was heard announcing
> that silvery, moon-lit jet, every reclining mariner started to his feet as
> if some winged spirit had lighted in the rigging, and hailed the mortal
> crew. "There she blows!" Had the trump of judgment blown, they could
> not have quivered more. (232–33)

A dreamy exegetical scene unfolds during this "moonlight night," in
which the sea is a "silvery scroll" that awaits interpretation. Fedallah, whose turban blends with the moon, is the first to detect the
sudden silvery jet and cry out "There she blows!" The customary

whaler cry sounds on this occasion like the blowing of the "trump of judgment" in messianic times. Chasing the ungraspable phantom of Moby Dick by day is mad enough; doing so at night is sheer madness, an undertaking not "one whaleman in a hundred" would venture to do. But the sheer madness of this somnambulist wild search makes it all the more alluring—"almost every soul on board instinctively desired a lowering."

Half celestial, half demonic, the "old Oriental" spurs the *Pequod*'s crew to venture a lowering, but the silvery jet vanishes. Fedallah's cry turns out to be a delusional cry that leads nowhere. The midnight spout is sighted again on the following nights but remains ungraspable. There were seamen "who swore that whenever and wherever descried; at however remote times, or in however far apart latitudes and longitudes, that unnearable spout was cast by one self-same whale; and that whale, Moby Dick. For a time there reigned too, a sense of peculiar dread at this flitting apparition, as if it were treacherously beckoning us on and on" (233).

Should Fedallah's misleading exegetical practices be seen as an expression of Melville's refusal to regard Orientals as privileged exegetical guides?[37] This is, it seems to me, a plausible reading of the "Spirit-Spout," though one should bear in mind that to begin with Fedallah is not quite the exegetical guide whose goal is to illuminate Christian truths. Dorothee Metlitsky Finkelstein associates Fedallah, whose Arabic name means "the Sacrifice (or Ransom) of God," with Islamic mysticism, primarily Ismailism.[38] Named after Ishmael, Ismailism speaks of a series of Imams (the revealed prophets of Islam who followed Mohammed) that would end with the climactic appearance of the seventh Imam, "the hidden prophet," Ishmael.[39] In one of the branches of the Ismailiya, the devotees were called "Fedais" for their willingness to sacrifice themselves for the sake of religious duty. Whether or not Fedallah's religion bears resemblance to Ismailism, the spirit spouts he discovers seem far closer to treacherous demonic apparitions than to the spirit of the Gospels.[40]

While pointing to the delusional qualities of Fedallah's reading of the silvery sea scrolls, Ishmael is at the same time wholly mesmerized by this exotic Oriental exegetical scene on a moonlit night and by the risky routes it displays. True or false, there is magic in Fedallah that inspires Ishmael to merge his own gaze with that of the old Parsee, much as the latter's turban unites with the moon, and turn his narrative into a spellbinding chain of s sounds—"silvery scrolls," "soft,

suffusing seethings," "silvery silence," "solitude"—all adding resonance to the double *s-p-t* of the "spirit-spout."

THE MASTHEAD OF THE PERPLEXED

There is a good deal of self-irony in Ishmael's depiction of Fedallah.
His own noncanonical exegesis, with its obtrusive departures from
Christian precepts and its imaginary qualities, may be as delusional
in its mesmerizing charm as that of the Parsee. Both, he seems to intimate, are Ishmael-like exegetes whose interpretations may vanish like
wild dreams. What makes Ishmael the narrator a markedly different
exegetical guide from Fedallah is the open skepticism forever evident in
his observations of the numinous. Ishmael is a perplexed guide to the
perplexed. In "The Mast-Head," he admits that he kept "sorry guard"
whenever he was assigned to be at the masthead to spot whales, or, in
whaler lingo, "whales [were] scarce as hen's teeth" when he was up
there. He never ventures, like Fedallah, to announce the coming of any
being, maritime or celestial. "With the problem of the universe revolv-
ing in me," asks Ishmael, "how could I—being left completely to myself at such a thought-engendering altitude,—how could I but lightly
hold my obligations to observe all whale-ships' standing orders, 'Keep
your weather eye open, and sing out every time'" (158). The masthead,
for Ishmael, becomes primarily the mast of the head, a post where one
may be lost in thought to the extent of losing all touch with reality, or
losing one's identity. "There is no life in thee, now, except that rock-
ing life imparted by a gently rolling ship; by her, borrowed from the
sea; by the sea, from the inscrutable tides of God. But while this sleep,
this dream is on ye, move your foot or hand an inch, slip your hold
at all; and your identity comes back in horror" (159). Ishmael "calls"
himself, only to hear the echoes of an unspeakable void as a response.
As "pilgrim-infidel," he experiences his exegetical voyage as taking
place on the horrifying, though unmistakably intoxicating, brink of
meaninglessness and death, where one runs the danger of falling, with
the slightest mistaken move, into the dizzying, inscrutable waters below. Drawn to the wild sublime seas by the "one hooded" grand white
whale, he often faces an epistemological vortex, never fully knowing
what the phantom stands for or whether his pilgrimage can lead to a
more substantive understanding of the "enigma of the whale." The
more Ishmael meditates on this enigma, the more abstract and undecipherable it becomes.

In "The Whiteness of the Whale," the riddle of the White Whale for Ishmael turns out to be the riddle of whiteness. Ishmael enumerates numerous, and at times contradictory, potential meanings of the color, thus experiencing whiteness, as Eyal Peretz suggests, as "an event that overflows with an overwhelming excess, or even explosion, of meaning, and at the same time lacks meaning altogether."[41] Whiteness in *Moby-Dick* touches on the same kind of obstinate "potentiality" Giorgio Agamben traces in Bartleby's "I would prefer not to."[42] If Bartleby opens a zone between "the potential to be (or do) and the potential not to be (or do)," whiteness, for Ishmael, is the ultimate principle of potentiality, so much so that it has the potential of being all colors and not being a color at all.[43] "Or is it," asks Ishmael, "that as in essence whiteness is not so much a color as the visible absence of color, and at the same time the concrete of all colors; is it for these reasons that there is such a dumb blankness, full of meaning, in a wide landscape of snows—a colorless, all-color of atheism from which we shrink?" (195).

THE QUESTION OF THE HOLY SEPULCHER'S AUTHENTICITY: WHALE SHRINES

Skepticism is not absent from American nineteenth-century Holy Land travel literature. Quite the contrary, a streak of doubt regarding the authenticity of holy sites in Palestine is one of its hallmarks. The question of what to do at sites where Oriental truths were obscured by the Catholic Church remained an ongoing preoccupation. Following American biblical geographers such as Edward Robinson, nineteenth-century Protestant travelers were no less eager to erase the stamp of Catholic monks in the Holy Land than to efface the realities of the Orient.

The Holy Sepulcher, Christianity's central shrine, was the most prominent site of uncertainty.[44] Nineteenth-century American travelers often address the question of its authenticity, but, reluctant to omit such a central station from their pilgrim's itinerary, they fashion alternative modes for constructing its holiness. Haight realizes that by entering the Holy Sepulcher one enters a "temple of ecclesiastical barbarism" replete with "monkish frauds," but she still believes in its potential as a true sacred site if one could rescue the authentic landscape of belief beneath the ornaments of the church. "The Sepulcher, as it now exists, is no longer the 'tomb hewn out in the rock' in which Joseph of

Arimathea laid the body of his Lord and master," writes Haight, but
if one were to "make bare the rock, strip it of its marble casing[,]
one then might *see,* and seeing, believe, if this is, in truth, that part of
the mount which, on that awful day 'when the earth did quake and
the rocks were rent,' was torn asunder as this stone is which they have
masoned up in marble."[45]

Twain's renowned debunking of the Holy Sepulcher's authenticity
in *Innocents Abroad* offers a similar strategy of rereading. "When
one stands where the Saviour was crucified, he finds that all he can
do to keep it strictly before his mind that Christ was not crucified
in a Catholic Church," writes Twain. "He must remind himself every now and then that the great event transpired in the open air, and
not in a gloomy, candlelighted cell in a little corner of a vast church,
up-stairs—a small cell all bejeweled and bespangled with flashy or-
namentation, in execrable taste."[46] But he goes beyond the customary
Protestant critique of Catholic idolatry to ridicule the inventiveness of
all sacred sites. While standing by the tomb of the first Adam, conve-
niently located by the tomb of the Second Adam in the Holy Sepulcher,
he bursts out in a mock-sentimental soliloquy (whose most immediate
target is Prime's *Tent Life in the Holy Land*):

> The tomb of Adam! How touching it was, here in a land of strangers, far
> away from home and friends and all who care for me, thus to discover
> the grave of a blood relation. True, a distant one, but still a relation. The
> unerring instinct of nature thrilled its recognition. The fountain of my
> filial affection was stirred to its profoundest depths, and I gave way to
> tumultuous emotion. I leaned upon a pillar and burst into tears. I deem
> it no shame to have wept over the grave of my poor dead relative. Let
> him who would sneer at my emotion close this volume here, for he will
> find little to his taste in my journeyings through Holy Land. Noble old
> man—he did not live to see me—he did not live to see his child. And
> I—I—alas, I did not live to see *him.* Weighed down by sorrow and dis-
> appointment, he died before I was born—six thousand brief summers
> before I was born. But let us try to bear it with fortitude. Let us trust
> that he is better off, where he is. Let us take comfort in the thought that
> his loss is our eternal gain.[47]

How does one account for the need to find distant relatives in Bible
lands? To what absurdities does such invented kinship lead? Twain
mocks the very attempt to construe biblical lineage—whether by biblical ethnographers or within typological frameworks. Given that all
humans can trace their origin back to Adam, there seems to be no
grounds for any definition of ethnic or spiritual specificity for biblical

lineage. And yet despite Twain's comic wailing at Adam's tomb, he ultimately finds the Holy Sepulcher moving, a site that has acquired religious significance through the history of thousands of pilgrims who regarded it as the culmination of their journeys: "With all its clap-trap sideshows and unseemly impostures of every kind, it is still grand, reverend, venerable—for a god died there; for fifteen hundred years its shrines have been wet with the tears of pilgrims from the earth's remotest confines."[48] Authenticity is thus redefined. It is now located in the history of the Holy Sepulcher rather than in its historicity.[49]

Melville's parodies of holy sites in *Moby-Dick* and later in *Clarel* avoid such final confirmation. In this respect, Obenzinger's juxtaposition of Twain and Melville blurs notable differences between the two.[50] It is not accidental that soon after its publication *Innocents Abroad* became a book that was carried by pilgrims in Palestine alongside the Bible, whereas Melville's work never attained such status.

The only sacred sites in *Moby-Dick* are whale shrines that appear on no pilgrim map. They are located in diverse corners of the world and are affiliated with a whole range of religious traditions. In the "Bower of the Arcasides," Ishmael provides a detailed account of his Jonah-like excursion within the skeleton of a Polynesian whale shrine. But he also ruminates on other sites of whale worship. In "The Honor and Glory of Whaling," he refers to Jaffa not as the central port through which nineteenth-century pilgrims (including Melville himself) reached the Holy Land but rather as the locus of an unknown "Pagan temple," where for many years stood the skeleton of a whale, "which the city's legends and all the inhabitants asserted to be the identical bones of the monster that Perseus slew."[51] What seems most significant, he adds, is that "it was from Joppa that Jonah set sail" (362). Perseus's monster and Jonah's big fish are thus commemorated by the same skeleton. Later, in "The Fossil Whale," Ishmael quotes the travel narrative of John Leo, according to which there is an African temple by the sea-shore whose rafters and beams are made of whale bones, and in it one can view a miraculous whale rib of incredible length whose arch is so high that its head cannot be reached, not even "by a Man upon a Camel's Back." From this temple, according to one tradition emerged a Prophet who "prophesy'd of Mahomet," and according to another tradition, this is where "the Prophet Jonas was cast forth by the Whale" (458).[52] Ishmael ridicules the limited scope of the exegetical world of Holy Land travel literature, in which any religion other than Christianity was given little mention, but, above all, he calls into question any attempt to identify bones—whether of whales or saints—and to regard them as venerable objects. Even if holy sites were constructed around whale skeletons (in the best of all Melvillean worlds) such sites, however intriguing, can at best offer only spicy tales.

When the Holy Sepulcher is mentioned explicitly in *Moby-Dick*, it is perceived, as we have seen, as a shrine of the past—the center of Crusade pilgrimages—a site that requires no pilgrimage at present, replaced as it is by an inscrutable White Whale whose ubiquity is part and parcel of his sublimity.[53] A real pilgrimage for Melville is one that avoids the seductions of fetishization, of fixed landscapes and fixed tombs, seeking to dive deep, to come daringly close to primary revelations in the oceanic wilderness, however deadly they may be.[54]

INTERTWINED DESTINIES AND DOOMS

Death in this oceanic pilgrimage is not limited to that of Christ alone. Tashtego's red hand, holding a hammer, is the very last sign of life to emerge from the sinking *Pequod*. Though death is inescapable, the hand of this Native American Ishmael is still out there against all, against all odds, trying to nail the flag to a subsiding spar, ending up nailing to the flag a sky hawk that "chanced to intercept its broad fluttering wing between the hammer and the wood" (572). That the final moment of the *Pequod* is devoted to Tashtego's defiant hand is a reminder that the ship is named after a "celebrated tribe of Massachusetts Indians, now extinct like the ancient Medes" (69).[55] Although Melville sets out to record the plight of all outcasts, he undoubtedly has a special need to bear witness to the cry of the Ishmaels of America. For Melville, the dispossession of Native Americans is one of the darker moments in American history, a moment that is relived in antebellum America through the horrors of slavery and the reinforcement of the Fugitive Slave Law.[56]

While most American travelers to Palestine were proud to post the American flag on their tents or caravans and happy to reaffirm America's Manifest Destiny through their encounter with the Land of the Bible (Stephens discovers on Mount Sinai, of all places, a Greek monk who sings the praises of America), Melville's *Pequod* offers a far more somber flag, one in which the American eagle and the sky hawk of Native American culture seem to be nailed together.[57] Melville, to be sure, lacks no passion in his preoccupation with American destiny, but he is, at the same time, a harsh critic of his contemporaries' understanding of the term and its so-called manifestations. If America will continue to turn a deaf ear to the afflictions of the dispossessed, the only end he can envision for it is as dark as that of the *Pequod*.[58]

Melville's exegetical voyage sets out to lay bare what American travelers failed to chart in their readings of Genesis: the fragile distinctions between Isaac and Ishmael, the interconnectedness of their lives. There are striking similarities between the story of the plight of Hagar and Ishmael in the wilderness (Gen. 21) and the following chapter on the binding of Isaac (Gen. 22). Both stories revolve around a child on the verge of death whose death is prevented at the very last moment through the intervention of an angel. Both stories end with a divine promise of future prosperity.

In Islamic exegesis, the interconnectedness of the two stories was taken a step further in renditions of Ishmael as the intended victim of the binding. According to Al-Tabarsī, Abraham had a vision regarding the sacrifice of Ishmael right after Sarah demanded the expulsion of Hagar and Ishmael. In this vision he was asked to sacrifice Ishmael during the Pilgrimage month in Mecca. With phenomenal devotion, Abraham brought Ishmael with him to perform the Ḥajj and informed him of the divine decree. He then laid him down for the Sacrifice at al-Jamra al Wustā.[59] This is but one of many Islamic commentaries that sought to shape a story of the sacrifice of Ishmael and to turn Mecca into the center of Islamic sacred geographies (the biblical Temple, as one recalls, was constructed on Mount Moriah, where the binding of Isaac took place).

The affinities between Ishmael and Isaac in Genesis resurge in Exodus and Numbers, inscribed in the lives of their descendants. As Phyllis Trible and Yair Zakovitch have noted, there are numerous textual links between the tale of Hagar and Ishmael and the history of ancient Israel.[60] If Hagar, the Egyptian bondwoman, was oppressed by her mistress, Sarah, the Israelites, in an inverted scene of affliction, are oppressed as slaves in Egypt. Hagar runs off to the desert, and so do the Israelites. The wandering Israelites will indeed cross her track on passing through the wilderness of Shur, and they too will find the desert not only a place of acute thirst but also one of divine revelation and intervention.

The boundaries between the chosen and the nonchosen in the biblical text are never as stable and decisive as the discourse of Manifest Destiny would have it.[61] From the very first vision of the nation to be, even before its emergence on the stage of history, it is doomed to exile and slavery. In the Covenant between the Parts, God tells Abraham, "Know of a surety that thy seed shall be a stranger in a land that is not theirs, and shall serve them, and they shall afflict them four hundred years. . . . But in the fourth generation they shall come hither again: for the iniquity of the Amorites is not yet full" (Gen. 15:13–15).[62] The fate of the Israelites is not radically different from that of other nations. Their chosenness does not exempt them from spending many years in the lowly position of oppressed exiles, nor does it assure their unconditional possession of the Promised Land. The divine plan takes into account other peoples as well, which is why the return of Israel to its land will depend, among other things, on the moral conduct of the Amorites. The Amorites have the right to reside in Canaan until their "iniquity" is "full." Only then will God deliver Abraham's descendants out of bondage and lead them back to Canaan.

There are moral flaws that make the nation's privileged position all the more questionable. On Mount Sinai, in the heart of the wilderness, in a grand scene of collective revelation, Israel is designated as a "kingdom of priests" and a "holy nation" (Exod. 19). Forty days later, however, the chosen people forge a Golden Calf and welcome it as the god who had brought them up from the land of Egypt (Exod. 32). God craves to obliterate the "stiffnecked nation" (one of the most resonant titles of ancient Israel) but ends up succumbing to Moses' plea for forgiveness. The covenant is preserved, though not without a series of severe divine punishments: the Calf is ground up and its dust scattered over water (which the people are required to drink), a group of Levites (the tribe of the official priests) massacres three thousand people, and a plague spreads within the camp.

The children of Israel are destined to take possession of the Land God had promised Abraham, Isaac, and Jacob. And indeed they do so after forty years of wandering in the wilderness. Yet their wanderings do not end on settling in Canaan. Their recurrent sins and failure to abide by the Law lead to new exiles. The dislocation that marks Ishmael from birth turns out to be the quintessential experience of Isaac's descendents as well. However central, chosenness remains one of the most obscure and fragile of all biblical concepts.

Melville will return to the question of chosenness and the Abraham cycle in *Billy Budd*. We are told that Captain Vere, the "austere devotee of military duty, letting himself melt back into what remains primeval in our formalized humanity, may in the end have caught Billy to his heart, even as Abraham may have caught young Isaac on the brink of resolutely offering him up in obedience to the exacting behest."[63] Through this hypothetical typology, Billy is likened to Isaac, a moment before the sacrifice. But he is also an untamed Ishmael, whose arm flies swiftly at those who infuriate him. The "binding" of Billy may thus be construed as yet another commentary on the interrelated lives of Abraham's sons. Whether an Isaac or an Ishmael, Billy, the chosen "Handsome Sailor," the center of attention and admiration, is not spared.[64] Captain Vere cherishes Billy's "Primary Nature," to use Deleuze's terms, but he cannot save the innocent, lawless sailor whom he loves, or avoid "the sacrifice of Abraham."[65]

THE FINAL SHOT

No God rescues the *Pequod*. There is but one wild whaler who has the privilege of being delivered like his biblical precursor: Ishmael the narrator. As the ship sinks down and the "great shroud of the sea" (572) rolls over it, the coffin Queequeg had built is "liberated by reason of its cunning spring, and, owing to its great buoyancy, rising with great force, the coffin life-buoy shot lengthwise from the sea, fell over, and floated by [his] side" (573). Queequeg's coffin seems to embody its maker's remarkable hunting skills, shot out of the closing vortex, like an arrow or a grand harpoon hitting its mark, floating by Ishmael as an unexpected gift of life. And Ishmael, who in "Loomings" speaks of his tendency to follow funerals and "pause before coffin warehouses," now finds himself floating on a coffin, trying to spring back to life after the catastrophe. Ishmael is a lonely pilgrim, cast away in "exiled waters," far from the holy sites of the Orient, far from any holy sepulcher. There is no turbaned guide by his side who could explicate the traces of the disaster in the "dirge-like main" or the miraculous phenomena that surround him: the sudden appearance of the buoyant coffin (a wild Ishmael-like version of Christ's resurrection?), the peculiar "unharming sharks," and the "savage sea-hawks" sailing with "sheathed beaks." But he needs no exegetical guide at this point; he is (almost) ready to become one himself. It is a circular ending that marks the emergence of Ishmael's voice as narrator-commentator. "Escaped alone," he now feels driven to tell the tale. Soon he will erupt from nowhere and demand that we call him Ishmael and hearken to tales no one else seems to hear.

CHAPTER 4

Ahab, Idolatry, and the Question of Possession

Biblical Politics

"Oh! He ain't Captain Bildad; no, he ain't Captain Peleg; *he's Ahab,* boy; and Ahab of old, thou knowest, was a crowned king!"

"And a very vile one. When that wicked king was slain, the dogs, did they not lick his blood?"

"Come hither to me—hither, hither," said Peleg, with a significance in his eye that almost startled me. "Look ye, lad; never say that on board the Pequod. Never say it anywhere. Captain Ahab did not name himself. 'Twas a foolish, ignorant whim of his crazy, widowed mother, who died when he was only a twelvemonth old. And yet the old squaw Tistig; at Gayhead, said that the name would somehow prove prophetic. And, perhaps, other fools like her may tell thee the same. I wish to warn thee. It's a lie. I know Captain Ahab well; I've sailed with him as mate years ago; I know what he is—a good man—not a pious, good man, like Bildad, but a swearing good man. . . . So good-bye to thee—and wrong not Captain Ahab, because he happens to have a wicked name. . . . No, no, my lad; stricken, blasted, if he be, Ahab has his humanities!"

"The Ship" (79)

Peleg's warning—not to think of Captain Ahab typologically—needs to be read as anything but literal. This tongue-in-cheek admonition is a self-reflexive moment, which, like "Call me Ishmael," is meant, above all, to urge us to meditate on the grand typological project at stake. Typologies, Melville reminds us, may seem transcendent, but they are finally nothing but the product of human whims and imagination and as such can be best explored within the domain of fiction. As an author, Melville has absolute, divinelike power to determine the fate of his characters and to decide whether or not their names will prove prophetic, whether or not "Ahab" will necessarily be "forever Ahab," forever as doomed as the biblical king whose blood was licked by dogs.[1] Indeed, Melville flaunts his authorial privilege as he supposedly suspends for a moment the possibility of reading Ahab as Ahab. But in ultimately choosing to render Ahab after his biblical namesake, he raises several questions: To what extent do we remain under the rule of scriptural texts, wittingly and unwittingly, with little freedom to escape them? To what extent are we all, like Ahab—who "did not name himself"—subjected to names bestowed upon us? Do commentators own the Bible, or are they possessed by it? Can a writer have impact in a culture saturated by biblical texts and names without responding to them?

The question of the typological affinity between the two Ahabs also calls attention to the complexity of Melville's debt to and departure from the Book of Kings. Melville models Captain Ahab on his notorious biblical namesake much as he endorses the sharp critique of royal rule in Samuel and Kings. But at the same time he ventures to complicate the definition of King Ahab's wickedness in reading the biblical portrayal of Ahab against the grain, spelling out in big strokes the charming and rebellious aspects of the ultimately vulnerable wicked king. Melville's Ahab, to use Peleg's terms, "has his humanities."

NABOTH'S VINEYARD AND THE BIBLE'S CIRCULATION IN POLITICAL DISCOURSE

Melville's reading of Ahab in *Moby-Dick* is inextricably connected with his metacommentary on the numerous evocations of Ahab and the story of Naboth's vineyard in the political discourse on American expansionism. In "*Moby-Dick* and American Political Symbolism," Alan Heimert offers an illuminating account of the common use of 1 Kings 21 in political writings against the imperial implications of America's Manifest Destiny. He quotes a congressman who accused Polk of committing Ahab's "sin of covetousness," reminding the American public that the king of Samaria had been "made to repent in sackcloth" for his "usurpation of another's rights."[2] In 1845 David Lee Child published a pamphlet against Texas annexation titled *The Taking of Naboth's Vineyard*. "So common was the likening of American invasion of other nations' rights to Ahab's aggressions," writes Heimert, "that by 1848 James Russell Lowell, attacking the Mexican War in the *Biglow Papers*, saw no need to amplify when he alluded in his notes to 'Neighbor Naboths.'"[3]

Theodore Parker, it seems to me, provides the sharpest reading of Naboth's Vineyard in this connection. He opens his 1848 sermon on the Mexican War with a "Scripture Lesson," quoting 1 Kings 21:1–19 as his exegetical point of departure. Though he does not refer to Ahab explicitly in the ensuing sermon, his wrath vis-à-vis the atrocities of the Mexican War are all colored by Elijah's memorable cry—"Hast thou killed, and also taken possession?" (1 Kings 21:19)—the final verse cited in the "Scripture Lesson." "It has been a war of plunder," Parker preaches, "undertaken for the purpose of seizing Mexican territory, and extending over it that dismal curse which blackens, impoverishes, and barbarizes half the Union now, and swiftly corrupts the other half."[4] Calling on the people to oppose the war, he imagines their refusal in these terms: "No. We will have no war! If we want more land, we will buy it in the open market, and pay for it honestly. But we are not thieves, nor murderers, thank God, and will not butcher a nation to make a slave-field out of her soil."[5] If in the case of the biblical Ahab one sin was piled upon another—the false accusation of Naboth was followed by his murder and finally by the usurpation of his vineyard—in the context of 1848 America, the plunder and murder were accompanied by the expansion of the "curse" of slavery to new lands.

Ahab is evoked once again in Parker's account of the nation's "chief sin": the notorious 1850 Compromise between the North and the South, following the Mexican War, and its disturbing reenactment of the Fugitive Slave Law. "If I am rightly informed, King Ahab made a law that all the Hebrews should serve Baal. . . . If they served Baal," Parker goes on to argue, "they could not serve the Lord. . . . We are told that Elijah gathered the prophets together; and he came unto all the people, and said, 'How long halt ye? If the Lord be God, follow him; but if Baal, follow him!' Our modern prophet says, 'Obey both. The incompatibility which the question assumes does not exist.' Such is the difference between Judge Elijah and Judge Peleg."[6] Parker calls for a higher ethical order that would not be susceptible to the idolatrous craving for money and material goods that had swept America. The inclination of politicians and judges to yield to their "chief desire," that is, "the desire for wealth," in endorsing the Fugitive Slave Law is in Parker's eye the equivalent of worshiping Baal. Any judge who like Judge Peleg considered a law that demanded the handing in of runaway slaves to their masters as compatible with divine justice did not hearken well to Elijah's warning in the Book of Kings. There are human laws, Parker declares (and he may have been implicitly referring to Naboth's mock trial as well), that one must consider a crime to follow.

Nineteenth-century America witnessed a certain decline in the use of the Bible in political discourse. Antebellum politicians did not evoke Scripture with the same kind of urgency that characterized their precursors. In fact, for the first time there were calls to refrain from regarding the Bible as the authoritative text in political matters. The abolitionist William Lloyd Garrison declared that slavery, the Mexican War, and women's suffrage were not biblical questions since "nothing in regard to controversial matters had ever been settled by the Bible." He was horrified by Zachary Taylor's use of the Bible to justify "giving the Mexicans Hell!" much as he was appalled by the use of Scripture in proslavery discourse. "The God," writes Garrison, "who, in America, is declared to sanction the impious system of slavery . . . is my ideal of the devil."[7]

Yet Garrison's voice was marginal in antebellum America, for biblical texts remained a privileged authoritative source in the major political debates of the period; no side was willing to give up the use of the Bible to reinforce its claims. Among those who opposed Garrison was Frederick Douglass. Douglass, who endangered himself by keeping a Sabbath school where he taught his fellow slaves to read the Bible against the master's prohibition, believed that ultimately scriptural texts offered an indispensable base for abolitionist theology.[8] In response to the use of biblical texts in proslavery rhetoric, he claimed that "[i]t is no evidence that the Bible is a bad book, because those who profess to believe the Bible are bad. The slaveholders of the South, and many of their wicked allies at the North, claim the Bible for slavery; shall we, therefore, fling the Bible away as a pro-slavery book? It would be as reasonable to do so as it would be to fling away the Constitution."[9] In a country in which the Bible is no less a founding text than the constitution, Douglass suggests, any struggle for political change must entail an exegetical battle over the right interpretation.

That the Bible can be recruited to bolster any political position is one of the most fascinating features of biblical reception in political discourse.[10] While proslavery advocates quoted the Pauline command in Ephesians 6:5, "Slaves, obey your earthly masters with fear and trembling," abolitionists preached on texts ranging from Exodus to Jesus' love of neighbor command in Matthew 22:39. Similarly, in the debate over woman's suffrage, each side underscored its own cherished verses. Suffragists such as Sarah Grimké regarded Genesis 1:27, with its depiction of the egalitarian creation of man and woman, as a hermeneutic key, while opponents cited the divine punishment of Eve in Genesis 3:16: "in sorrow thou shalt bring forth children; and thy desire shall be to thy husband, and he shall rule over thee." As for the Mexican War, at variance with those who evoked the story of Naboth's Vineyard to oppose the American invasion, there were many others who quoted biblical passages glorifying war to justify it.

In rendering Ahab as a key figure in *Moby-Dick,* Melville joins such exegetical debates, following those who called American expansionism into question.[11] Several critics in the 1960s sought to read *Moby-Dick* as a political allegory with specific political references. Charles Foster suggested that Webster, who sold his soul to the devil by supporting the Fugitive Slave Law, was the figure behind Melville's Ahab.[12] Alan Heimert preferred the southern fanatic Calhoun, who was as keen an advocate of slavery as of expansionism, to Webster.[13]

In *Subversive Genealogy,* Rogin succinctly suggests that such readings "politicize *Moby-Dick* at the expense both of Melville's political imagination and of his actual subject. Were *Moby-Dick* simply a political allegory, then nothing would be lost by translating its representations back into their referents, for that would have been the purpose of writing it. Yet, as a political allegory *Moby-Dick* remains, paradoxically, above politics. . . . It points to no political truth above and outside its own story."[14] Rogin highlights the power of Melville's fiction to fathom certain features of political dynamics that transcend a given political situation while being deeply embedded in it. *Moby-Dick* does not "flee history"—it does indeed offer a penetrating critique of antebellum America—but the critique is delivered with the force of an imaginative prophecy, which allows for a broader reflection on America's past and future.

Although previous readings of Ahab—primarily those of Heimert and Rogin—touch on Melville's debt to the biblical political tradition, their primary interest lies in American politics rather than in aesthetic-hermeneutic issues. Thus, Melville's great admiration for the Bible's critical suspicion of political authority and willingness to explore the darker aspects of the seductions of power receive but little attention. What makes the biblical critique of kingship even more compelling for a literary exegete, I would suggest, is its imaginative oscillation between private lives and the public sphere. Samuel and Kings do not offer a dry chronicle but rather a remarkable mélange of royal history and literature, replete with well-wrought nuanced dialogues, that provides a close study of the inner worlds of those who preoccupy the political stage and a metaphorical base through which to explore the intricacies of political institutions.

Alter defines biblical narrative (royal historiography in particular) as a mode of "fictionalized history" analogous to Shakespeare's historical plays. Like Shakespeare, Alter claims, the biblical writers felt free to probe the minds of historical figures, "to ascribe feeling, intention, or motive to them[,] . . . to supply verbatim dialogue . . . for occasions when no one but the actors themselves could have knowledge of exactly what was said."[15] To be sure, the Bible, far more than Shakespeare's plays, maintains a historical drive to document past events and a theological commitment to convey the Truth, but the similarities between the two oeuvres are intriguing and must have been especially intriguing for Melville, who describes (in a letter to Evert Duyckinck) his discovery of Shakespeare at the age of twenty-nine as a discovery of a new Bible: "Dolt & ass that I am I have lived more than 29 years, & until a few days ago, never made the close acquaintance with the divine William. Ah, he's full of sermons-on-the-mount, and gentle, aye, almost as Jesus."[16]

I would go so far as to argue that the Books of Samuel and Kings are Melville's primary literary touchstones for the exploration of political imagination, which is why he does not merely evoke the outline of Ahab's story (as do James Russell Lowell, Theodore Parker, and other opponents of the Mexican War) but rather follows the intricate details of Ahab's character and rule, joining the biblical authors in their attempt to understand the political impact of individual desires and anxieties, the ways in which the intimate dramas of rulers shape public conduct.[17] His study of biblical political imagination, in turn, allows him to deepen his reflection on the character of imperial drives in the American context and beyond.

THE BIBLICAL CRITIQUE OF KINGSHIP

The critique of royal rule looms large already in the foundation story of biblical kingship. When the people request that Samuel select a king for them so that they may be "like all other nations," the angry prophet, upon yielding, enumerates the abuses that kingship entails: "He will take your sons, and appoint them for himself, for his chariots, and to be his horsemen; and some will run before his chariots. . . . And he will take your daughters to be confectionaries, and to be cooks, and to be bakers. And he will take your fields, and your vineyards, and your oliveyards, even the best of them, and give them to his servants. And he will take the tenth of your seed, and of your vineyards, and give to his officers, and to his servants" (1 Sam. 8:11–15). From Samuel's point of view, the king is something of a colonizer who can only oppress the people and rob them of their goods rather than provide them with any real sense of security. The rhythmic anaphoric repetitions of the expression "and he will take" augment his claim that royal rule excels at taking rather than giving.[18] God too opposes kingship on this occasion. He interprets the people's craving for an earthly king as a rejection of his rule as the ultimate King. "Hearken unto the voice of the people," says God to Samuel, "for they have not rejected thee, but they have rejected me, that I should not reign over them" (1 Sam. 8:7).[19]

Royal rule is construed as a menace to divine rule, as a competing political system that threatens the exclusivity of God as sovereign. Accordingly, on agreeing to establish a monarchy, God sets limits to the king's power, emphasizing the subjugation of human kingship to divine law. "Within the Bible," as Moshe Halbertal puts it, "there is a struggle between two understandings of the idea of God's kingship. The one claims that *God is king;* the other claims that the king *is not god.*"[20] The danger, then, lies in the reversal of the metaphor "God is King" in the tendency to deify human power and attribute absolute traits to fallible agents.

The divine precautions, however, prove futile. Biblical historiography throughout Samuel and Kings abounds in intriguingly unflattering accounts of the diverse ways in which different kings failed to abide by the Law. Martin Buber regards failure as the very hallmark of biblical leadership: "This existence in the shadow, in the quiver, is the final word of the leaders in the biblical world; this enclosure in failure, in obscurity, even when one stands in the blaze of public life."[21] Buber does not refer to "wicked" leaders, nor does he devote much attention to moral flaws, but his emphasis on failure is relevant to the understanding of the Bible's reluctance to idealize and idolize political rule.

Ahab is but one in a long list of biblical kings who failed to do "what is right in God's eye." His failure is exemplary, tied as it is to an unwillingness to accept the limits set on royal dreams of grandeur, the very phenomenon that troubled Samuel and God. Ahab, who initially sets out to buy Naboth's vineyard, thinking it an offer no one can refuse, is agonized by the latter's refusal to sell his patrimony or receive another lot in its stead. He returns to the palace, "heavy and displeased," and lies down in bed, turning away his face, refusing to eat a thing, not even bread (1 Kings 21:4). One may well wonder why a king who excelled both as warrior and city builder should be obsessed with such a trifle. But this is precisely the power of biblical narrative. Expansionist drives are studied through the small-scale desire of the king to annex his neighbor's vineyard and turn it into the royal "garden of herbs." However minute the issue of the vineyard may be, it is an unbearably painful reminder for Ahab that there is a Law above him—in this case, the law according to which patrimonies are not transferable. The vineyard is tantalizingly close, and the temptation to simply "take" it by force (not unlike Samuel's dire depiction of royal encroachment) or to get rid of Naboth lurks between the lines. But all Ahab actually does is to repeat Naboth's refusal to provide the craved-for "food" by fasting in bed. This intimate view of the royal bedroom exposes Ahab's melancholy wrath and vulnerability and sheds light on his subsequent silent acquiescence to Jezebel's schemes.

What makes the abuse of power more luring for kings is the privilege of having agents who are willing to execute their desires, wittingly and unwittingly. Jezebel sets out to do what Naboth would not: to regard royal desire as her own. Better still, she regards Ahab's latent violent fantasies as her own. "Dost thou now govern the kingdom of Israel?" she says to her husband (on entering the bedroom, one would assume), "arise, and eat bread, and let thine heart be merry: I will give thee the vineyard of Naboth the Jezreelite" (21:7). The cunning Jezebel (Shakespeare's source of inspiration for Lady Macbeth) oscillates between being maternal (offering food) and seductive (making his heart merry), promising to heal Ahab's inner wounds by restoring his sense of royal omnipotence and virility.[22]

The character of the trial she fashions is not without significance. She summons two false witnesses and demands that they accuse Naboth for committing the grave double sin of cursing God and king. Biblical law lists the two forbidden types of blasphemy together in Exodus 22:27 as similar offenses vis-à-vis sanctified hierarchies, but here the linking of the two seems to serve as a specific darker strategy, to bolster Ahab's rule by placing him at God's side. No words are allotted to Naboth. Even if he did speak, the lacuna seems to suggest, his discourse would be synonymous with silence, lacking the power to dismantle Jezebel's schemes. He is stoned to death outside the city, according to the customary legal procedures.

After Naboth's death, Ahab, without asking any questions about Jezebel's moves or Naboth's trial, goes down to the vineyard to inherit it. It is there that Elijah finds him and delivers God's scathing rebuke: "Hast thou killed, and also taken possession? . . . In the place where the dogs licked the blood of Naboth shall dogs lick thy blood, even thine" (21:19). Samuel's critique of kingship is but the first note in the prophetic critique of royal conduct. The conflict between kings and prophets remains a central dramatic line throughout Samuel and Kings. Elijah lays bare Ahab's accountability for Naboth's death (alongside Jezebel's), making clear that sins do not go unnoticed even if one tries to efface their traces or hide behind agents. Divine justice ultimately manifests itself when human courts fail. In a symmetrical punishment, Ahab is doomed to have his blood licked by dogs, much as his victim did, and his house is doomed to fall.

Why some biblical kings acquire the title of "wicked" while others do not remains something of a mystery. Ahab's usurpation of Naboth's vineyard is not a darker crime than that of David, who lay with his neighbor's wife and then made sure that Uriah would be killed in the war (here too via an agent, Joab).[23] What seems to augment the wickedness in the case of Ahab from a monotheistic point of view is the fact that political idolatry—regarding his desire as the Law—is accompanied by idolatrous religious practices: "And he did very abominably in following idols, according to all things as did the Amorites, whom the Lord cast out before the children of Israel" (21:26). In his idolatrous conduct, Ahab proves unworthy to replace the pagans whom God cast out of Canaan on behalf of his people.

The representation of Ahab, however, is not entirely devoid of empathy. There is something moving in the intimate, desperate way he addresses Elijah in the vineyard: "Hast thou found me, O mine enemy?" (21:20).[24] What is more, Ahab's deep repentance over his sins—he fasts and puts "sackcloth upon his flesh"—leads God to mitigate some aspects of the punishment, namely, postponing the final fall of the House of Ahab to the days of his sons.

CAPTAIN AHAB AND THE IDOLIZATION
OF POWER: THE DOUBLOON

Melville's Ahab is an intensified version of his biblical precursor. King Ahab's craving to take possession of Naboth's vineyard is magnified in *Moby-Dick* by means of the obsessive, violent, blasphemous quest of

Captain Ahab to "own" the White Whale, to master what lies beyond possession, to cross the boundaries set on human dreams.

Although there are no kings aboard the American ship of state, the problem of deification, the manipulation and abuse of power, and the insatiability of possessive drives, Melville seems to suggest, have hardly disappeared from the political scene. The democratic typology that allows Ishmael to regard a "poor old whale hunter" as "King Ahab" (150) reflects not only on the ways in which common people may hold royal grandeur but also on the ways in which democracy has not rid itself of the drawbacks of monarchic rule.[25]

Political rule for Captain Ahab ultimately means what it meant to his biblical namesake: approaching the position of the divine King, having the privilege of total mastery, total possession. He lures those who surround him to make the object of his desire their own, to see the world the way he does, to make his pain their grudge. With striking demagoguery, accompanied by the promise of a Spanish golden doubloon, he recruits the crew, in the memorable "Quarter-Deck" chapter, to join in his monomaniac search for Moby Dick:

> "All ye mast-headers have before now heard me give orders about a white whale. Look ye! d'ye see this Spanish ounce of gold?"—holding up a broad bright coin to the sun—"it is a sixteen dollar piece, men,– a doubloon. . . . Whosoever of ye raises me a white-headed whale with a wrinkled brow and a crooked jaw . . . whosoever of ye raises me that same white whale, he shall have this gold ounce, my boys!"
>
> "Huzza! Huzza!" cried the seamen, as with swinging tarpaulins they hailed the act of nailing the gold to the mast. (161–62)

Body and soul, the seamen "are one and all with Ahab, in the matter of the whale" (164). His hunt becomes theirs; his insatiable craving to take possession of the monster that dismembered him becomes their own craving, sharing as they do both the wound and the revenge of their captain.

In "The Doubloon," we discover that the golden glittering coin has become an idol, seen and revered by all, at all times, as the amulet of the whale. "For it was set apart and sanctified to one awe-striking end; and however wanton in their sailor ways, one and all, the mariners revered it as the white whale's talisman" (431). Halbertal and Margalit distinguish between three modes of idolatry: the first is based on similarity (on the assumed shared attributes between the representation and what it stands for), the second is metonymic (as when an object that is associated with God—the Ark of the Covenant or the Temple—is

endowed with divine powers), and the third is a convention-based representation wherein a symbol (be it linguistic, visual, or other) substi-
tutes for the deity.[26] The doubloon pertains to the third category. It
does not resemble the White Whale, nor does it maintain a metonymic
relation with it. Rather, it is an object that allegedly bears the magical
powers of the sought-for Moby Dick.

This scene of idolatry on board the *Pequod* entails a curious improvisation on the primal scene of idolatry in Exodus 32: the merry feast
around the Golden Calf at the foothills of Mount Sinai. The "sin,"
however, is graver. The golden doubloon, the *Pequod*'s equivalent of
the Golden Calf, is not merely an erroneous substitute for God (the
Children of Israel welcome the Calf as the God who had brought them
out of Egypt) or an erroneous metonymic representation of his chariot
(some scholars construe the Calf as such); rather, it is a fetish of a fetish, a talisman of a White Whale, who from a monotheistic point of
view is nothing but a gigantic idol of sorts.

No less relevant are the golden calves of King Jeroboam (the gam
with the *Jeroboam* reinforces this exegetical link). "Behold thy gods, O
Israel, which brought thee up out of the land of Egypt" (1 Kings 12:28),
declares Jeroboam on setting up two golden calves in Bethel and Dan.
Jeroboam ventures to reinvent and even duplicate the notorious image
of the Golden Calf in his attempt to consolidate the Kingdom of Israel
as a separate political entity and sway his people from regarding the
Temple in Jerusalem as the sole site of worship. The construction of
idols in the Bible is never solely a theological event. There are always
political underpinnings that are part and parcel of the scene. King
Ahab continues in the footsteps of his predecessor (the two are the
most prominent wicked kings of Israel) in using idolatry as a political
tool. In Ahab's case, the objective is not quite to compete with Jerusalem but rather to weaken the power of Elijah and his prophets.

This same phenomenon, the centralization and deification of power,
may be traced in Captain Ahab's idolatry. The doubloon is, among
other things, an implicit icon of Captain Ahab, nailed to the mainmast
as a visible symbol of his rule. On pausing before the doubloon, Ahab
can only see his own reflection, interpreting every single shape on the
coin as the mirror image of himself: "The firm tower, that is Ahab; the
volcano, that is Ahab; the courageous, the undaunted, and victorious
fowl, that, too, is Ahab; all are Ahab" (431). "Ahab sees only himself in
the doubloon," writes Rogin, "and imposes that self on the crew."[27] But
how successful is Ahab in doing so? Igniting the crew's imagination, the

doubloon generates an array of interpretations that proliferate beyond the captain's control.

Each crew member holds a different view of the glittering coin. Ishmael marches them, as it were, to the mainmast one by one, according to rank, and observes their response to its different features.[28] After Ahab comes the pious Starbuck, who discerns an allegorical battle between good and evil in the molten landscapes of the doubloon: the "devils' claws" and "a dark valley between three mighty, heaven-abiding peaks, that almost seem the Trinity, in some faintly earthly symbol" (432). Stubb tries to fathom the exceptional "signs and wonders" of the doubloon and finds the key to them not in the deeds of the apostles—Acts 2:24 and 5:12—but rather in the signs of the zodiac. The following renderings of the doubloon are construed from Stubb's perspective as he hides behind the try-works and watches his shipmates. Flask, he observes, is a literalist who insists that the doubloon is only a doubloon worth sixteen dollars ("that's nine hundred and sixty cigars"). Reading the doubloon as inseparable from a horseshoe that is also nailed to the mast, the Manxman tries to predict the date of the *Pequod*'s momentous encounter with the White Whale. Queequeg, who cannot decipher the signs on the coin (or so Stubb surmises) and "looks like the signs of the Zodiac himself," regards the coin as an "old button of some king's trowsers" (434), hinting, perhaps, that even kings may lose their trouser buttons and find themselves naked, without their customary symbols of power (a heathen version of "The Emperor's New Clothes," or a comment on Queequeg's own fate as dispossessed king?). The "ghost-devil" Fedallah "only makes a sign to the sign and bows himself; there is a sun on the coin—fire worshipper, depend upon it." And the mad Pip offers a split vista of the doubloon—"I look, he looks, you look"—seeing nothing but the baffling multiplicity of different perspectives.

This is one of the most palpable ars poetic–hermeneutic moments in *Moby-Dick,* not only because it displays the unending routes of exegesis through the rapid transitions from one beholder to another, but also because Ishmael moves from commentary on the exegetical excursions of different crew members to a reflection on Stubb's commentary on the other commentators. Stubb, Ishmael seems to intimate, is not always a perceptive reader of his shipmates' minds or half utterances—the second mate's speculative observations seem to disclose his own disposition and interests. But what could be more intriguing than to hide behind another metacommentator and follow his ruminations?

Interpretation for Ishmael—and by extension for Melville—always means thinking through other interpreters, watching the exegetical obsessions of others—be they whalers, scholars, or politicians.

The crew members appear before the doubloon in hierarchical order—from the captain to the lowest in rank, Pip. But no interpretation is given clear priority. Ahab cannot dictate the associations that run through the minds of his crew members. Neither can Ishmael dictate them, but somehow, without quite explaining how, he seems at this point (and elsewhere) to hold the position of an omniscient narrator who can read the thoughts of his characters and hear what they "murmur" to themselves as they gaze at the doubloon or as they watch their shipmates watch the doubloon. Lacking no self-irony, however, Ishmael realizes that he too, like Stubb, his double in this scene (note that the term *doubloon* comes from the Spanish *doblón,* derived from *doble,* "double"), may be imagining the voices he hears.

"FAST-FISH AND LOOSE-FISH": POETIC POWER

In "Fast-Fish and Loose-Fish," Ishmael provides an incredibly humorous account of the American legislation on the question of fast and loose fish that entails a sharp reflection on the dynamics of possessive drives. His initial remark provides the elementary definition of the distinction only to show that it does not hold, for possession, regardless of the numerous commentators who strive to pin it down, is more often than not determined by physical force rather than by code or legal commentary:

> I. A Fast-Fish belongs to the party fast to it.
> II. A Loose-Fish is fair game for anybody who can soonest catch it.
> But what plays the mischief with this masterly code is the admirable brevity of it, which necessitates a vast volume of commentaries to expound it.
> First: What is a Fast-Fish? Alive or dead a fish is technically fast, when it is connected with an occupied ship or boat, by any medium at all controllable by the occupant or occupants. . . . Likewise a fish is technically fast when it bears a waif, or any other recognized symbol of possession; so long as the party waifing it plainly evince their ability at any time to take it alongside, as well as their intention so to do.
> These are scientific commentaries; but the commentaries of the whalemen themselves sometimes consist in harder words and harder knocks. (396)

The small legal code regarding fast fish–loose fish turns out to be the ultimate hermeneutic key to the understanding of all "human jurisprudence" and, above all, to the central position of possession within it. Swept away by his own rhetoric, Ishmael declares that the very "Temple of the Law" relies on these two cherished concepts. His mock sanctification of the code ridicules the tendency of legal institutions to idolize their power and demand reverence. The Temple of the Law is not all that different from the Temple of the Philistines, whose two columns were brought down by Samson as his final act of courage.[29]

Once possession is defined as "the whole of the law," Ishmael juggles a wild stream of associations, opening up numerous possibilities of what may count as fast or loose fish. Special attention is given to colonial enterprises as a whole and to their manifestation in the American context in particular. "What was America in 1492," he playfully asks, "but a Loose-Fish, in which Columbus struck the Spanish standard by way of waifing it for his royal master[?] . . . What at last will Mexico be to the United States? All Loose-Fish" (398). Much as whalemen solve their legal debates over loose fish via blows, so in America—from Columbus's "waifing" to the annexation of Mexico—rights of ownership have often been determined by force.

American leaders may have imagined their lives as construed on the model of Moses or Nehemiah—John Winthrop is exemplary in this connection—but in practice, Melville's countertypology suggests, they were at times closer to following in the footsteps of King Ahab in their relentless quest for "loose" lands.[30]

In his comments on the readings of "Cold War critics" (Matthiessen's *American Renaissance* in particular), Donald Pease points to their problematic tendency to position Ahab as the embodiment of totalitarian tyrannical power while hailing Ishmael's free spirit, thus securing in "Ishmael's survival a sign of the free world's triumph over a totalitarian power."[31] For Pease, this dichotomy does not do justice to the complexity of the two characters, for Ahab offers an articulation of a quest for freedom along with his tyrannical inclinations and Ishmael's rhetoric is far from being uninvolved in the displays of power. "Ishmael uncouples the actions that occur from the motives giving rise to them," Pease writes, "thereby turning virtually all events in the narrative into an opportunity to display the powers of eloquence capable of taking possession of them. Indeed, nothing and no one resists Ishmael's power to convert the world he sees into the forms of rhetoric that he wants."[32] Pease somewhat exaggerates Ishmael's power, or rather, he overlooks Ishmael's oscillation between a sense of authorial omnipotence and omniscience to crises of authorship,

but his call for a reassessment of the interrelations of the two characters is vital.

Ishmael is all too ready to implicate himself in the wild world of
possessive drives. He ends "Fast-Fish and Loose-Fish" with the realms
of thought, religion, and verbalization, pointing to the relevance of
power and possession to all. In the final line of the chapter, in an unexpected self-reflexive move, he lays bare his own dominant position
as writer on addressing his readers: "What are the Rights of Man and
the Liberties of the World but Loose-Fish? What all men's minds and
opinions but Loose-Fish? What is the principle of religious belief in
them but a Loose-Fish? What to the ostentatious smuggling verbalists
are the thoughts of thinkers but Loose-Fish? What is the great globe
itself but a Loose-Fish? And what are you, reader, but a Loose-Fish
and a Fast-Fish, too?" (398). Writers too turn out to be Ahabs of sorts
in their eagerness to seize their readers, to magnetize them, as if they
were "Loose-Fish and Fast-Fish, too." They too aspire to shape "men's
minds and opinions" and capture their souls.

And what is the Bible, I would follow suit and ask, but a canonical,
evasive Loose-Fish, which each interpreter tries to hook and own? Like
other opponents of the Mexican War who took part in the exegetical
politics of his time, Melville yokes the story of Naboth's Vineyard to
American expansionism, but his momentous literary "waif" is somewhat different. He is not only interested in exposing the crude desire
for plunder and power underlying American policies. His Ahab is both
a "wicked" tyrannical captain, with maddening possessive dreams,
and a daunting charming rebel, who sets out to dismember his dismemberer in an attempt to reverse the divine punishment.

Unwilling to accept the prophecy that envisions the wrenching
apart of his body in the mouths of dogs (or whales), Captain Ahab delivers his own counterprophecy against heaven. "The prophecy was,"
he cries, "that I should be dismembered: and—Aye! I lost this leg. I
now prophesy that I will dismember my dismemberer. Now, then, be
the prophet and the fulfiller one. That's more than ye, ye great gods,
ever were" (168). Assuming the roles of king, prophet, and God at
once (the wild dream of every biblical king), Ahab offers a compel-
lingly bold promise to redress the all too painful lack of fulfillment in
the world.[33]

Similarly, Melville's reading of idolatry entails a notable departure
from the biblical text. His sharp critique of the fetishization of power is
accompanied by a radically blasphemous fascination with the aesthetic

potential of idolatrous practices. In opposition to the monotheistic prohibition on images, Melville endorses an aesthetic in which words try
to approach the visual (in other cases they approach music), to become
images, as visible as the idols they depict. The idol in *Typee,* which
flies toward heaven in the dark forest, Queequeg's Yojo, the inscrutable
White Whale, and his talisman, the golden doubloon—all open up new
reaches of the imagination, generating new mixtures of words and images that the stifling mores of Christianity, especially in their institutional expression, fail to acknowledge.

Melville is eager to comment on the political concerns of his time
through Kings and vice versa, but he also strives to carve out a politi-
cally unaffiliated poetic space where power, among other things, is an
aesthetic-hermeneutic enigma, where only the imagination determines
the value of things, where loose fish can become "the globe itself,"
where doubloons dazzle their beholders with their unending shapes and
forms.[34] The Spanish inscription on the doubloon, "REPUBLICA DEL
ECUADOR: QUITO," may call our attention to the interconnections of
the different imperial enterprises in the Americas (something Melville
would explore more extensively in "Benito Cereno"), but it does not
preclude other uses of the coin beyond the economic and the political.[35]
The "Spanishly poetic" doubloon, with its esoteric symbols, is the navel
of an enchanting dream world. The foreign language of the inscription
and the foreign landscapes of the Andes seem to reinforce the coin's
poetic-oneiric qualities: "this bright coin came from a country planted
in the middle of the world, and beneath the great equator, and named
after it; and it had been cast midway up the Andes, in the unwaning
clime that knows no autumn. Zoned by those letters you saw the like-
ness of three Andes' summits; from one a flame; a tower on another;
on the third a crowing cock; while arching over all was a segment of
the partitioned zodiac, the signs all marked with their usual cabalis-
tics, and the keystone sun entering the equinoctial point at Libra" (431).
Melville supposedly detaches the doubloon from its assigned cultural
inscriptions, inviting his readers to "nail" it, to momentarily suspend its
customary semiotic definition and normative circulation and explore its
poetic grandeur. Put differently, he calls on his readers to follow the *Pe-*
quod whalers, whose cravings for the material and political benefits of
the coin did not prevent them from plunging into its molten imaginary
landscapes in an attempt to decipher its riddles.

In my introduction I suggested that the definition of *Moby-Dick*
as a "mighty book" reveals Melville's more specific aspiration to hold

the power of the biblical writers, to compose an all-encompassing text that would touch on every imaginable realm of human experience. "The Scripture stories," claims Erich Auerbach in the renowned opening chapter of *Mimesis*, "do not, like Homer's, court our favor, they do not flatter us. . . . [T]hey seek to subject us, and if we refuse to be subjected we are rebels."[36] Through his Ahabs (Ishmael as Ahab included, of course), Melville investigates this desire to write the kind of text that would subject its readers in unparalleled ways, that would become, with its multiplicity of discourses, part and parcel of their everyday life, but he never ceases to complicate the question of authority and subjection or to wonder whether his "mighty book" with its "mighty theme" could truly approach the capacity of biblical texts—and biblical names—to shape lives and destinies. "What's the use of elaborating what, in its essence, is so short-lived as a modern book?" writes Melville to Hawthorne in early June 1851. "Though I wrote the Gospels in this century, I should die in the gutter."[37] What is more, he is always well aware of the limits of the power of literature and commentary in a world in which the distinction between fast and loose fish is often determined by "harder knocks."

THE POLITICS OF WAGING WAR:
TRUE PROPHETS VERSUS FALSE PROPHETS

With characteristic exegetical virtuosity, Melville goes beyond the normative scope of biblical allusions in the political discourse of his time. He further complicates his reading of the Book of Kings by evoking, along with Naboth's Vineyard, a less known episode in Ahab's history—1 Kings 22—where the politics of waging wars is at the center of attention.

In the opening scene of this chapter, Ahab, king of Israel, and Jehoshafat, king of Judah (in a rare moment of cooperation), seek prophetic advice in their attempt to determine whether to join forces and wage war against Syria (Aram). They summon four hundred prophets to deliver their prophecies before them in a public, highly theatrical setting by the city gate. "And the king of Israel and Jehoshafat the king of Judah sat each on his throne, having put on their robes, in a void place in the entrance of the gate of Samaria; and all the prophets prophesied before them. And Zedekiah the son of Chenaana made him horns of irons: and he said, Thus saith the Lord, With these shalt thou push the Syrians, until thou have consumed them. And all the prophets prophesied so, saying, Go up to Ramoth-gilead, and prosper: for the Lord shall deliver it into the king's hand" (22:10–12).

But the unanimous assertion of the four hundred prophets that victory is at hand does not fully convince Jehoshafat, who asks for additional prophetic visions. Yielding to his ally's request, if reluctantly, Ahab summons Micaiah, son of Imla, and urges him to answer the cardinal question: "Shall we go against Ramoth-gilead to battle, or shall we forebear?" (22:15). Micaiah's initial response, "Go, and prosper: for the Lord shall deliver it into the hand of the king," must have been delivered in an ironic tone for it provokes Ahab's anger: "How many times shall I adjure thee that thou tell me nothing but that which is true in the name of the Lord?" (21:16). In mimicking the discourse of the false prophets, Micaiah mocks the public spectacle by the gate, run by kings who are not interested in the Truth but rather in a prophetic stamp to approve their policies.

When Micaiah finally moves from irony to true prophetic discourse, he delivers a prophecy of death and defeat: "And he said, I saw all Israel scattered upon the hills, as sheep that have not a shepherd. . . . I saw the Lord sitting on his throne, and all the host of heaven standing by him on his right hand and on his left. And the Lord said, Who shall persuade Ahab, that he may go up and fall at Ramoth-gilead? And one said on this manner, and another said on that manner. And there came forth a spirit, and stood before the Lord, and said, I will persuade him. And the Lord said unto him, Wherewith? And he said, I will go forth, and I will be a lying spirit in the mouth of all his prophets. And he said, Thou shalt persuade him, and prevail also: go forth, and do so. Now therefore, behold, the Lord hath put a lying spirit in the mouth of all these thy prophets, and the Lord hath spoken evil concerning thee" (22:17–23).

Micaiah fleshes out the metaphor of God as king and ridicules the earthly kingdoms of Ahab and Jehosafat. Whereas in the heavenly kingdom the divine ruler has full mastery over the future and shapes it at his will, human kings (despite their theatrical display of power by the gate, sitting with royal robes on elevated thrones) prove flawed and blind, mere pawns in a divine game they are unaware of.

It comes as no surprise that Ahab and Jehoshafat prefer Zedekiah's gimmick of iron horns to Micaiah's bleak prophecy. In the final scene by the gate, Zedekiah slaps Micaiah on his cheek, as if to transfer the evil lying spirit to Micaiah: "Which way went the Spirit of the Lord from me to speak unto thee?" (22:24). Micaiah's insistence on the validity of his vision is of no avail. The kings march off to the battlefield, and Micaiah is sent to prison, where he is given nothing but "bread of affliction and water of affliction" (22:27). The Book of Kings supports no democratic principle. The four hundred prophets are nothing but misleading; the one opposing prophet, Micaiah, is the sole representative of the true way.

Melville renders his Ahab as blind to true vision as the biblical king, though in *Moby-Dick,* as Wright points out, the balance between false and true prophets is reversed.[38] Captain Ahab defies the warning of a number of true visionaries, from Gabriel to Pip, and chooses to hearken to the one false prophet aboard the *Pequod,* Fedallah.

Martin Buber defines false prophets as

> politicians who foster illusions [who] use the power of their wishful thinking to tear a scrap out of historical reality and sew it into their quilt of motley illusions. . . . False prophets are not godless. They adore the god "success." They themselves are in constant need of success and achieve it by promising it to the people. . . . The craving for success governs their hearts and determines what rises from them. . . . The true prophets know the little, bloated idol that goes by the name of "success" through and through. They know that ten successes that are nothing but successes can lead to defeat, while on the contrary ten failures can add up to a victory, provided the spirit stands firm. . . . The false prophet feeds on dreams, and acts as if dreams were reality. . . . [A]t every street corner you are likely to run into Hananiah, or standing slightly to the right, his colleague Zedekiah, the son of Chenaanah, with horns of iron or cardboard on his temples, and empty air issuing from his mouth. Brilliant or insignificant—he is always the same.[39]

Fedallah, like Buber's false prophet, is one who feeds on dreams. He knows just how to lure Ahab to pursue his wild fantasies of grandeur and regard his possessive drives as realizable. On hearing Fedallah's oracular reassurance that Moby Dick cannot kill him, Ahab cries, "I am immortal then, on land and on sea," ecstatically merging with the seer who has made him a god.

Such illusion politics, Melville intimates, were no less relevant to the politics of waging wars in the context of American expansionism. It was as impossible to prevent American leaders from sallying out to war once their minds were set on such a move as it was to stop King Ahab and King Jehoshafat from doing so. And there were always plenty of illusion politicians who were ready to bolster dreams of victory, providing the American public with the necessary justification for Manifest Destiny, concealing the dangerous consequences of such military success.

Buber wants to "startle" false prophets "out of their fantasies." Melville is not only iconoclastic. With Faustian fervor, he wishes to probe these deadly dreams, to allow them to run their full course, and to explore their intoxicating power from within.

Melville's reading of 1 Kings 22 has distinct antithetical features. Its fascination with the evil seductive dimension of Ahab and Fedallah is but one such feature. The other notable antithetical line is antitheodician in character. In shaping the *Pequod*'s captain as both an Ahab and a Job, Melville lays bare the striking resemblance between the heavenly consultation regarding Ahab's fate in Micaiah's vision and the prologue in heaven in the Book of Job, with its dramatic account of the wager between God and the Adversary. Melville sees 1 Kings 22, no less than Job 1, as a springboard for antitheodician contemplation. How can Ahab be accountable for his so-called wicked deeds when the divine King is the one who sends an "evil spirit" via a false prophet to lure him to wage war? Why does Ahab deserve to die?

Within the framework of Hobbes's political theology, God's kingship and the covenant he made with his people are perfect models for political rule (*Leviathan,* chaps. 31 and 35 in particular).[40] In Melville's hands, the metaphor of God as King points to the sinister possibility that God may be imitating the arbitrary malicious bullying of human kings rather than serving as an immaculate primary standard for kingship.

Melville does not refer to divine kingship as such but tackles the question through the malevolently majestic Moby Dick who dismembers Ahab with no apparent reason. There are numerous points in *Moby-Dick* where whales are associated with royalty. Already in the anonymous "Whale Song" of the "Extracts," the whale is depicted as the "King of the boundless sea," echoing God's final words regarding Leviathan in Job 41:34: "he is a king over all the children of pride."[41] Another case in point is the treatment of the whiteness of the White Whale as royal in "The Whiteness of the Whale" (188). Melville turns the biblical insistence on the superiority of divine kingship to human kingship into an agonizing power game in which the majestically omnipotent white Moby Dick cannot but prevail over Captain Ahab, remaining the only ruler in the "boundless sea."

JEZEBEL

Jezebel is never mentioned in *Moby-Dick*. P. Adams Sitney finds traces of her (inseparable from those of Delilah) in the unnamed sensuous feminine air that merges in "The Symphony" with the "man-like sea," whose waves heave "as Samson's chest in his sleep" (542).[42] But a more pronounced mark of Jezebel may be found in the figure of Fedallah. Jezebel and Fedallah share much in common: both are foreigners, advocates of false prophecy and idolatry (bearing theophoric names that underscore their affinity with forbidden worship) whose seductiveness proves deadly.

In Kings the Phoenician queen is described as the one who sponsors the worship of Baal in Ahab's kingdom, serving as the matron of four hundred prophets of Baal (the target of Elijah's wrath). In Revelation 2:20, she is not only the benefactress of such prophets but also one who shares their profession, calling herself a "prophetess," teaching God's "servants to commit fornication, and to eat things sacrificed unto idols." Her designation as an advocate of fornication in the New Testament has made her the archetypal lethal seductress in later exegetical contexts. "Jezebel" was the worst tongue-lash a Puritan could give a woman, and in antebellum America epithets such as "Jezebel woman" were hurled at women who dared to exceed the limits of their domestic sphere.[43]

Fedallah crops up one day from heathen regions—the product of the "mundane amours" of devils (of the kind depicted in the account of "the uncanonical Rabins" in the Book of Enoch and the Book of Jubilees)—and becomes, before anyone quite knows how, Ahab's most intimate and influential adviser. A mysterious combination of court prophet, consort, and co-captain of sorts, he turns the *Pequod* in no time into a cultic site of moon and fire worship. Idolatry, power, and seduction are inextricably connected both in Kings and in *Moby-Dick*. If Jezebel entices King Ahab to fulfill his dreams and usurp Naboth's land (though she executes the deed herself), promising him, albeit implicitly, a future of absolute rule and ultimate manhood, Fedallah's luring of Ahab to pursue Moby Dick seems to entail a similar double promise.

The only biblical queen who is mentioned in *Moby-Dick* is Queen Maachah. Her idolatrous rituals are evoked in "The Cassock," where the whale's enormous penis, his "enigmatic object," is likened to the idol "that was found in the secret groves of Queen Maachah in Judea, and for the worshipping which, king Asa, her son, did depose her, and destroyed the idol, and burnt it for an abomination at the brook of Kedron, as darkly set forth in the 15th chapter of the first book of Kings" (419). The "darkly" language of the Bible does not specify the nature of the idol but Ishmael/Melville reads between the lines, imagining the idol at stake as some kind of grand phallus. Jezebel's dubious sexual reputation seems to color his rendition of Maachah's idolatry, or perhaps his interpretation of the idol as phallic is a response to the previous verse, where Asa is said to have taken "the sodomites out of the land" (1 Kings 15:13).[44]

The whale's "enigmatic object" is adored by the whalers much as Maachah's idol was worshiped in the "secret groves of Judea," but it is doomed. It appears on board in the course of a process of "post-mortemizing." Its foreskin is pealed off in a mock-ritual (a grand circumcision?) and made into the mincer's cassock (two slits are cut for armholes).[45] The idolization of earthly virility—whether of kings, captains, or whales—can provide no absolute power, nor can it prevent dismemberment or death. The only one who surely transcends such earthly limitations is the ungraspable Moby Dick.

AHAB'S HEROIC DEATH AND THE
SINKING OF THE SHIP OF STATE

King Ahab is granted a heroic death. It is one of the rare moments in the Book of Kings in which more favorable aspects of his character are brought to light. Wounded severely by a stray arrow, Ahab insists on staying up in his chariot so that his troops will not be devastated by his condition (1 Kings 22:34–35). He dies in the evening, bleeding to death in his carriage. Elijah's prophecy is fulfilled for the bloodstained carriage is washed at the pool of Samariah after the troops withdraw, and the dogs lick up Ahab's blood.

Melville follows the biblical text in fashioning a heroic tragic death for Captain Ahab. The *Pequod*'s captain leaps at his enemy even when the jaws of death are about to close on him, hurling his spear at the monster with his very last breath.

But in a sense the crazed Captain Ahab is also something of a Saul (Macbeth—the Shakespearean blend of the two biblical kings—hovers in the background).[46] Saul too, like Ahab, dies heroically, falling on his own sword in a battle doomed to fail (1 Sam. 31). More than any other king in biblical historiography, Saul represents the vulnerability of those in power, the extent to which power and madness may go hand in hand. In his mad jealousy of David, Saul is often struck by an "evil spirit," so much so that he hurls a spear at his young rival time and again, wishing him dead rather than playing the harp before him.

Having tremendous power at hand, as kings do, can make any limit on royal illusions of absolute power maddening.[47]

The tragedy of governance is a topic that occupies central stage in *Billy Budd* as well, though the principal biblical reference in this case is the story of the Binding of Isaac. Vere is a tormented Abraham who loses his mind after allowing the execution of Billy Budd to take place. Interestingly, Vere's tragic flaw lies not in setting himself above the Law but in following the letter of the Law too closely.

Melville bolsters the empathetic touches in the biblical representation of Ahab in rendering Captain Ahab's "humanities." He strives to tackle further the more complicated, but all too human situations, in which victimizers are also victims, but he does not let his readers forget that regardless of his charm and vulnerability, the charismatic captain of the *Pequod* plays a major role in the disastrous sinking of the ship. Captain Ahab after all does not die alone. His mistaken war (and this is true of King Ahab as well) leads to the death and defeat of many others.

Melville "may have hoped," claims Rogin, "like the biblical prophets, that by dramatizing the course on which the nation was embarked, he could alter its destiny."[48] He tried, I would add, to set limits to the Ahabs of the world through a number of prophetic figures—from Jonah, who is defined in Father Mapple's sermon as one who ultimately ventures to "pluck" the truth "out from under the robes of Senators and Judges," to the strange-looking Elijah, who insinuates to Ishmael and Queequeg, as they embark on the *Pequod,* that its captain is mad, to the maddened Pip, who delivers fragmentary warnings, and Gabriel, who "hurl[s] forth prophecies of speedy doom," urging the blasphemous Ahab to heed his bleak end—"Think, think of the blasphemer—dead, and down there!—beware of the blasphemer's end!" (317).[49]

That Gabriel delivers a prophecy of doom from the *Jeroboam* is not without significance. Through the allusion to Jeroboam Melville predicts not only the imminent sinking of the American ship of state but also the very dismantling of the Union. The account on the rule of Jeroboam marks the primary moment of split between the kingdoms of Judah and Israel and as such serves as a relevant admonition against civil war.

By the year of the Compromise, Heimert writes, "'Conscience Whigs' had forsworn all association with the South, and a few younger prophets were advocating a separate and holier confederacy. For their policy of moral secession they found a precedent in the Old Testament separation of Israel and Judah. When Israel repudiated the 'arbitrary sway' of Rehoboam, such extremists recalled and divided itself 'forever from the house of David,' God indicated his approval by giving them 'Jeroboam for King.'"[50] Unlike the "Conscience Whigs," Melville is no advocate of secessions. He follows the biblical authors in seeing the splitting of nations as inseparable from bloodshed and violence, having the potential to lead to colossal catastrophe.

FROM TOCQUEVILLE TO MELVILLE

In *Democracy in America,* Tocqueville speaks of the highly influential role of religion in American politics and everyday life. "I do not know if all Americans have faith in their religion," he comments, "for who can read the secrets of the heart?—but I am sure that they think it necessary to the maintenance of republican institutions. That is not the view of one class or party among the citizens, but of the whole nation; it is found in all ranks. . . . For the Americans the ideas of Christianity and liberty are so completely mingled that it is almost impossible to get them to conceive of the one without the other."[51]

To make a political impact in antebellum America while insisting on the indispensability of liberty one could not afford to ignore the political traditions of the biblical text. In rewriting Ahab's story, Melville attempts to challenge the interpretations of those who use Scripture to sanctify false political agendas—whether slavery or Manifest Destiny. But he also departs from the politicians whose opinions he does cherish in exploring the imaginary base of political beliefs, in trying to "read the secrets of the heart," which Tocqueville and other political thinkers left untold, and in using the biblical text as a point of departure for a study of the human dimension of the political sphere. Yet Melville's attempt to fathom inner realities, here as elsewhere, never leads to terra firma. Many questions remain unresolved or partially open. Does Ahab impose himself on the crew, or is he the one who best articulates certain aspects of the crew's inner life? Does Ahab lead his ship of state, or is he the agent of the desires of others? Who possesses whom? "Who aint a slave?" (6). These questions are all the more puzzling in a Melvillean world in which characters are split or duplicated, where all crew members are Ahabs of sorts.

Moby-Dick is embedded in its times—it is set against the background of the Mexican War and the 1850 Compromise—but its political imagination like that of the Bible has the power to be strikingly relevant to other political contexts as well. Like Micaiah's dark prophecy, *Moby-Dick* was largely ignored in its own time, but it has lasted as a grand political vision, for all times, in America and beyond.

In my epilogue, I will discuss more extensively the ways in which the reception of *Moby-Dick* repeats the dynamics of biblical reception—circulating as it does in diverse cultural realms, from political discourse to musical adaptations and literary exegesis. Suffice it to suggest at this point that if *Moby-Dick* has had resonance in the political debates of the twentieth century up to our own times, it is because, like the Bible, it touches on the personal while trying to grasp the political, because, like the Bible, it invites its readers to dive into the big questions of power, desire, possession, evil, and violence, avoiding the all-too-common tendency to idealize or idolize political constructs.

CHAPTER 5

Rachel's Inconsolable Cry

The Rise of Women's Bibles

Rachel is the only female biblical character who looms large in *Moby-Dick*. Melville's Rachel is primarily a ship named *Rachel* that appears toward the end of the voyage in "The Pequod Meets the Rachel," a chapter devoted to one of the most striking gams in *Moby-Dick*. What is a gam? "You might wear out your index-finger running up and down the columns of dictionaries," Ishmael warns us, "and never find the word"—not even in "Noah Webster's ark." With that in mind, he provides his own "learned" definition of one of the everyday practices of whalers: "GAM. Noun—*A social meeting of two (or more) Whale-ships, generally on a cruising-ground; when, after exchanging hails, they exchange visits by boats' crews. The two captains remaining, for the time, on board one ship, and the two chief mates on the other*" (240). Melville's ethnographies of the unrecorded, unlexicalized practices of the whaling world, here as elsewhere, are in many ways biblical ethnographies: for the gam with the *Rachel* is not merely an encounter between two whaleships; it is at the same time an exegetical event, a momentous encounter with Jeremiah's weeping Rachel that leads to a different reading of the *Pequod*'s voyage and to a different reading of Jeremiah. In the course of this unusual gam, the *Rachel*'s Captain Gardiner pleads for help, asking Ahab to join him in the search for his missing son: "My boy, my own boy is among them. For God's sake—I beg, I conjure . . . For eight-and-forty hours let me charter your ship—I will gladly pay for it . . . you must, oh, you

must, and you *shall* do this thing" (531–32). Eager to proceed with
his maddened hunt for the White Whale, Ahab icily refuses, and the
"two ships diverged their wakes." In a woeful fulfillment of her name,
Gardiner's ship now captures in her wake the vast, inconsolable cry of
Jeremiah's Rachel: "But by her still halting course and winding, woeful way, you plainly saw that this ship that so wept with spray, still
remained without comfort. She was Rachel, weeping for her children,
because they were not" (533).

Rachel's inconsolable cry is one of many cries and dirges in Jeremiah. "Oh that my head were waters, and mine eyes a fountain of
tears," cries Jeremiah, "that I might weep day and night for the slain of
the daughter of my people!" (9:1). Crying seems to be the only means
to express something of the horror and pain of the forthcoming destruction, to warn backsliding Jerusalem of the outcome of her sins,
but it does not quite suffice in its normative mode: a hyperbolic leap
is required. If only the entire head were waters so that the eyes could
be fountains supplying an interminable flow of tears. In his quest for
the unattainable cry that would pierce the air and force his audience to
face the horrors that lie ahead, Jeremiah summons the wailing women,
women whose trade was to deliver dirges: "Call for the mourning
women, that they may come . . . and let them make haste, and take up
wailing for us that our eyes may run down with tears, and our eyelids
gush out with waters . . . For death is come up into our windows"
(9:17–21). That dirge singing was primarily a female trade in ancient
Israel (as well as in Mesopotamia and Greece) attests to an underlying
assumption that women are far less inhibited than men in expressing
grief and misery.[1] Relying on such gender configurations of mourning,
Jeremiah urges the wailing women to "take up wailing" to facilitate
and release the tears of those who cannot find the key to crying, whose
eyelids block tears much as they block the vision of death crawling,
like a demon, up their windows.

Rachel's weeping continues the female wailing that preceded it
while marking a new departure. Her voice, as Jeremiah envisions it,
rises time and again from the dead, from her tomb in Ramah, to cry on
behalf of her exiled children: "A voice was heard in Ramah, lamentation and bitter weeping; Rachel weeping for her children refused to be
comforted for her children, because they were not" (Jer. 31:15). She is
an aggrandized version of Rachel of Genesis—a national mother who
cries over many children, the descendants of her own offspring (Joseph
and Benjamin) as well as of other tribes. First, she cried on witnessing

the fall of the Kingdom of Israel and the Assyrian exile, but her ghostly cry emerges yet again, declares Jeremiah, now that the wretched exiles of Jerusalem pass by her tomb, as they are forced to march off to Babylon. Positioned after the disaster has already taken place, her cry not only touches on the inexpressible horror of catastrophic times but also offers a bold refusal to be consoled for what remains inconsolable; it protests against the unjustified harshness of divine punishment, unwilling to accept the immeasurable pain of destruction and exile, of losing children. It is an unyielding maternal cry that has the power to cross the insurmountable boundaries between life and death, going beyond grief and mourning to call out for mercy and compassion, to demand a redeeming change.

Melville, I believe, is compelled by Rachel's impatience. Indeed, he intensifies her impatience much as he intensifies the blasphemous lines in Job and Jonah. But he also shares Jeremiah's fascination with the quintessentially feminine power of Rachel's weeping. The matriarch's relentless lament allows Melville to underscore a primary cry whose echoes are but rarely heard in the predominantly male hunt for the White Whale: the cry for the maternal, the cry for the maternal cry, the yearning for feminine love and compassion that have been almost utterly repressed throughout the *Pequod*'s voyage but seem to break forth, cracking the masks, as the ship heads toward its tragic end.

Through Rachel, other biblical women enter the scene. In a tale told by a narrator who asks to be called Ishmael, Rachel's inconsolable cry cannot but encapsulate the cry of Hagar in the wilderness on seeing her son on the verge of death (Gen. 21:16). And given that Christian exegesis is also at stake, Melville's Rachel shares much in common with Mary, whose escape with Jesus from Herod's massacre of the innocents is read in Matthew 2 in light of Jeremiah 31. As they blend with each other, these maternal cries deliver an urgent plea for an opening of hearts, eyes, and ears in the face of the imminent sinking of the *Pequod*. Their cries may be as futile as all Jeremiah's cries, Melville seems to intimate, as ephemeral as a trail of tears in the sea, but they must be delivered against the monomaniacal worlds of male voyagers whose very definition of voyage means leaving mothers, wives, and homes behind.

Ultimately, I would add, the *Rachel* calls for a different definition of gender distinctions, which like any other category of identity in *Moby-Dick*—ethnic, national, or religious—is construed as forever evasive and necessarily shifting. "Oh, man! admire and model thyself after the whale," exclaims Ishmael in one of his playful heretical variations of the traditional *imitatio dei* (307). But the whale "by the rare virtue" of its "thick walls" and by "the rare virtue" of its "interior spaciousness" is at once the epitome of masculinity and a vast womb (307). The tragedy of the *Pequod,* and, above all, of its captain, seems to lie in a failure of imitation, in the excessive irreversibly destructive worship of walls that barely leaves space for the longings of the heart.[2]

Only one whaler, Ishmael, the one who survives to tell the tale, to bear witness to the *Pequod'*s tragic fall, seems to fully embrace the *Rachel'*s call. Ishmael devotes the final line of his tale, the very final line of the "Epilogue," to the dreamy unexpected moment in which the *Rachel* reappears out of nowhere, after the *Pequod* had sunk into the black vortex, and rescues him, showing the mercy Ahab refused to show: "A sail drew near, nearer, and picked me up at last. It was the devious-cruising Rachel, that in her retracing search after her missing children, only found another orphan" (573).

THE FEMINIZATION OF BIBLICAL EXEGESIS

In Melville's rendition of Jeremiah's Rachel, I trace a response to the burgeoning corpus of exegetical writings by women, evident in diverse cultural spheres in nineteenth-century America, exhibiting a wide range of religious, aesthetic, and political stances, which I call "women's Bibles," in light of Elizabeth Cady Stanton's influential *The Woman's Bible,* though such writings were not always thus named. This exegetical trend set out to highlight and reinterpret female characters in the Bible—among them, Rachel—positioning at the center a biblical feminine realm that previous interpreters had regarded as marginal. Committed as he was to reflecting on the changing role of the Bible in American culture, Melville, as I have argued throughout, had a particular, even obsessive interest in every new exegetical trend of his time. The feminization of biblical exegesis, I believe, was no exception.

If this line of metacommentary has not been acknowledged before it is because the predominant tendency in Melville criticism has been to see Melville's oeuvre as detached from feminine culture or even as opposed to it.[3] What has made it even more difficult to follow this hermeneutic move is the fact that Melville's Rachel is not as visible as the other biblical texts I have discussed. She is, more often than not, present in tone, gesture, emotional response, and diction rather than in person and scene. Similarly, the concomitant response to women's exegetical writings nowhere becomes as elaborate or explicit as is the

case with Melville's response to biblical criticism in "Jonah Historically Regarded." But the fact that Rachel appears through partially
hidden traces does not make her presence less vital to the understanding of Melville's exegetical imagination.

Melville's cultural horizons, we keep on discovering, were far
broader than suspected at first. Sterling Stuckey has called attention
to Melville's exposure to the rhythms and music of African culture,
too pervasive in the streets of New York for Melville to have ignored.
"In his genius and moral courage," writes Stuckey, "Melville gives primary attention in *Moby-Dick*" (he refers in particular to Pip's dance
in "Midnight, Forecastle") to an "African aesthetic" that prefigures
jazz and jazz dance, thus "capturing in the process of their formation, music and dance that are now emblematic of American culture."[4]
The same holds for women's Bibles. This exegetical trend would become progressively more noticeable in the late nineteenth century and
throughout the twentieth century, but it was already making its mark
in antebellum America in ways that could not but intrigue someone as
steeped in exegetical matters as was Melville and as capable as he of
anticipating the cultural emblems of the future.

The increasing involvement of women in the exegetical scene was one
of the major shifts in the Bible's cultural position in nineteenth-century
America. This shift, as Carolyn De Swarte Gifford shows, was initially
inseparable from the rise of a new perception of women as the chief
educators and guardians of religious values. Their distance from the
political and financial spheres was construed as an asset that made them
especially suitable to assume the duty of providing moral education for
children at home and in the newly developed Sunday schools.[5]

For Sarah Grimké, however, the role of the domestic moral arbiter did
not suffice. Seeking an exegetical route that would have political impact,
she published a series of letters in 1837 in response to the Pastoral Letter of the Massachusetts clergy, against the latter's claim that Scripture
supports the subjugation of women to men and sanctifies the boundaries between their respective spheres. "My dear friend," she writes, "in
examining this important subject I shall depend solely on the Bible to
designate the sphere of woman, because I believe that almost every thing
that has been written on this subject, has been the result of a misconcep-
tion of the simple truths revealed in the Scriptures." Relying on Genesis
1:27 as her principle proof text, she goes on to argue, "Men and women
were CREATED EQUAL: they are both moral and accountable beings,
and whatever is *right* for man to do, is *right* for woman."[6]

The link between women's right to reinterpret the Bible and the struggle for women's rights became pronounced in 1848, when Grimké joined forces with Elizabeth Cady Stanton to organize the first women's rights convention in Seneca Falls, New York. The two, who were initially active in the abolition movement, now implemented abolitionist interpretive strategies in the context of woman's suffrage. Here, as in the context of slavery, they engaged in an exegetical battle against the misuse of Scriptures to advance social wrongs. The "Declaration of Sentiments," produced by the convention organizers, condemned the exclusion of women from the ministry and church governance and suggested that "woman has too long rested satisfied in the circumscribed limits which corrupt customs and a perverted application of Scriptures have marked out for her. . . . [I]t is time she should move in the enlarged sphere which her great Creator has assigned her."[7]

In the late nineteenth century, Stanton edited *The Woman's Bible* (1895, 1898), a series of essays on the Bible by women designed to offer extensive commentaries on principal biblical women. Informed by the findings of biblical criticism, Stanton suggested that instead of treating the Bible as fetish, readers need to regard it as a composite historical text of differing accounts, in part worthy of endorsement—when compatible with cherished principles of liberty and equality—and in part unacceptable.[8] The book was criticized both by clergymen, who regarded it as "the work of women and the devil," and by the members of the National American Woman Suffrage Association, who by then were unwilling to risk antagonism and hurt the campaign for suffrage.

Within the realm of belles lettres, women poets and writers offered new renditions of a whole gallery of biblical women, from Eve and Vashti to Esther and Judith. Shira Wolosky calls attention to the variegated character of this project. While Lydia Sigourney (1791–1865) was rereading Scripture within conservative religious frameworks, other women poets took an irreverent anticlerical position.[9] No one was as blunt as Emily Dickinson, who wryly declared that the Bible was an "antique Volume—Written by faded Men," lacking the charm of Orpheus's sermon, which "did not condemn" (poem no. 545).

Along with such poetic activity, one finds a growing participation of women in the exegetical realms of Holy Land travel literature and missionary writings. Indeed, missionary work became in the nineteenth-century a way for women "to have an adventure in a good cause," and for some who ventured to publish their letters and diaries it served as a springboard for a literary career.[10]

The feminization of biblical exegesis was led by women but not exclusively. Nathaniel Hawthorne and Theodore Parker were two notable male advocates.[11] In the closing paragraphs of *The Scarlet Letter* (1850), Hester, whose cottage on the outskirts of Salem has turned into a refuge for the wretched (wretched women in particular), is represented as a cross between a new female savior and a prophetess of sorts, although ironically her acceptance of Puritan notions of sin does not allow her to regard herself as such. She dreams of a "brighter period" in the future with unstinting conviction that "the angel and apostle of the coming revelation must be a woman, indeed, but lofty, pure, and beautiful; and wise, moreover, not through dusky grief, but the ethereal medium of joy."[12] For Parker, the challenge was to redefine the godhead. In "A Sermon of the Public Function of Women" (1863) he spoke of the "need for female virtues, particularly the lack of materialism, and finding these virtues in a godhead which embodied all the symbols of mother's mercy along with father's justice." Thus, his radical views in the realm of biblical scholarship and the slavery question intersect with his position on gender and religion.

In more diffuse ways, the new focus on femininity was evident in the format of the great nineteenth-century family bibles. Responding to the new trends of their time with a keen sense of business acumen, the publishers of these bibles were eager to include not only a variety of drawings of Holy Land sites but also a substantive number of representations of biblical women. Harper's *Illuminated Bible,* one of the most widely circulated bibles in the 1840s (the number of copies sold, 75,000, was astronomical for the time), a sort of Ur-text for the large family bibles, was one of the first to include a vast selection of illustrations of biblical female figures, geared in part to a growing audience of female readers and educators who were playing a more prominent role in the exegetical and religious spheres.

Rachel, I want to argue, was among the prominent biblical female figures in this burgeoning exegetical trend. Substantive sections in *The Woman's Bible* are devoted to Rachel of Genesis—from a commentary by Clara Bewick Colby, in which the matriarch's position vis-à-vis Jacob is regarded as anything but subordinate, to a commentary by Elizabeth Cady Stanton that sheds unfavorable light on Jacob's dismissal of the name Ben-Oni, the name the dying Rachel sought to bestow on her son (Jacob names him "Benjamin" instead).[13] Stanton's critique is

FIGURE 6. New Testament title page foregrounding Rachel
weeping, from Harper's *Illuminated Bible*. Courtesy of the
University of Iowa Libraries, Iowa City, Iowa.

not only directed toward the "injustices" in the scriptural texts, but
also at the tendentious presuppositions of earlier interpretations, according to which Rachel's untimely death is a punishment for her "un-
due" craving to have sons.

Jeremiah's Rachel is also present in a variety of forms. Harper's *Illuminated Bible* chooses, as Paul Gutjahr points out, to present a large
illustration of Rachel weeping, rather than of Jesus, in its New Testament title page (alluding to Matt. 2:17–18 in particular, one would assume; see fig. 6).[14] The illustration offers a combination of Jeremiah's

Rachel and the Pietà: weeping Rachel is caressed by another sobbing woman at her side and by a sad child behind her, all crying, it seems, over the dead child who lies on the ground before them.

In Holy Land travel literature the weeping Rachel was evoked in references to her tomb, a holy site on the way to Bethlehem. Rachel's tomb was not a central station in the Holy Land but one that is noted in almost every Holy Land travel narrative: from Sarah Haight to John Lloyd Stephens and William Thomson. "All that we know in regard to this tomb," claims Stephens in *Incidents of Travel in Egypt, Arabia Petraea, and the Holy Land,* "is that Rachel died when journeying with Jacob . . . and whether it be her tomb or not, I could not but remark that, while youth and beauty have faded away and the queens of the East have died and been forgotten and Zenobia and Cleopatra sleep in unknown graves, year after year thousands of pilgrims are thronging to the supposed last resting place of a poor Hebrew woman."[15] Melville himself would refer to Rachel's tomb in *Clarel:* "Far, in upland spot/A light is seen in Rama paling;/But Clarel sped, and heeded not,/At least recalled not Rachel wailing."[16]

The inconsolable Rachels of *Uncle Tom's Cabin* are of special relevance here, but I begin with another book by Harriet Beecher Stowe, largely forgotten today, *Woman in Sacred History: A Celebration of Women in the Bible* (1873), one of the most notable nineteenth-century women's Bibles (sales exceeded 15,000). The text was later condensed and retitled *Bible Heroines,* enjoying yet another successful circulation.[17] The book consists of a collection of essays on biblical women from the "Patriarchal Ages," the "National Period," and the "Christian Period," which are accompanied by chromolithograph illustrations of biblical women by different artists. Most of the paintings, including *Hagar the Slave, Leah and Rachel,* and *Jezebel, the Heathen Queen,* are painted by Orientalist artists such as Jean-François Portaels and Charles Brochart who imagined biblical women in shiny Oriental costumes (see figures 7–9). This is but one example of the ways in which the orientalization and the feminization of the Bible intersect.

Stowe regards biblical women as exemplary models of family life and, above all, as exemplary maternal models (of course, there is a certain discrepancy between the modest maternal models she writes of and the luscious female figures in the accompanying paintings). In her commentary on Rachel, she focuses on the matriarch's barrenness, spelling out her misery with special attention to the historical significance of infertility in biblical times: "Rachel murmurs and

FIGURE 7. *Hagar and Ishmael,* by Christian
Kowhler, from Harriet Beecher Stowe's *Woman
in Sacred History.* Courtesy of the University of
Michigan, Making of America.

pines, and says to her husband, 'Give me children, or I die.' The desire for offspring in those days seemed to be an agony. To be child-
less, was disgrace and misery unspeakable." Lamenting the scarcity
of details on women provided in the Bible and beyond, she exclaims,
"How many such women there are, pretty and charming, and holding
men's hearts like a fortress, of whom a biographer could say nothing
only that they were much beloved!" Jeremiah is regarded as a com-
pensation of sorts for the limited account of the matriarch's history
in Genesis. The "sacred poet," Stowe comments, "has made the name
of this beloved wife a proverb, to express the strength of the motherly
instinct. . . . 'Rachel weeping for her children' is a line that immortal-
izes her name to all time."[18]

FIGURE 8. *Leah and Rachel,* by Jean-François
Portaels, from Harriet Beecher Stowe's *Woman
in Sacred History.* Courtesy of the University of
Michigan, Making of America.

While *Woman in Sacred History* highlights Stowe's commitment
to the feminization of the Bible, it mitigates some of the bolder aspects of Stowe's abolitionist hermeneutic line in *Uncle Tom's Cabin,*
where Rachel crosses racial lines and serves as a typological figure for
both black and white women. Chapter 12, "Select Incident of Law-
ful Trade," one of the most moving chapters of the book, opens with
a slightly modified quotation from Jeremiah 31:15: "In Rama there
was a voice heard,—weeping, and lamentation, and great mourning;
Rachel weeping for her children, and would not be comforted."[19]
There are two black Rachels in this chapter. Both are slaves who are
forced to part from their loved sons in the course of a slave auc-
tion conducted by the slave trader, Haley. The first woman, Hagar,

FIGURE 9. *Jezebel,* by Charles Brochart, from
Harriet Beecher Stowe's *Woman in Sacred
History.* Courtesy of the University of Michigan,
Making of America.

who "might have been sixty, but was older than that by hard work
and disease," follows in the tearful track of Jeremiah's inconsolable
Rachel as well as that of her biblical namesake, the Egyptian bondwoman, Hagar, as her request to be sold with her only remaining son
is turned down:[20] " 'Couldn't dey leave me one?' . . . she repeated over
and over, in heartbroken tones. 'Trust in the Lord, Aunt Hagar,' said
the oldest of the men, sorrowfully. 'What good will it do?' said she,
sobbing passionately."[21]

The other heartbroken Rachel-like mother is Lucy, whose baby is sold
behind her back. Lucy does not cry at first. "The shot had passed too
straight and direct through the heart, for cry or tear." But when night
comes on Tom can hear "a smothered sob or cry from the prostrate

figure—'O! what shall I do? O Lord! O good Lord, do help me!'" Finding no heavenly help, Lucy ends up jumping into the water as a last defiant move, escaping, as the narrator wryly remarks, "into a state which *never will* give up a fugitive,—not even at the demand of the whole glorious Union."[22] While supporters of slavery regarded the verse, "Cursed be Canaan, a servant of servants shall he be unto his brethren," in Genesis 9:25 as a justification of the treatment of blacks as an inferior race, doomed by Providence to serve as slaves (Haley too quotes this verse), Stowe sets slaves in the canonical roles of the chosen, of the agonized Rachel in this case, using Scripture as a text through which to question the sacred racial hierarchies of antebellum America.

In chapter 13, we encounter a white Rachel: Rachel Halliday, the grand matriarch of the Quaker community, who follows her biblical precursor in her unwillingness to accept human suffering as an unchangeable given. Taking on the role of female savior, she ventures to offer her home as refuge to runaway slaves. She thus helps Eliza and George escape from "the house of bondage" and discover salvation in a true pious "home" like her own. "This, indeed, was a home—*home,*—a word that George had never yet known the meaning for; and a belief in God, and trust in his providence, began to encircle his heart."[23] Stowe, as Elizabeth Ammons suggests, "heartily embraced the Victorian idealization of motherhood and channeled it into an argument for widespread social change. . . . [S]he concurred in the culture's insistence on the importance, even sacredness of maternal values, and . . . argued from that premise that, rather than segregate maternal ethics into some private domestic realm, motherhood—the morality of women—should be made the ethical and structural model for all of American life."[24] Rachel Halliday is exemplary of Stowe's use of domestic theology to oppose slavery.

When Theodore Parker, in a sermon condemning the reenactment of the Fugitive Slave Act in 1852, likened the Negro mothers of Boston to Jeremiah's Rachel, claiming that they "wept like Rachel for her first-born, refusing to be comforted," he may have been inspired by Stowe, but perhaps the association of Jeremiah's Rachel with questions of abolition was at that point an almost irresistible exegetical move.[25]

Melville, to be sure, was not uncritical of the Victorian idealizations and idolizations of motherhood that often characterized his contemporaries' renditions of biblical women and female saviors. Nor was he uncritical of the role American women were playing in missionary projects both abroad and at home. The missionary woman in *Typee*

who travels to the Pacific to educate the "heathen" refuses to get off
the carriage when the old man who carries it sinks in the sand. Similarly, Bildad's sister, Aunt Charity, who distributes "spare" bibles to
whalers before they set sail, is far more preoccupied with the profit-
ability of the whaling ship, "in which she herself owned a score or two
of well-saved dollars" (96), than with the well-being of the *Pequod*'s
castaways and renegades.

   And yet, Melville did, I believe, sense along with Hawthorne, to
whom *Moby-Dick* is dedicated, the revolutionary potential of this burgeoning exegetical corpus, its capacity to generate new imaginings of
love, compassion, and equality, both in the individual sphere and in the
collective one. Camille Paglia reads *Moby-Dick* as Melville's ambivalent response to the "female-centered" world of *The Scarlet Letter*.[26]
What she does not take into account is the extent to which the two
books are complementary. Both writers are disturbed by the oppres-
sive aspects of normative gender roles and strive for a change: whereas
Hawthorne is primarily preoccupied with the possibility of imagining
a more liberated and liberating cultural position for women, Melville
is primarily concerned with the pitfalls of masculine monomaniacal
obsessions with mastery (there is no less ambivalence in *Moby-Dick*
vis-à-vis the male-centered world of Ahab). Their exegetical paths,
however, merge in the *Rachel*. The vision of the dreamy *Rachel* in the
final line of *Moby-Dick* is, among other things, Melville's homage to
Hawthorne's final vision of a redeeming female angel in the closing
paragraphs of *The Scarlet Letter*.

   But insofar as Melville renders his new female savior as a particular
embodiment of Jeremiah's Rachel he comes closer to the inconsolable
Rachels of *Uncle Tom's Cabin*. Melville could not have read chapters
12 and 13 of *Uncle Tom's Cabin,* published in the *National Era* in
August 1851 (only a few months after he had submitted his manuscript of *Moby-Dick*), but unknowingly he shares Stowe's perception
of Jeremiah's Rachel as vital for a redefinition of one's responsibility
to the suffering of others.[27] More specifically, he shares her conviction that to translate Rachel (and Hagar by extension—both authors
choose, astonishingly, to link the two) into the world of antebellum
America would mean to use the inconsolable matriarch to rethink
questions of both gender and race. The respective revisionary aesthetics and theology of Melville and Stowe, however, as we shall see, do
clash at several points.[28]

AHAB'S TEAR

To better understand Melville's renditions of Rachel and their position within the new exegetical writings of his time one needs to bear in mind that there are numerous half-hidden traces of Rachel throughout *Moby-Dick,* among them, traces in the fluid character constructs of the *Pequod* whalers. In previous chapters, I offered an extensive consideration of the ways in which Melville, in his insatiable craving to play out hermeneutic possibilities and in his challenge to the American school of ethnology (aligned at the time with the justifications for African American slavery and Native American dispossession), split Ishmael, Jonah, Job, and Ahab among the multiethnic crew members of the *Pequod,* insisting that biblical typologies are relevant to all—be they Polynesian, white American, Native American, African American, Asian, or European. His treatment of Rachel relies on the same hermeneutic principle, only in this case not only racial and ethnic consistencies are questioned, but also gender ones. Gender boundaries, for Melville, are as fluid as all other boundaries, which is why he does not hesitate to project different aspects of Rachel onto the male crew of the *Pequod,* calling on us to explore the enigma of what being a Rachel may be like in unexpected ways.

Surprising as it may seem at first, it is, above all, Captain Ahab who becomes something of a Rachel in the closing chapters of *Moby-Dick.* To be more precise, Ahab oscillates between becoming a Rachel, seeking a Rachel-like embrace, and withdrawing sharply, torn as he is between a growing compassion for human misery and an attempt to block it, as well as between a growing need for human compassion and a desire to repress it. Just before the *Rachel* appears, Ahab, who never shows mercy to his crew, and is not in the least preoccupied with their suffering, softens up toward Pip, the lowliest of all, railing against the heavens for bringing on the luckless black boy such immense misery:

> "There can be no hearts above the snow-line. Oh, ye frozen heavens! look down here. Ye did beget this luckless child, and have abandoned him, ye creative libertines. Here, boy; Ahab's cabin shall be Pip's home henceforth, while Ahab lives. Thou touchest my inmost center, boy; thou art tied to me by cords woven of my heart-strings. . . . Lo! Ye believers in gods all goodness, and in man all ill, lo you! See the omniscient gods oblivious of suffering man; and man, though idiotic, and knowing not what he does, yet full of the sweet things of love and gratitude." (522)

Countering all those who deserted Pip in the midst of seas and spurning the gods who did not intervene on behalf of this castaway, who were blind to his sweet love and gratitude, Ahab adopts him as a son. The blasphemous Ahab is no advocate of pious domestic theology, but in offering his cabin as a home and shelter to the forlorn black Pip he assumes a role that is strangely analogous to that of Stowe's Rachel Halliday. Melville's typologies, however, are far more tantalizing than those of Stowe: not so much because his Rachel is a man (Stowe too experiments with gender fluidity, at least in her rendition of Uncle Tom as a feminized Christ), but primarily because Ahab keeps shifting. In the following episodes he is far closer to the oblivious heartless gods he had condemned (or to Haley, the slave trader) than to Jeremiah's Rachel.[29]

Shortly after adopting Pip, Ahab's heart is lured by the zones beneath "the snow-line." He laughs at his crew for being startled and moved by the "wild and unearthly" cry that pierces the air "like half-articulated wailings of the ghosts of all Herod's murdered Innocents" (523). Ridiculing this wailing as the sobbing of "seals that had lost their dams, or some dams that had lost their cubs" (524), Ahab distances himself from the possibility that human lives are at stake (as the Manxman suggests) and from the pain entailed in dams and cubs losing each other. Unwittingly, already here he distances himself from the tragedy of the *Rachel*, whose precursor's cry in Matthew 2 is construed as a cry on behalf of the massacred innocents.

Once the *Pequod* meets the *Rachel*, Ahab's withdrawal from the realm of compassion becomes clear-cut. He refuses to help the *Rachel*'s captain search for his missing son and does not even respond to the latter's final heartbreaking plea: "'I will not go . . . till you say *aye* to me. Do to me as you would have me do to you in the like case. For *you* too have a boy, Captain Ahab—though but a child, and nestling safely at home now. . . . Yes, yes, you relent; I see it" (532). Standing like an "anvil," Ahab forgives himself in a mock-Christian gesture of forgiveness: "Captain Gardiner, I will not do it. Even now I lose time. Good buy, good buy. God bless ye, man, and may I forgive myself, but I must go" (532).

Ahab's rejection of Gardiner is followed by a sharp rejection of Pip. He can no longer bear Pip's clinging to him, or his own deep attachment; he does not want to be cured of his blasphemous maddened obsessions or turned into a reformed "healthy" believer by the boy's unconditional fidelity:

Lad, lad, I tell thee thou must not follow Ahab now. The hour is coming when Ahab would not scare thee from him, yet would not have thee
by him. There is that in thee, poor lad, which I feel too curing to my
malady. Like cures like; and for this hunt, my malady becomes my most
desired health. . . . Oh! spite of million villains, this makes me a bigot
in the fadeless fidelity of man!—and a black! And crazy!—but methinks
like-cures-like applies to him too; he grows so sane again. . . . Weep so,
and I will murder thee! Have a care, for Ahab too is mad. (534)

Ahab is ready to murder Pip for weeping, but then, in "The Symphony," in yet another abrupt turn, he shifts back to the realm of the
heart and even sheds a tear. The gam with the *Rachel* has left a mark
on his body and soul after all. "That glad, happy air, that winsome
sky, did at last stroke and caress him; the step-mother world, so long
cruel—forbidding—now threw affectionate arms round his stubborn
neck, and did seem to joyously sob over him, as if over one, that however willful and erring, she could yet find it in her heart to save and
to bless. From beneath his slouched hat Ahab dropped a tear into the
sea; nor did all the Pacific contain such wealth as that one wee drop"
(543). For once, the "cruel step-mother world" becomes a caressing,
maternal air with affectionate arms. If in the opening of the chapter
the sensuous air was likened implicitly to lethal Delilah (and to Jezebel
by extension), copulating with the sea that heaved "as Samson's chest
in his sleep" (542), now a different feminine spirit, a Rachel-like spirit,
emerges, with a redeeming passionate heart and teary eyes, providing
love and forgiveness, even to errant Ahab. Ahab is beside himself. For
a fleeting moment, he yields and melts. His "stubborn neck" is made
pliable, and a tear rolls down from his eye, a tear that seems to merge
with the teary sea "spray" the *Rachel* leaves behind in her search for
her lost son, a tear whose wealth, Ishmael assures us, surpasses the
wealth of the entire Pacific.

In *Literature, Disaster, and the Enigma of Power,* Eyal Peretz offers
a reading of *Moby-Dick* as a whale/wail book that revolves around
the experience of catastrophe, primarily Ahab's recurrent cries over
the wound inflicted on him by Moby Dick. Evoking one of Ahab's
most striking cries on springing up from a nightmarish dream, Peretz
suggests that "the address of the whale, by remaining an unknowable,
inassimilable, and unmasterable event which cannot be understood as
unified meaning, keeps infinitely repeating in dreams as the attempt of
the wounded subject to restore its mastery and to regain knowledge,
that is, to heal the wound at its heart."[30] Let me suggest that in "The

Symphony" Ahab's cry acquires a new form. It turns from a shout into a "wee drop" of oceanic proportion, revealing a more primary cry, over a far more unknowable and unassimilable catastrophic event: the cry of an abandoned child. Being hugged at last (however imaginary this airy embrace may be), Ahab seems to sense the ineffable pain of his own orphanhood—his "crazy widowed" mother died when he was only a twelve-month-old (79)—the immense agony of "cubs losing their dams" that he denied so bluntly, his own lonely desperate cry for compassionate maternal care (not the cruel treatment of a stepmother world).[31] The closer Ahab gets to the traumatic zone where he was initially wounded, the closer he gets to the final grand encounter with Moby Dick, the more he discovers other yearnings and cries he had repressed all along.

The very possibility of touching on such primary pain seems to allow him at this point to have compassion for others. He now cries for the wife he has left behind, "a widow with her husband alive," and the child he has forsaken. He can now see his wife and child in the "human eye" of Starbuck and venture to doubt, for the first time in his life, the value of his long exile at sea, in "the walled-town of a Captain's exclusiveness" (543), away from home. He now resembles the narrator of "Bartleby" who cries out, "Ah humanity!" as he breaks up at the very end, no longer capable of justifying the walls of Wall Street (and beyond) in which he is trapped.

But ultimately Ahab cannot shed more than one tear. He can neither remain in the posture of a Rachel nor return to his family in Nantucket, as Starbuck urges him to do. He must follow his destined road and pursue his dismemberer.[32] "What is it, what nameless, inscrutable, unearthly thing is it; what cozening, hidden lord and master, and cruel, remorseless emperor commands me; that against all the natural lovings and longings, I so keep pushing, and crowding, and jamming myself on all the time; recklessly making me ready to do what in my own proper, natural heart, I durst not so much as dare? Is Ahab, Ahab? Is it I, God, or who, that lifts this arm? . . . By heaven, man, we are turned round and round in this world, like the yonder windlass, and Fate is the handspike" (545). It is Ahab's tragic fate to be forever drawn by his maddening drive to hunt. He is split at the core ("Is Ahab, Ahab?"), acutely perplexed, colonized by his obsessive desires, subject to their cruel remorseless inscrutable tyranny, not quite the master of his arms or heart. The White Whale—which Ahab defines in "The Quarter-Deck" as a wall or mask that he, as a prisoner, must strike through—has blocked his "own natural heart," robbing him of the freedom to follow his "natural lovings and longings."[33]

QUEEQUEG'S ARM

If Ishmael regards Ahab's tear as possessing wealth greater than the Pacific it is because this "wee drop" touches on his own primary wounds. In "Moby Dick" he shouts with the rest of the sailors, swept by a "wild, mystical, sympathetical feeling," accepting Ahab's "quenchless feud" with Moby Dick as his own. In "The Symphony" Ishmael's "sympathetical" feeling is only intimated through his depiction of Starbuck's response to the weeping captain. Starbuck "seemed to hear in his own true heart the measureless sobbing that stole out of the center of the serenity around" (543), remarks Ishmael from an omniscient point of view that seems to reflect his own experience as well. Ishmael, after all, like Ahab, is an orphan (their biographies intersect at this point) who can hardly approach the enigmatic pain of his orphanhood. Such wounds remain only half-articulated, almost invisible, like the fathomless "stranger world" of "watery vaults" where nursing mothers of whales roam about, where the breasts of nursing whales, when cut "by chance" by a hunter's lance, discolor the sea by "rivaling" milk and blood (387–88).

In a rare moment, however, in one of the opening chapters of the book, Ishmael has a nightmare in which he relives the horror of being locked up in his bedroom by his stepmother. On waking, he finds refuge in Queequeg's arm, which reminds him of the "supernatural hand" of the benevolent imaginary phantom that finally rescued him from the cruelty of his stepmother. "Now, take away the awful fear," he says, "and my sensations at feeling the supernatural hand in mine were very similar, in their strangeness, to those which I experienced on waking up and seeing Queequeg's pagan arm thrown round me" (26). Later, he explicitly regards his "bosom friend" as an invaluable redeemer: "I felt a melting in me. No more my splintered heart and maddened hand were turned against the wolfish world. This soothing savage had redeemed it" (51). In chapter 3 I construed this passage as a trace of the Ishmael-like character of the wild Polynesian. Now I would like to suggest that Queequeg's bosom and arms also embody a trace of Rachel. Indeed, Queequeg's redeeming body and soul seem to pave the way for Ishmael's willingness to be redeemed by the *Rachel* and to become her own orphan. It is, then, no coincidence that in the end Queequeg's buoyant coffin serves as Ishmael's life preserver until the *Rachel* picks him up.[34]

In his cross-racial redemptive benevolence, Queequeg too may be compared to Rachel Halliday, though to be sure there are notable differences. Queequeg does not define mercy in Christian terms. He is not an Uncle Tom who, as Buell puts it, "essentially just mirrors in idealized form the Christian virtues that the dominant culture values in principle."[35] Quite the contrary, the wild pagan accentuates the lack of morality and compassion in the Quaker world of New England. And if this were not enough, his hug has a distinct homoerotic bent.[36] He would never have found his place within the devout traditional Quaker kitchen of Rachel Halliday, where heterosexual matrimonial ties are reaffirmed.

PROPHETIC LEAPS: THE QUESTION OF CONSOLATION

Should the scene of Ishmael's deliverance by the *Rachel* be construed as Melville's grand final jeremiad (in this case, a political sermon that is based literally on Jeremiah's prophecies)? Does the *Rachel* offer a redeeming consoling vision of a different ship of state, an alternative to the sinking *Pequod?* To probe into the political allegories embedded in the final scene of *Moby-Dick,* let us go back to Jeremiah. Jeremiah's Rachel appears in a sequence of consolation prophecies, called the "Book of Consolation," presumably delivered during the time of destruction or shortly after. In this context, Jeremiah, who more often than not depicts Israel as the adulterous-idolatrous Wife of God in his visions of disaster, now uses the prophetic marital metaphor to envision redemption.[37] Imagining redemption requires no less of a poetic-prophetic leap than imagining disaster. In searching for unconventional ways to envision a scene of reconciliation and reunion in which the initial passion between God and the nation, the passion of their primary courtship in the wilderness, would be rekindled, Jeremiah goes so far as to imagine redemption in terms of an unusual reversal of gender roles: "Set thee up waymarks, make thee high heaps: set thine heart toward the highway . . . turn again, O virgin of Israel, turn again to these thy cities. How long wilt thou go about, O thou backsliding daughter? for the Lord hath created a new thing in the earth, A woman shall compass a man" (31:21–22). It is precisely the prophet's task to insist on imagining the unimaginable, to foresee "new things in the earth": to envision disaster against the

smug delusional promises of false prophets and then, in turn, to envision the grand return of Israel as a woman who can "compass a
man" against the backdrop of the wretched exiles forced to leave
Jerusalem.

Rachel anticipates this redemptive reversal of the normative power
relations between God and the nation. God, according to Jeremiah,
yields to Rachel's inconsolable cry and delivers a grand promise of an
era of return and redemption that will put an end to crying: "Thus
saith the Lord; Refrain thy voice from weeping, and thine eyes from
tears: for thy work shall be rewarded, saith the Lord; and they shall
come again from the land of the enemy. And there is hope in thine end,
saith the Lord, that thy children shall come again to their own border"
(Jer. 31:16–17). In wresting from God a promise for a better future,
Rachel, like the "backsliding" beloved (and in a sense, as her personi-
fication) takes part in bringing forth a "new thing on earth," whereby
men (or God in his metaphorical male configuration) may be "compassed"—compelled by a woman to have mercy and compassion.[38]

But why, one may well ask, does Jeremiah choose to turn Rachel
into a national metaphor? And why is Rachel the matriarch who is best
suited for this redeeming role? Several explanations have been raised.[39]
Rachel is the legendary beloved for whom Jacob waited seven years,
seven years that seemed but a few days in his eyes, so great was his
love. Such passionate love would seem to reinforce the consolatory dimension of the prophetic marital metaphor. What is more, her acute
maternal suffering—first as a desperate barren wife and later on dying
in the prime of her life while giving birth to Benjamin, "the son of her
sorrows"—makes her (far more than the other matriarchs) the most
appropriate speaker on behalf of the wretched. But no less important is
her lawless boldness. Rachel hesitates neither to trick her father while
stealing the household gods nor, later on, to strike a dubious deal with
her sister Leah, whereby Jacob is exchanged for mandrakes.[40] Daring
as Rachel was, she could, Jeremiah seems to imagine, even dare to
challenge the harshness of divine punishment.

Through Jeremiah, Melville cries over the horrors of his age, holding up a mirror to an antebellum America that is blind to its immense
backsliding, to its crimes in every possible realm, and to the catastrophe that lies ahead. But Melville, it seems to me, is also interested in
imagining, with Jeremiah, a consoling political vision. In halting the
search for her own missing son in order to pick up another forlorn "orphan," the "devious-cruising" *Rachel* has the audacity to deviate from

the common routes of the whaling world and introduce a radically "new thing" at sea: a ship of state that insists on mercy and compassion—traits that both in Jeremiah's times and in antebellum America were construed as primarily feminine—in the face of disaster.

True to the heretical line of his hermeneutics, however, Melville also offers substantive departures from Jeremiah. First, he bolsters Rachel's boldness by having the ship *Rachel*—rather than a divine hand—venture to perform the act of deliverance. Second, wherever the *Rachel* may be sailing to, Melville refrains from fashioning a scene of Ishmael's final return to "his border." The *Rachel* remains in "exiled waters," away from the fixed borders of the "slavish shore," relying on a far more pliable notion of member-ship: she does not rescue her own children but rather adopts the son of the rival nation—Ishmael! Rogin reads this scene of deliverance as foretelling the future deliverance of slaves, given that Ishmael is the son of a slave.[41] But the *Rachel* offers more than a craving for a change in American society. Her cross-national adoption whereby Rachel merges with Hagar and Ishmael with the exiled Israelites also sketches the possibility of remodeling relations between nations and religions. Third, set against the rise of the women's movement and the growing visibility of women on the cultural stage, Melville's Rachel intimates a need to go beyond experimental gender relations on the national metaphoric sphere and seek an actual cultural-political redefinition of gender roles within this new construct of member-ship.

But how hopeful is Melville's closing vision of the *Rachel?* The bulk of the book is, after all, devoted to the fall of the *Pequod,* a fall the *Rachel* does not succeed in preventing. She rescues only one whaler. In *The American Jeremiad,* Bercovitch argues that what distinguishes the American jeremiad from its European precursors is its insistence on an uplifting ending with a momentous drive toward a transformed dynamic future. In Melville's writings, Bercovitch traces a move from a more traditional rendition of the jeremiad in *White-Jacket* to a somber antijeremiad in *Moby-Dick,* where there seems to be no future but the future of failure and doom, where cherished American constructs prove false: "If Ahab is a distortion of the 'political Messiah' celebrated in *White-Jacket,* that may be because the messianic promise, the dream of knowledge, power, and the spirit, is itself a distortion."[42]

In *Moby-Dick* Melville does indeed reject the devout triumphalist rhetoric of the American jeremiad. But following the tantalizing combination of prophecies of doom and consolation in the primary model of such jeremiads—the Book of Jeremiah—he does not give up the possibility of consolatory visions, of advancing scenes of unimaginable social change. Melville's approach to America is inextricably intertwined with his paradoxical approach to religion: his scathing, dark critique undoubtedly discloses a great passion (this is, of course, true of biblical prophets as well; their dire visions are by no means devoid of love for the people). Even if the grand dream of America as the embodiment of an exemplary "political Messiah" is shattered, the quest for alternative redeeming routes, however fragmentary and tentative, never ceases: it becomes all the more urgent after the *Pequod*'s sinking. And yet the question of how to deliver a prophecy of consolation in modern times that would not ring false remains one of the greatest challenges of all.[43]

Stowe's black Rachels find no salvation, reminding us that however successful Rachel Halliday may be, she cannot rescue all. And yet in the final scene of *Uncle Tom's Cabin,* Stowe chooses a more traditional American jeremiad and envisions a grand release of slaves at George's estate that is dramatized as a grand new Christian jubilee. Hawthorne is more irreverently ironic and cautious in the ending of *The Scarlet Letter.* Hester's cottage is a marginal site in a Salem that for the most part remains blind to its hypocritical notions of sin and to its oppression of women. What is more, even Hester, the bearer of the promise for a new female savior, is ironically blind to her redeeming powers.

Melville, like Hawthorne, offers only partial hope in his final vision. He sees in nations what he sees in Ahab: a reluctance to be cured, an immense fascination with the charm and power of maladies. "There is that in thee, poor lad, which I feel too curing to my malady" says Ahab to Pip. The consoling *Rachel* remains inconsolable even as she rescues Ishmael. Her "devious-cruising" in the "Epilogue" continues her earlier woeful winding, making clear that the crying over what has been lost and the crying for what will be lost never really stops. She can offer only a fragmentary, fleeting consolatory image whose power lies in the very refusal to endorse too facile a notion of salvation. Cruising between possible and impossible worlds, between the redeemable and the irredeemable, the *Rachel,* above all, sketches a wondrous dreamy potentiality, a dim glittering beginning of another route, no less unknown and no less evasive than the route of the White Whale.[44]

Lest this dreamy image seem too promising or benevolent, even in its fragmentary form, let me point to the darker shades of the word *devious,* that is, "misleading" or "erring."[45] There still lurks the possibility that the *Rachel,* like her cunning namesake in Genesis, holds dubious attributes as well. Could she too—via her "devious cruising"—lure her crew members to the brink? But what is the point—from a Melvillean perspective—of following any ship that bears no mark of the wicked? "I have written a wicked book," claims Melville in a famous letter to Hawthorne on November 17, 1851, "and feel spotless as the lamb."[46]

THE *RACHEL*'S POETIC LEGACY

The *Rachel* has one more role, perhaps her most consoling, that of poetic midwife. She serves as the final note in a spellbinding scene of rebirth through which Ishmael springs back to life and assumes the poetic-prophetic mantle:[47]

> So, floating on the margin of the ensuing scene, and in full sight of it, when the half-spent suction of the sunk ship reached me, I was then, but slowly, drawn towards the closing vortex. When I reached it, it had subsided to a creamy pool. Round and round, then, and ever contracting towards the button-like black bubble at the axis of that slowly wheeling circle, like another Ixion I did revolve. Till, gaining that vital centre, the black bubble upward burst; and now, liberated by reason of its cunning spring, and, owing to its great buoyancy, rising with great force, the coffin life-buoy shot lengthwise from the sea, fell over, and floated by my side. Buoyed up by that coffin, for almost one whole day and night, I floated on a soft and dirge-like main. The unharming sharks, they glided by as if with padlocks on their mouths; the savage sea-hawks sailed with sheathed beaks. On the second day, a sail drew near, nearer, and picked me up at last. It was the devious-cruising Rachel, that in her retracing search after her missing children, only found another orphan. (573)

The rhythmic hypnotic repetition of words and sounds, moving "round and round" in dizzying alliterations—"button-like black bubble . . . burst"—attest not only to the great buoyancy of Queequeg's coffin but also to the liberating force of language, to the intoxicating force of a bubbling, nascent voice, ready to leap out from a "contracting," deadly, black vortex.[48]

The "soft dirge-like main" on which Ishmael floats before the *Rachel* actually turns up is already an invitation on her part to follow in her poetic-prophetic wake, to invent a new dirge, with and beyond Jeremiah. And the "unharming sharks" with "padlocks on their mouths" and the savage sea-hawks whose beaks seem momentarily "sheathed" already intimate, before the *Rachel* appears, that even in a world whose gods are oblivious, utopian prophetic scenes of consolation in which predatory animals become harmless and swords are broken need not be entirely relinquished.[49]

On drawing "near, nearer," as if in a cinematic close-up that brings us closer into the scene, the *Rachel*'s legacy becomes more tangible. She seems to call upon Ishmael to bear witness, to tell the tale, against the overwhelming whirlpool of disaster; she seems to urge him to raise his voice beyond the buoyant coffin, much as she raised her voice from her tomb, and to cry, inconsolably, on behalf of the outcasts. But she also seems to urge him to view his orphanhood not only as a wound but also as a potential poetic blessing in the freedom it provides to imagine a new mother (the very antithesis of the "cruel step-mother world") and a new "society of orphans," as Deleuze puts it, that would venture to go beyond conventional constructs of familial and national ties.[50]

Epilogue

It is no coincidence that in each chapter I read the "Epilogue" of *Moby-Dick* anew. This is, as it were, Melville's grand finale of biblical juggling. Here Ishmael assumes at once the role of Job's messenger (the epigraph), of a Jonah who has just emerged from the belly of the fish, of his own namesake, spared from death at the very last moment, of a Micaiah insisting on a prophecy of doom, of a crying Jeremiah who refuses to relinquish the possibility of partial consolation, and of one of Rachel's exiled sons. But as Ishmael floats on Queequeg's buoyant coffin, he also resembles two other biblical castaways I have not yet mentioned: he is a Noah in the ark, the sole survivor of the flood, and a Moses borne in an ark on the Nile, escaping Pharaoh's decree, on the first stage of becoming his people's deliverer.[1] The implicit association of the buoyant chest with the arks of Noah and Moses extends to the ultimate biblical ark: the Holy Ark of the Covenant, where scriptural writings were preserved. I would go so far as to suggest that this scene, which follows the momentous encounter with Moby Dick, not only marks Ishmael's semimythical (re)birth as narrator but also serves as the final act in the dramatization of the birth of a new Bible, or rather the birth of a new Ark.[2]

In a famous passage in *White-Jacket*, Melville evokes the Holy Ark in imagining America's role and destiny:

> And we Americans are the peculiar, chosen people—the Israel of our time; we bear the ark of the liberties of the world. . . . God has given to us, for a future inheritance, the broad domains of the political pagans,

that shall yet come and lie down under the shade of our ark, without
bloody hands being lifted. God has predestinated, mankind expects,
great things from our race; and great things we feel in our souls. . . .
Long enough have we been sceptics with regard to ourselves, and
doubted whether, indeed, the political Messiah had come. But he has
come in *us,* if we would but give utterance to his promptings.[3]

This passage has often been quoted as an exemplary formulation of
America's Manifest Destiny. *White-Jacket* is far more critical of American politics than this passage may suggest but nowhere as critical
as *Moby-Dick.* In *Moby-Dick* Melville undoubtedly offers his most
penetrating critique of traditional American typologies and messianic
dreams of grandeur. With the fervor of Elijah, Jonah, Micaiah, and Jeremiah, he ventures time and again throughout the *Pequod*'s voyage to
lift up a mirror to the Ahabs of America, intimating that a nation that
endorses slavery, whose Manifest Destiny is too closely intertwined
with expansionism, and whose industries rely on massive exploitation
cannot regard itself as the bearer of "the ark of the liberties of the
world." Instead of assuming the role of a "political Messiah," it comes
closer to being a "cannibal of a craft," decked out in "the chased bones
of her enemies."

Yet as a true prophet-poet-pilot, Melville is propelled to imagine new
things in the sea. The sharp skepticism with which he regards every
American ideal in *Moby-Dick* is accompanied by a passionate attempt
to envision a new "outlandish" or "orphaned" (in Deleuze's terms) ark
that would be quintessentially American but at the same time capable
of drifting beyond normative national distinctions, calling into question every imaginable convention—whether political, religious, scientific, or literary. In *Moby-Dick*'s unmoored ark nothing remains fixed.
Biblical characters are forever split and shifting, continuously merging
with each other in unexpected ways. The very definition of what counts
as Scripture remains equally shifty. The ark/coffin on which Ishmael
floats bears no familiar texts but rather the hieroglyphic inscriptions of
a Polynesian seer who had written a "complete theory of heavens and
the earth, and a mystical treatise on the art of attaining truth" (480).
Queequeg copies these inscriptions from his tattooed body onto the lid
of the chest (much as Ishmael in "The Bower of the Arsacides" ventures
to copy the inscriptions of the whale shrine onto his body). This is not
the kind of ark that would make the idol Dagon, the Philistine fish god,
fall off the pedestal, nor is it the kind that Winthrop would imagine carrying.[4] Although Melville is primarily indebted to the Judeo-Christian

Bible he never ceases to insist that any esoteric symbol demands interpretation, that any scriptural writing, monotheistic or heathen, needs
to be preserved—against the sharks that surround it and the oblivions
that endanger it—whether on one's body or in arks, chests, and coffins
of all sorts.

To deliver such an ark means to fashion a new poetic sublime. A
memorable footnote in "The Whiteness of the Whale," dealing with
the white albatross, is illuminating in this connection:

> I remember the first albatross I ever saw. It was during a prolonged
> gale, in waters hard upon the Antarctic seas. From my forenoon watch
> below, I ascended to the overclouded deck; and there, dashed upon the
> main hatches, I saw a regal, feathery thing of unspotted whiteness,
> and with a hooked, Roman bill sublime. At intervals, it arched forth
> its vast archangel wings, as if to embrace some holy ark. Wondrous
> flutterings and throbbings shook it. Though bodily unharmed, it ut-
> tered cries, as some king's ghost in supernatural distress. Through its
> inexpressible, strange eyes, methought I peeped to secrets which took
> hold of God. As Abraham before the angels, I bowed myself; the white
> thing was so white, its wings so wide, and in those for ever exiled
> waters, I had lost the miserable warping memories of traditions and of
> towns. (190)

The albatross is likened to a white cherub with "archangel wings"
that supposedly embraces "some holy ark" in its flight.[5] The sight of
the creature is utterly sublime—horrifyingly ghostly and wondrous at
once. Ishmael is shaken by its "flutterings and throbbings," so much
so that he finds himself bowing as "Abraham before the angels." He
seems to eagerly follow the biblical traditions of his namesake's father, but then in a wild turn he relinquishes them—first in bowing
before a white albatross (rather than an angel) and then in relinquishing all "the miserable warping memories of traditions and towns,"
plunging into a whirlpool of "exiled waters" where everything seems
to dissolve in an alliterative stream of *w* sounds—"white," "was,"
"white," "wings," "wide," "waters," "warping." Here as elsewhere,
Melville's overriding aesthetic-hermeneutic principle is to go with
Scripture beyond Scripture. His literary ark never remains on ground:
it either floats on water or is carried off to heaven on the wings of
a strange white albatross, the winged harbinger of the inscrutable
White Whale.

The grand finale of biblical texts that intersect in the "Epilogue"
is accompanied by a final juggling of metacommentaries. The genesis
of a new ark, for Melville, is inextricably connected with reflections

on other Bibles and other commentaries: Job's messenger reminds us of the privileged position of the Book of Job among the advocates of the literary Bible; Queequeg's buoyant coffin calls to mind the scholarly hypotheses in Kitto's *Cyclopedia of Biblical Literature* regarding Jonah's "historical" means of deliverance; the miraculous phenomena that surround Ishmael call for a pilgrimage where the Book and the Sea replace the Book and the Land; the sinking ship of state in the background evokes the use of the story of Ahab in the political discourse of the time; and the *Rachel* welcomes aboard the different women's Bibles of nineteenth-century America.

But there is also something strikingly mundane about the coffin/ ark on which Ishmael floats. It is a buoyant wooden chest that literally saves Ishmael from drowning. He floats on it in a very primary, physical way, trying to catch his breath after the long journey and the catastrophic loss of the ship. When Queequeg "had changed his mind about dying" (480), he turned this coffin into a sea chest, using it for daily purposes while inscribing on its lid the treatises of his island's seer. In doing so, Queequeg unabashedly rejects all prejudices regarding death and artifacts that supposedly belong only to the realm of the dead. The same kind of "wild whimsiness," Melville seems to intimate, is called for in one's treatment of arks. They need not remain untouchable, unchangeable, canonical items whose use is determined by custom: their very capacity to serve as a gift of life depends on the wild imagination of readers who are willing to follow the radicality of the biblical authors and think anew.

To what extent has *Moby-Dick* become the new Ark that it strives to be? I want to end with a few fragmentary thoughts about the circulation of *Moby-Dick*.

MOBY-DICK AS BIBLE

"When my critics find a message about the assassination of a prime minister encrypted in *Moby-Dick*, I'll believe them," claimed Michael Drosnin, author of the controversial *The Bible Code*, in a *Newsweek* interview in June 1997. His critics soon picked up the gauntlet and did indeed find the same kind of encrypted codes Drosnin discovered in the Bible between the lines of *Moby-Dick*.[6] Let me suggest that Drosnin's choice of *Moby-Dick* as a potential test case is not without significance. It is the one book in American culture that has acquired the status of a Bible of sorts and could be offered as a counterpart.

Interestingly, *Moby-Dick* has its own history of readers who have searched for encrypted prophetic codes in it. Otter suggests that this phenomenon may be traced back to 1856, to the March issue of *Frederick Douglass's Paper,* where James McCune Smith detected signs in the text regarding the maneuverings in the House of Representatives in the context of the upcoming presidential elections.[7] But this practice became much more prominent in the frequent evocations of *Moby-Dick* in responses to the events of September 11, 2001. One such case is the Internet discussion group alt.paranormal. The exchanges within this group in October 2001 regarding the hidden codes of *Moby-Dick* revolved around three lines in the first chapter, "Loomings," where Ishmael, just before he embarks on his voyage, envisions the following sensational poster:

> "*Grand Contested Election for the Presidency of the United States.*
> "WHALING VOYAGE BY ONE ISHMAEL.
> "BLOODY BATTLE IN AFFGHANISTAN."
>
> (7)

"What intrigued—and 'intrigued' is a mild word—what transfixed them," writes Otter, "was Ishmael's imagining of the 'grand program of Providence' that would announce his decision to go to sea. . . . And they were preoccupied, of course, by what they saw as 'an astounding synchronicity' with the events of September 11th, 2001, and their aftermath."

While the members of alt.paranormal were debating the significance of such codes, scholars were using *Moby-Dick* as a source of insight with which to interpret the political consequences of September 11. As is the case with the political uses of the Bible, the interpretations were highly diverse. Andrew Delbanco suggested that Osama bin Laden needs to be construed as analogous to Ahab: a demagogue who knows how to "fuse his personal need for vengeance with the popular will by promising his followers a huntable enemy in which evil was made practically assailable." Edward Said, in turn, drew a comparison between bin Laden and Moby Dick. "Captain Ahab in Melville's great novel *Moby-Dick,*" he writes, "was a man possessed with an obsessional drive to pursue the white whale which had harmed him, which had torn his leg out, to the ends of the Earth, no matter what happened. . . . And it would seem to me that to give Osama bin Laden—who has been turned into Moby Dick, he's been made a symbol of all that's evil in the world—to give him a kind of mythological proportion

FIGURE 10. Photograph of Laurie Anderson reading
Melville's bible, by Clifford Ross, from the collection of
Clifford Ross. Courtesy of Clifford Ross.

is really playing his game. I think we need to secularize the man, we
need to bring him down to the realm of reality, . . . [n]ot to bring down
the world around him and ourselves."[8]

These quests for prophetic codes and insights in *Moby-Dick* are
but three incidents in which the reception of Melville's work resembles
that of the Bible. My larger claim is that the vast circulation of *Moby-Dick* in diverse cultural realms repeats the dynamics of biblical reception. *Moby-Dick*, like the Bible, is a cultural text whose traces may be
found in an array of modes and forms—from children's adaptations to
musical interpretations (Laurie Anderson is but one prominent example; see figure 10), literary modes of homage—by writers as different

as D.H. Lawrence, Albert Camus, William Faulkner, and, more recently, Sena Jeter Naslund, author of *Ahab's Wife*—artworks (Jackson Pollock, Mark Milloff, Clifford Ross, and Guy Ben-Ner, among others), Hollywood films (most notably, John Huston's 1956 film starring Gregory Peck and Orson Welles), television productions, political discourse, academic research, "The Melville Trail" in Berkshire County, the Starbucks cafés all over the world, and the numerous boats and seafood restaurants called "Moby Dick."⁹

Both the Bible and *Moby-Dick,* I should add, have acquired pivotal cultural positions even though few of their readers have read them from cover to cover. How many readers have endured the long, detailed depictions of the tabernacle in Exodus or the long lists of laws in Leviticus? How many readers have endured the detailed anatomical representations of whales or the elaborate accounts of the different ship parts in *Moby-Dick?* But the grand impact of these two books does not depend on such thorough readings: it seems to lie in their astounding power to ignite the imagination, to generate new interpretations and new adaptations in every possible realm in each and every generation. They are the kind of big cultural narratives one knows and responds to even without having read them.

To be sure, there are notable differences. Nor did Melville lack self-irony in his treatment of *Moby-Dick* as a "mighty book." The Bible does have a significantly longer and broader history of exegesis than *Moby-Dick* and a far wider range of readers. What is more, as Buell puts it, "no community of devotees has ever received [*Moby-Dick*] as a spiritual authority, nor was that Melville's intent, though he did think of his vocation as truth telling rather than tale telling."¹⁰

In *Mariners, Renegades, and Castaways: Herman Melville and the World We Live In* (1953), the Trinidadian writer C.L.R. James asks what he defines as "the question of questions": "How could a book from the world of 1850 contain so much of the world of the 1950s?"¹¹ While writing *Melville's Bibles,* I found myself asking a similar question: How could *Moby-Dick* have such immense relevance to my life in Jerusalem in the first years of the new millennium? Melville's prophetic warnings and urgent call for a change could be uttered (if differently) in contemporary Jerusalem. What is more, his insights regarding the circulation of the Bible in antebellum America shed much light on the Bible's role in Israeli culture—in the political sphere, in popular and canonical art and music, in travel guides, and in many other realms, among them, modern Hebrew literature with its impressive gallery of biblicists, such as Bialik, Bat-Miriam, and Agnon. Having wandered to and fro between Jerusalem and the United States and given that I am deeply indebted to both Israeli and American culture, *Moby-Dick* also sharpened my understanding of the points of intersection between the two exegetical settings.

But the world I lived in while writing this book was in many ways that of the *Pequod*. Leviathans kept popping up in my thoughts or dreams, and my obsessions with exegetical pursuits (quite substantive to begin with) only deepened. There is nothing, it seems to me, as exhilarating as following a Melvillean exegetical line—it often leads to a black, bubbly vortex, overwhelming in its excess, but a moment later it can offer an exegetical springboard by which to chase yet another "portentous" enigma beyond the domain of the knowable. I will not try to spell out further the experience of what writing a book on *Moby-Dick* was for me. I can only hope that I have conveyed something of the excitement of this adventure throughout the book, while luring you, dear shipmates, to pursue the "Loose-Fish" on your own.

Notes

INTRODUCTION

1. Ralph Waldo Emerson, *The Journals and Miscellaneous Notebooks of Ralph Waldo Emerson*, vol. 8, ed. William H. Gilman (Cambridge, MA: Harvard University Press, 1960–82), July 16, 1843, 438.

2. Herman Melville, *Moby-Dick; or, The Whale* [1851], vol. 6, *The Writings of Herman Melville*, ed. Harrison Hayford, Hershel Parker, and G. Thomas Tanselle (Evanston and Chicago: Northwestern University Press and the Newberry Library, 2001), xix. Subsequent references to the Northwestern-Newberry edition are given in parentheses in the text.

3. Melville endorses the traditional attribution of Ecclesiastes to King Solomon.

4. In later works such as *The Confidence-Man* and *Billy Budd*, the Christian Bible is far more central than the Hebrew Bible.

5. On *Moby-Dick*'s aspiration to be Scripture, see Lawrence Buell, "*Moby-Dick* as Sacred Text," in *New Essays on Moby-Dick*, ed. Richard H. Brodhead (Cambridge: Cambridge University Press, 1986), 53–72. See also Andrew Delbanco, "Melville's Sacramental Style," *Raritan* 12, no. 3 (Winter 1993): 69–92.

6. On Melville and the heterogeneity of the biblical text, see Craig Svonkin, "Melville and the Bible: *Moby-Dick; Or, The Whale*, Multivocalism, and Plurality," *Letteratura D'America* 21, nos. 88–89 (2001): 53–73.

7. Nathalia Wright, *Melville's Use of the Bible* (New York: Duke University Press, 1949; rpt. 1969); Lawrence Thompson, *Melville's Quarrel with God* (Princeton, NJ: Princeton University Press, 1952); Sacvan Bercovitch, *The American Jeremiad* (Madison: University of Wisconsin Press, 1978) and *The Rites of Assent: Transformations in the Symbolic Construction of America* (New York: Routledge, 1993); Lawrence Buell, *New England Literary Culture:*

From Revolution through Renaissance (Cambridge: Cambridge University Press, 1986), Elisa New, "Bible Leaves! Bible Leaves! Hellenism and Hebraism in Melville's *Moby-Dick*," *Poetics Today* 19, no. 2 (1998): 281–303; Michael Paul Rogin, *Subversive Genealogy: The Politics and Art of Herman Melville* (Berkeley: University of California Press, 1979); Hilton Obenzinger, *American Palestine: Melville, Twain, and Holy Land Mania* (Princeton, NJ: Princeton University Press, 1999).

   8. Wright, *Melville's Use of the Bible*, 27.

   9. One of the only critics to provide an extensive consideration of Melville's hermeneutics is Bainard Cowan, *Exiled Waters: Moby-Dick and the Crisis of Allegory* (Baton Rouge: Louisiana State University Press, 1982). Cowan, however, does not focus on the implications of Melville's hermeneutics within the realm of biblical exegesis.

   10. Robert Alter, *Canon and Creativity: Modern Writing and the Authority of the Canon* (New Haven, CT: Yale University Press, 2000); Harold Fisch, *New Stories for Old: Biblical Patterns in the Novel* (New York: St. Martin's Press, 1998); Northrop Frye, *The Great Code: The Bible and Literature* (San Diego: Harcourt Brace Jovanovich, 1982). See also Chana Kronfeld, "Theories of Allusion and Imagist Intertextuality: When Iconoclasts Read the Bible," in *On the Margins of Modernism: Decentering Literary Dynamics* (Berkeley: University of California Press, 1996), 114–40.

   11. Mieke Bal, *Lethal Love: Feminist Literary Interpretations of Biblical Love Stories* (Bloomington: Indiana University Press, 1987); Elizabeth Castelli, Stephen D. Moore, Garry A. Phillips, and Regina M. Schwartz, eds., *The Postmodern Bible: The Bible and Culture Collective* (New Haven, CT: Yale University Press, 1995); Paul C. Gutjahr, *An American Bible: A History of the Good Book in the United States, 1777–1880* (Stanford, CA: Stanford University Press, 1999); Jonathan Sheehan, *The Enlightenment Bible: Translation, Scholarship, Culture* (Princeton, NJ: Princeton University Press, 2005).

   12. The "Vaticans" are vast libraries such as that of the Vatican in Rome. The choice of a theological library in particular is of course no coincidence.

   13. William M. Thomson, *The Land and the Book: or, Biblical Illustrations Drawn from the Manners and Customs, the Scenes and Scenery of the Holy Land*, vol. 2 (New York: Harper and Bros., 1859), xv.

   14. Sheehan, *The Enlightenment Bible*, xi.

   15. On the Bible in American culture, see Perry Miller, *Errand into the Wilderness* (Cambridge, MA: Harvard University Press, 1956); Sacvan Bercovitch, *The Puritan Origins of the American Self* (New Haven, CT: Yale University Press, 1975); Nathan O. Hatch and Mark A. Noll, eds., *The Bible in America: Essays in Cultural History* (New York: Oxford University Press, 1982); Avihu Zakai, *Exile and Kingdom: History and Apocalypse in the Puritan Migration to America* (Cambridge: Cambridge University Press, 1992).

   16. Lawrence Buell, *Emerson* (Cambridge, MA: Harvard University Press, 2003); Donald Pease, "C.L.R. James, *Moby-Dick*, and the Emergence of Transnational American Studies," *Arizona Quarterly: A Journal of American Literature, Culture, and Theory* 56, no. 3 (Autumn 2000): 93–123.

17. Herman Melville, "Hawthorne and His Mosses," in the Norton Critical Edition of Herman Melville, *Moby-Dick,* ed. Hershel Parker and Harrison Hayford (New York: Norton, 2002), 527.

18. For a consideration of the mixed reviews *Moby-Dick* received on its publication, see Brian Higgins and Hershel Parker, eds., *Herman Melville: The Contemporary Reviews* (New York: Cambridge University Press, 1995); and Hershel Parker, *Herman Melville: A Biography,* vol. 2 (Baltimore, MD: Johns Hopkins University Press, 2002), 1–30.

19. Herman Melville, *The Confidence-Man: His Masquerade,* ed. Hershel Parker, Norton Critical Edition (New York: Norton, 1971), 59.

20. On typologies in *The Confidence-Man,* see Shira Wolosky, "Melville's Unreading of the Bible: *Redburn* and the *Confidence Man,*" *Letterature D'America* 21, nos. 88–89 (2001): 31–52. For more on Melville's treatment of the inconsistencies of character, see Elizabeth Renker, "'A___!': Unreadability in *The Confidence-Man,*" in *The Cambridge Companion to Herman Melville,* ed. Robert S. Levine (Cambridge: Cambridge University Press, 1998), 114–34.

21. Ursula Brumm, *American Thought and Religious Typology,* trans. John Hoagland (New Brunswick, NJ: Rutgers University Press, 1970), 177.

22. For studies that complicate Melville's perception of democracy, see Larzer Ziff, *Literary Democracy: The Declaration of Cultural Independence in America* (New York: Viking, 1981); David S. Reynolds, *Beneath the American Renaissance: The Subversive Imagination in the Age of Emerson and Melville* (New York: Knopf, 1988), 275–308; Nancy Ruttenburg, *Democratic Personality: Popular Voice and the Trial of American Authorship* (Stanford, CA: Stanford University Press, 1998); Myra Jehlen, "Melville and Class," in *A Historical Guide to Herman Melville,* ed. Giles Gunn (New York: Oxford University Press, 2005), 83–104.

23. See Frank Kermode, *The Genesis of Secrecy: On the Interpretation of Narrative* (Cambridge, MA: Harvard University Press, 1979); Geoffrey H. Hartman, "The Struggle for the Text," in *Midrash and Literature,* ed. Geoffrey H. Hartman and Sanford Budick (New Haven, CT: Yale University Press, 1986), 3–18; Joshua Levinson, "Dialogical Reading in the Rabbinic Exegetical Narrative," *Poetics Today* 25, no. 3 (2004): 497–528.

24. Andrew Delbanco, *Melville: His World and Work* (New York: Knopf, 2005), 21. For more on Melville's religious background and religious thought, see William Braswell, *Melville's Religious Thought: An Essay in Interpretation* (Durham, NC: Duke University Press, 1943); Zephyra Porat, *Prometheus among the Cannibals: Adventures of the Rebel in Literature* (Tel Aviv: Am Oved, 1976), 82–114 (in Hebrew); T. Walter Herbert, *Moby-Dick and Calvinism: A World Dismantled* (New Brunswick, NJ: Rutgers University Press, 1977); Rowland A. Sherrill, *The Prophetic Melville* (Athens: University of Georgia Press, 1979) and "Melville and Religion," in *A Companion to Melville's Studies,* ed. John Bryant (New York: Greenwood Press, 1986), 481–513. See also Gail H. Coffler, *Melville's Allusions to Religion: A Comprehensive Index and Glossary* (Westport, CT: Praeger, 2004).

25. I am referring to Melville's famous words on Hawthorne in "Hawthorne and His Mosses," 521.

26. Randall Stewart, ed., *The English Notebooks by Nathaniel Hawthorne* (New York: Russell and Russell, 1941), 432–33.

27. The expression "pilgrim-infidel" is used in *Clarel* to define the ambiguities of its protagonist (1.6.15–19):

> If little of the words he knew,
> Might Clarel's fancy forge a clue?
> A malediction seemed each strain—
> Himself the mark: O heart profane,
> O pilgrim-infidel, begone!

Clarel: A Poem and Pilgrimage in the Holy Land (1876), vol. 12, *The Writings of Herman Melville,* ed. Harrison Hayford, Alma A. MacDougall, Hershel Parker, and G. Thomas Tanselle (Evanston and Chicago: Northwestern University Press and the Newberry Library, 1991).

28. Jenny Franchot, "Melville's Traveling God," in Levine, ed., *The Cambridge Companion to Herman Melville,* 160. For more on Melville's spiritual restlessness, see Emory Elliott, "'Wandering To-And-Fro': Melville and Religion," in Gunn, ed., *A Historical Guide to Herman Melville* (New York: Oxford University Press, 2005), 167–204.

29. For the full list of Melville's bibles, see Merton M. Sealts, *Melville's Readings: A Check-list of Books Owned and Borrowed* (Madison: University of Wisconsin Press, 1966), nos. 60–65. See also Mary K. Bercaw, *Melville's Sources* (Evanston, IL: Northwestern University Press, 1987).

30. See Walker Cowen, *Melville's Marginalia* (New York: Garland, 1987); Mark Heidmann, "The Markings in Herman Melville's Bibles," *Studies in the American Renaissance* (1990): 341–98.

31. Wright, *Melville's Use of the Bible,* 9–10.

32. See Gutjahr, *An American Bible,* 89–111; David Daniell, *The Bible in English* (New Haven, CT: Yale University Press, 2003), 624–58.

33. Laurie Anderson, "Songs and Stories from Moby Dick," *HomePage of the Brave,* 1999, www-static.cc.gatech.edu/~jimmyd/laurie-anderson/performances/mobydick/programnotes.html.

34. Maurice Blanchot, "The Song of the Sirens," in *The Station Hill Blanchot Reader: Fiction and Literary Essays,* trans. Lydia Davis, Paul Auster, and Robert Lamberton, ed. George Quasha (New York: Station Hill Press, 1999), 448.

35. Proverbs, much like Ecclesiastes, was attributed to King Solomon.

36. Blanchot, "The Song of the Sirens," 448.

I. PLAYING WITH LEVIATHAN

1. Thompson, *Melville's Quarrel with God,* 147.

2. Ibid.

3. C. Hugh Holman, "The Reconciliation of Ishmael: Moby-Dick and the Book of Job ," *South Atlantic Quarterly* 57 (1958): 478–90; Janis Stout,

"Melville's Use of the Book of Job," *Nineteenth-Century Fiction* 25 (1970): 69–83. See also Nathalia Wright, "Moby Dick: Jonah's or Job's Whale?" *American Literature* 37 (May 1965): 190–95.

4. Buell, *New England Literary Culture,* 166–90.

5. Melville's alignment with continental genealogies is also apparent in "The Try-Works," where he hails Cowper, Young, Pascal, and Rousseau as true readers of Eccelesiastes.

6. In *Emerson,* Buell claims that "the most striking qualities of Emerson's work often tend to get lost when we yield too quickly to the temptation of casting him as epitomizing the values of nation or regional tribe, instead of conceiving him in tension between such a role and a more cosmopolitan sense of how a writer-intellectual should think and be" (4). This description holds for Melville's work as well.

7. Sheehan, *The Enlightenment Bible.*

8. Robert Lowth, *Lectures on the Sacred Poetry of the Hebrews* (Hildesheim: Georg Olms Verlag, 1969), 2:345–435. David Norton discusses Robert Lowth's contribution to the rise of the literary Bible in *A History of the Bible as Literature: From 1700 to the Present* (Cambridge: Cambridge University Press, 1993), 59–73.

9. For more on the question of Joban sublimity in the English Enlightenment, see Jonathan Lamb, *The Rhetoric of Suffering: Reading the Book of Job in the Eighteenth Century* (New York: Oxford University Press, 1995).

10. For an illuminating consideration of Herder, see Hans W. Frei, *The Eclipse of Biblical Narrative: A Study in Eighteenth- and Nineteenth-Century Hermeneutics* (New Haven, CT: Yale University Press, 1974).

11. J. G. Herder, "God and Nature in the Book of Job" (from *The Spirit of Hebrew Poetry*), in *The Dimensions of Job: A Study and Selected Readings,* presented by Nahum N. Glatzer (New York: Schocken Books, 1969; rpt. 1975), 154.

12. Jonathan Sheehan, "Theodicy in Translation: Writing the Book of Job in the Enlightenment," *Prooftexts* 27, no. 2 (Spring 2008).

13. Thomas Carlyle, *On Heroes, Hero-Worship, and the Heroic in History* [1840], ed. Carl Niemeyer (Lincoln: University of Nebraska Press, 1966), 49.

14. The Book of Job opens with a folkloric prose Prologue (chaps. 1, 2) and ends with a stylistically similar prose Epilogue (chap. 42). The majority of the text comprises the poetic Dialogues between Job and his friends/comforters (chaps. 3–37). God's whirlwind poem comes after the Dialogues and before the Epilogue (chaps. 38–41). For an extensive account of the structure of the Book of Job, see Marvin Pope, *Job,* the Anchor Bible (Garden City, NY: Doubleday, 1977).

15. The one notable precursor of this exegetical move is Shakespeare's *King Lear.* For a remarkable reading of the antitheodician Joban qualities of Lear, see Ruth Nevo, *Tragic Form in Shakespeare* (Princeton, NJ: Princeton University Press, 1972).

16. On "The Tyger" and Job, see Harold Fisch, *The Biblical Presence in Shakespeare, Milton, and Blake: A Comparative Study* (New York: Oxford University Press, 1999), 318–25. For more on Blake and the Romantic sublime,

see Thomas Weiskel, *The Romantic Sublime: Studies in the Structure and Psychology of Transcendence* (Baltimore, MD: Johns Hopkins University Press, 1976).

17. Readers in the nineteenth century were well aware of the Joban character of *Faust*. In an essay on Goethe published in the *Dial,* Margaret Fuller suggests, "The Jewish demon assailed the man of Uz with physical ills, the Lucifer of the middle ages tempted his passions, but the Mephistopheles of the eighteenth century bade the finite strive to compass the infinite, and the intellect attempt to solve all the problems of the soul." Quoted in Johann Wolfgang von Goethe, Norton Critical Edition of *Faust,* trans. Walter Arndt, ed. Cyrus Hamlin (New York: Norton, 2001), 565.

18. Franchot, "Melville's Traveling God," 158.

19. For more on the multiplicity of genres in Melville's work, see Nina Baym, "Melville's Quarrel with Fiction," *PMLA* 94 (1979): 903–23. On the relation of Melville's mixed genres to the literary practices of his time, see Sheila Post-Lauria, *Correspondent Colorings: Melville in the Marketplace* (Amherst: University of Massachusetts Press, 1996), 101–22.

20. Melville offers an explicit discussion of the Oriental origins of Job in *Clarel* 2.27.74–79. Melville, I should emphasize, was not necessarily familiar with all the readings of Job I have listed. We know he read Burke, Goethe, and Carlyle, and one may add Shelley's *Prometheus Unbound* to the list. I suspect that he was exposed to Herder's work either directly (he mentions Herder in his journal on April 21, 1856; *Journals,* vol. 15, *The Writings of Herman Melville,* ed. Holward C. Horsford with Lynn Horth [Evanston and Chicago: Northwestern University Press and the Newberry Library, 1989], 520) or through the writings of Carlyle and Coleridge (on Coleridge's debt to Herder, see E. S. Shaffer, *'Kubla Khan' and the Fall of Jerusalem: The Mythological School in Biblical Criticism and Secular Literature, 1770–1880* [Cambridge: Cambridge University Press, 1975]). He probably was not familiar with Blake's interpretations while writing *Moby-Dick,* though the similarities between the two are rather striking. In *Melville's Readings,* Sealts lists Alexander Gilchrist's *Life of William Blake* (London: Macmillan, 1863), acquired by Melville in 1870.

21. John Lloyd Stephens, *Incidents of Travel in Egypt, Arabia Petraea, and the Holy Land,* ed. Victor Wolfgang von Hagen (Norman: University of Oklahoma Press, 1970), 294.

22. Melville, among other things, debunks Calvin in this passage. Calvin construed God's response to Job as a humbling lesson: "And if a saint like Job, who humbled himself under His majesty, needed to be checked, what about us? . . . God speaks to us out of a whirlwind because we did not hear Him when he spoke to us graciously and in a humane and fatherly manner. For a time He lets us run like horses, yet in the end we shall experience His terrible majesty to be frightened by it" (Sermon 147, *The Dimensions of Job,* 33). For more on Calvin's commentary on Job, see Susan E. Schreiner, *Where Shall Wisdom Be Found? Calvin's Exegesis of Job from Medieval and Modern Perspectives* (Chicago: University of Chicago Press, 1994).

23. Cowan provides a reading of Ishmael's Joban "unveilings" in *Exiled Waters,* 151.

24. On Job and "Cetology," see Samuel Otter, *Melville's Anatomies* (Berkeley: University of California Press, 1999), 133–34.

25. According to Ps. 104:26, Leviathan is God's pet: "There is that leviathan, whom thou hast made to play therein" (quoted in the "Extracts," xx).

26. Eyal Peretz, *Literature, Disaster, and the Enigma of Power* (Stanford, CA: Stanford University Press, 2003), 45. Original emphasis removed.

27. Edmund Burke, *A Philosophical Enquiry into the Origin of our Ideas of the Sublime and the Beautiful* (London: Routledge and Kegan Paul, 1958), 63. For more on Burke's notion of the sublime, see Andrew Ashfield and Peter de Bolla, eds., *The Sublime: A Reader in British Eighteenth-Century Aesthetic Theory* (Cambridge: Cambridge University Press, 1996), 131–43.

28. René Girard, *Job: The Victim of His People,* trans. Yvonne Freccero (Stanford, CA: Stanford University Press, 1987).

29. Gustavo Gutiérrez, *On Job: God-Talk and the Suffering of the Innocent,* trans. Matthew J. O'Connell (New York: Orbis Books, 1987), 31.

30. In making the distinction between the two modes of the sublime, I rely on Marc C. Conner's observations in "From the Sublime to the Beautiful: The Aesthetic Progression of Toni Morrison," in *The Aesthetics of Toni Morrison: Speaking the Unspeakable* (Jackson: University of Mississippi Press, 2000), 50–51. On Ishmael as witness, see Peretz, *Literature, Disaster, and the Enigma of Power.* Peretz highlights the power of Ishmael's narrative as testimony but overlooks the transcendent playful mode of sublimity that intersects with it.

31. W. M. L. De Wette, *A Critical and Historical Introduction to the Canonical Scriptures of the Old Testament,* trans. Theodore Parker (Boston: C. C. Little and J. Brown, 1843), 555.

32. Richard B. Sewall, *The Vision of Tragedy* (New Haven, CT: Yale University Press, 1959), 9–24. For more on the debate regarding Job's tragic bent, see Harold Fisch, *Poetry with a Purpose: Biblical Poetics and Interpretation* (Bloomington: Indiana University Press, 1990), 26–42. For new considerations of Job as tragedy, see Ariel Hirschfeld, "Ha'im 'Iyov' hu Tragedia," in *Iyov baMikra baHagut baOmanut,* ed. Lea Mazor (Jerusalem: Magnes Press, 1994), 54–88; and Ed Greenstein, "Bdiduto shel Iyov," in Mazor, ed., *Iyov baMikra baHagut baOmanut,* 43–53.

33. Melville critics have overlooked the fact that sea monsters and the mythical divine struggle against them in primeval times is a recurrent theme in Job. The portrayal of Leviathan in Job 41, in other words, is the climactic moment of a principal metaphoric line in the text.

34. On Job's cursing as turning point, see my *Countertraditions in the Bible* (Cambridge, MA: Harvard University Press, 1992), 145–51.

35. See Robert Alter, *The Art of Biblical Poetry* (New York: Basic Books, 1985), 76–84.

36. See Exod. 22:27 and Lev. 24:13–16. This is the law Job's wife has in mind when she cries "curse God and die."

37. See S. Foster Damon, *Blake's Job: William Blake's Illustrations of the Book of Job* (New York: E. P. Dutton, 1966), 26.

38. Goethe, in the Norton Critical Edition of *Faust,* 43. Melville is also indebted to Goethe in shaping his tragic Job. Goethe himself defines *Faust*

as tragedy, but the salvation of Faust at the end has led Benjamin Bennett, among others, to regard it as an "interrupted" tragedy. See Benjamin Bennett, *Goethe's Theory of Poetry: Faust and the Regeneration of Language* (Ithaca, NY: Cornell University Press, 1986), 19–39.

39. F. O. Matthiessen, *American Renaissance: Art and Expression in the Age of Emerson and Whitman* (New York: Oxford University Press, 1941), 441.

40. Quoted in Shira Wolosky, *Emily Dickinson: The Voice of War* (New Haven, CT: Yale University Press, 1984), 66. Wolosky provides an examination of Dickinson's treatment of theodicy that is relevant to the understanding of Melville's position.

41. Melville, "Hawthorne and His Mosses," 522.

42. The Book of Job is one the books that Melville marked profusely: forty-five markings, among them, the Leviathan sequence in Job 41 and this verse, 13:15.

43. The Joban quality of this line is discussed in Stout, "Melville's Use of the Book of Job," 78.

44. Immanuel Kant, "On the Miscarriage of all Philosophical Trials of Theodicy," in *Religion and Rational Theology*, trans. Allen W. Wood and George Di Giovanni (Cambridge: Cambridge University Press, 1996), 33. For more on Kant's reading of Job, see Glatzer, *The Dimensions of Job*, 37–39.

45. Alter, *The Art of Biblical Poetry*, 109. I provide an extensive consideration of Alter's reading of Job in "Job's Leviathan: Between Melville and Alter," *Prooftexts* 27, no. 2 (Spring 2008).

46. Herman Melville, "Bartleby," in *The Piazza Tales*, ed. Harrison Hayford, Alma A. MacDougall, and G. Thomas Tanselle (Evanston, IL: Northwestern University Press, 2000), 45. On Bartleby as Job, see Rogin, *Subversive Genealogy*, 200–201.

47. Thompson, in *Melville's Quarrel with God*, 235, traces the Joban echoes of this scene. Michael Gilmore reads Ahab's death as an inversion of Christ's successful triumph over Satan in *The Middle Way: Puritanism and Ideology in American Romantic Fiction* (New Brunswick, NJ: Rutgers University Press, 1977), 147–48.

48. See Cowan, *Exiled Waters*, 134–35.

49. In *The Confidence-Man*, Melville further explores the wager scene. See Stout, "Melville's Use of Job," 81.

50. Martin Buber, "Job," in *On the Bible: Eighteen Essays by Martin Buber*, ed. Nahum N. Glatzer (New York: Schocken Books, 1982), 190.

51. Thomas Hobbes, *Leviathan* (London and Oxford: Basil Blackwell Oxford, 1946), 209. Melville refers to *Leviathan* in the "Extracts" (xxii).

52. In tracing the marks of the devil under the robes of high officials, Melville shares Hawthorne's concern with the drawbacks of any mode of rule, including democracy. "Young Goodman Brown," "My Kinsman, Major Molineux," and *The Scarlet Letter* all attest to the intriguingly complex ties majors, deacons, and reverends have with their respective devils in disguise.

53. Melville may also be referring to talmudic lore according to which the righteous are granted the privilege of eating the flesh of Leviathan (Baba Batra 74b–75a). Stubb's dinner is an inverted version of the righteous one. On the

Talmudic perception of Leviathan, see Moshe Idel, "Livyatan u-Vat zugo," in *haMitos baYahadut,* ed. Moshe Idel and Itamar Gruenwald (Jerusalem: Zalman Shazar Center for Jewish History, 2003), 145–88 (in Hebrew).

54. For more on *The Trial* as a rereading of Job, see Harold Fisch, *New Stories for Old: Biblical Patterns in the Novel* (New York: St. Martin's Press, 1998), 81–99; Schreiner, *Where Shall Wisdom Be Found?* 183–90. The affinity between "Bartleby" and Kafka has been noted earlier but not in relation to Job. See Gilles Deleuze, "Bartleby; Or the Formula," in *Essays Critical and Clinical,* trans. Daniel W. Smith and Michael A. Greco (Minneapolis: University of Minnesota Press, 1997), 68. Giorgio Agamben offers a similar observation in *Potentialities: Collected Essays in Philosophy,* trans. Daniel Heller-Roazen (Stanford, CA: Stanford University Press, 1999), 243.

55. Quoted in Schreiner, *Where Shall Wisdom Be Found?* 186.

56. Jacques Derrida, "Devant la Loi," in *Kafka and the Contemporary Critical Performance,* trans. Avital Ronell, ed. Alan Udoff (Bloomington: Indiana University Press, 1987).

2. "JONAH HISTORICALLY REGARDED"

1. On Mapple's sermon, see Thompson, *Melville's Quarrel with God,* 153–66; Cowan, *Exiled Waters,* 81–86; and Jay A. Holstein, "Melville's Inversion of Jonah in *Moby-Dick," Illif Review* 42 (1985): 13–20. These studies contribute much to the understanding of Melville's parody of Calvinist dogma. What they overlook is the ars poetic–hermeneutic qualities of the sermon.

2. This midrash appears in Midrash Jonah and in *Pirke de Rabbi Eliezer,* chap. 10. It is quoted in Pierre Bayle's entry on Jonah in *Dictionnaire historique et critique.*

3. Sterling Stuckey, "The Tambourine in Glory: African Culture and Melville's Art," in *The Cambridge Companion to Herman Melville,* ed. Robert S. Levine (New York: Cambridge University Press, 1998), 37–64.

4. Howard P. Vincent, *The Trying-Out of Moby-Dick* (Carbondale: Southern Illinois Press, 1949), 271.

5. New, "Bible Leaves! Bible Leaves!" 294.

6. Otter, *Melville's Anatomies,* 4.

7. For more on Strauss, see Frei, *The Eclipse of Biblical Narrative,* 233–44.

8. Jerry Wayne Brown, *The Rise of Biblical Criticism in America, 1800–1870* (Middletown, CT: Wesleyan University Press, 1969), 7. For more on biblical criticism in America, see Philip F. Gura, *The Crossroads of American History and Literature* (University Park: Pennsylvania State University Press, 1996).

9. Quoted in Brown, *The Rise of Biblical Criticism,*158.

10. Quoted in Brown, *The Rise of Biblical Criticism,* 157.

11. Theodore Parker, *A Discourse of Matters Pertaining to Religion,* vol. 1, *The Collected Works of Theodore Parker* (London: Trubner & Co., 1863), 244.

12. Theodore Parker, "A Sermon of Slavery," vol. 5, *The Collected Works of Theodore Parker* (London: Trubner & Co., 1863), 14.

13. Albert J. Harrill, "The Use of the New Testament in the American Slave Controversy: A Case History in the Hermeneutical Tension between Biblical Criticism and Christian Moral Debate," *Religion and American Culture: A Journal of Interpretation* 10, no. 2 (2000): 149–86.

14. Quoted in Obenzinger, *American Palestine,* 52.

15. Gutjahr, *An American Bible,* 64.

16. J. E. Rayland, ed., *Memoirs of Dr. John Kitto* (Edinburgh: William Olphant & Sons, 1856), 572–75.

17. *New Englander* 5 (January 1847): 144.

18. For more on Kitto's role in the British exegetical scene, see Eitan Bar-Yosef, *The Holy Land in English Culture, 1799–1917* (Oxford: Oxford University Press, 2005),113–29.

19. Among John Eadie's writings is a "critical estimate" of John Kitto's work; see Rayland, *Memoirs of Dr. John Kitto.*

20. John Eadie, "Jonah," in *Cyclopedia of Biblical Literature,* ed. John Kitto (Edinburgh: Adam and Charles Black, 1845), 142.

21. On zoological readings of Jonah's fish, see Yvonne Sherwood, *A Biblical Text and Its Afterlives: The Survival of Jonah in Western Culture* (Cambridge: Cambridge University Press, 2000), 32–41. Note that in Kitto's zoological account of Job's Leviathan, the creature is classified as crocodile rather than the traditional designation whale. "There can be no doubt," claims Kitto, "that the description in Job applies to the crocodile."

22. Eadie, "Jonah," 143.

23. Ibid.

24. The parody on sacred geography in this passage is indebted to Pierre Bayle's sharp critique of Sulpicius Severus's "geographical blunder" regarding Jonah's unidentified coast. Pierre Bayle, *The Dictionary Historical and Critical, 1734–1738,* 2d ed. (New York: Garland, 1984), 579.

25. See *New Englander* 7 (May 1849): 326–27. For more on Layard's *Nineveh and Its Remains,* see David Damrosch, *What Is World Literature?* (Princeton, NJ: Princeton University Press, 2003).

26. A. H. Layard, *Nineveh and Its Remains: With an Account of a Visit to the Chaldaean Christians of Kurdistan, and the Yezidis, or Devil Worshippers; and an Inquiry into the Manners and Arts of the Ancient Assyrians* (New York: Putnam, 1849), 242–43.

27. Eadie, "Jonah," 143.

28. Bruce H. Franklin, *The Wake of the Gods: Melville's Mythology* (Stanford, CA: Stanford University Press, 1963), 3.

29. Buell, *New England Literary Culture,* 181.

30. Elizabeth Castelli, Stephen D. Moore, Garry A. Phillips, and Regina M. Schwartz, eds., *The Postmodern Bible: The Bible and Culture Collective* (New Haven, CT: Yale University Press, 1995), 1–3.

31. Otter, *Melville's Anatomies,* 147–53.

32. Biblical scholars from De Wette on have defined the psalm as an interpolated text, claiming that its contents are incompatible with the prophet's position. Eadie goes so far as to suggest that this psalm of thanksgiving was delivered only after Jonah's safe arrival on shore. But, for Melville, this change

of locus is unacceptable. The canticle emerges from the belly of the big fish because this is one of the ultimate sites of poetic-prophetic vision. For more on
the relation between the psalm and narrative in Jonah, see Steve Weitzman,
*Song and Story in Biblical Narrative: The History of a Literary Convention in
Biblical Narrative* (Bloomington: Indiana University Press, 1997), 109–13.

33. Robert Lowth, *Lectures on the Sacred Poetry of the Hebrews*
(Hildesheim: Georg Olms Verlag, 1969), 2:18.

34. On Melville's debt to Gnostic traditions, see Thomas Vargish, "Gnostic Mythos in *Moby-Dick*," *PMLA* 81, no. 3 (1966): 272–77.

35. Gershom Scholem, *Kabbalah* (Jerusalem: Keter Publishing House,
1974), 17. According to Scholem, an early Hellenized version of such specula-
tion appears in the description of the "body of truth" in the Gnostic Markos.
Other references are to be found in the Slavonic Book of Enoch and in Origen,
who was aware of the role of these teachings in the midrashic interpretations
of the Song of Songs. For more on *Shi'ur Koma,* see Joseph Dan, *Hamistika
ha-'ivrit hakduma* (Tel Aviv: Oniversita Meshuderet, 1989).

36. Deleuze, *Essays Critical and Clinical,* 72.

37. Eadie, "Jonah," 142.

38. Ibid., 144.

39. On Melville's treatment of madness, see Paul McCarthy, *The Twisted
Mind: Madness in Melville's Fiction* (Iowa City: University of Iowa Press,
1990).

40. "Castaway" is the title of the chapter dealing with the desertion of
Pip in the midst of seas. Note that the verb *cast* is a keyword in the first two
chapters of the King James Version of Jonah. For more on Pip as castaway, see
Viola Sachs, *The Game of Creation: The Primeval Unlettered Language of
Moby-Dick* (Paris: Editions de la Maison de Sciences de l'Homme, 1982).

41. Melville reexamines the question of violence in Jonah's story in *Billy
Budd,* where the narrator speaks of the temptation of sailors to give "Jonah's
toss" to "aggravating" objects. *Billy Budd, Sailor, and Selected Tales* (Oxford: Oxford University Press, 1998), 308.

42. Quoted in Lawrence Levine, *Black Culture and Black Consciousness*
(New York: Oxford University Press, 1977), 51.

43. Carolyn Karcher, *Shadow over the Promised Land: Slavery, Race,
and Violence in Melville's America* (Baton Rouge: Louisiana State University
Press, 1980), 89.

44. See James Ackerman, "Jonah," in *The Literary Guide to the Bible,* ed.
Robert Alter and Frank Kermode (Cambridge, MA: Harvard University Press,
1987), 234–43; E. M. Good, *Irony in the Old Testament* (Philadelphia: West-
minster Press, 1965); Terry Eagleton, "J. L. Austin and the Book of Jonah," in
The Book and the Text: The Bible and Literary Theory, ed. Regina Schwartz
(Cambridge: Basil Blackwell, 1990), 231–36. For an extensive consideration of
Jonah and genre, see J. M. Sasson, *Jonah,* Anchor Bible (New York: Double-
day, 1990), 331–51.

45. Eagleton, "J. L. Austin and the Book of Jonah," 233. Eagleton relies on
Austin's speech-act theory in defining the paradoxical status of prophetic discourse. Let me add that Eagleton is not strictly speaking a biblical critic. The

essay on Jonah is his only piece on the Bible, but it has had much resonance in the field. Thus, for example, it has been included in David Jobling, Tina Pippin, and Ronald Schleifer, eds., *The Postmodern Bible Reader* (Oxford: Blackwell, 2001).

46. Eagleton, "J. L. Austin and the Book of Jonah," 234.

47. Ibid., 236.

48. See Yehuda Liebes, "Yona Ben Amitai as Messiah Ben Yosef," *Jerusalem Studies in Jewish Thought* 3 (1984): 269–311 (Hebrew); Gershom Scholem, "On Jonah and the Concept of Justice," *Critical Inquiry* 25 (Winter 1999): 353–62; Uriel Simon, *Jonah*, JPS Bible Commentary, trans. Lenn J. Schramm (Philadelphia: Jewish Publication Society, 1999); Bruce Vawter, *Job and Jonah: Questioning the Hidden God* (New York: Paulist Press, 1983).

49. Parker, "Sermon of Slavery," 3.

50. On *Moby-Dick*'s prophetic envisioning of the Civil War, see Rogin, *Subversive Genealogy*, 102–51. For a discussion of the apocalyptic quality of Melville's prophecy, see Michael Gilmore, "Melville's Apocalypse: American Millennialism and *Moby-Dick*," *Journal of the American Renaissance* 21, no. 1 (1975): 154–61.

3. "CALL ME ISHMAEL"

1. I use Kitto's translation of the name "Ishmael." Robert Alter offers a more accurate translation: "God has heard"; see Robert Alter, *The Five Books of Moses* (New York: Norton, 2004), 79.

2. On the blurring of boundaries between the testimonial and the fictional in this opening address, see Peretz, *Literature, Disaster, and the Enigma of Power*, 35–45.

3. Wright, *Melville's Use of the Bible*, 46–59, regards Ishmael as one of Melville's central "types."

4. On Ishmael's spleen, see Robert Zoellner, *The Salt-Sea Mastodon: A Reading of Moby-Dick* (Berkeley: University of California Press, 1973), 118–45.

5. Ralph Waldo Emerson, *The Collected Works of Ralph Waldo Emerson*, vol. 1, ed. Robert E. Spiller, Alfred R. Ferguson, Joseph Slater, Jean Ferguson Carr, Wallace E. Williams, and Douglas Emory Wilson (Cambridge, MA: Harvard University Press, 1971). For more on "The Divinity School Address," see Buell, *Emerson*, 158–69.

6. Redburn explicitly identifies with Ishmael at the end of chapter 12: "So that at last I found myself a sort of Ishmael in the ship, without a single friend or companion; and I began to feel a hatred growing up in me against the whole crew." Herman Melville, *Redburn* (New York: Penguin Books, 1986), 114.

7. Melville, *Redburn*, 46.

8. On Stephens as Melville's "Arabian traveler," see Victor Wolfgang von Hagen's introduction to Stephens, *Incidents of Travel*, xxxii–xxxiv.

9. Obenzinger, *American Palestine*, 3.

10. Ibid., x.

11. To be sure, *Moby-Dick* has often been defined as pilgrimage but not in relation to Holy Land travels. For other notable contributions to the

understanding of *Clarel* in the context of Holy Land travel literature in addition to Obenzinger's work, see John Davis, *Landscape of Belief: Encountering the Holy Land in Nineteenth-Century America* (Princeton, NJ: Princeton University Press, 1996); and Basem L. Ra'ad, "Ancient Lands," in *A Companion to Herman Melville,* ed. Wyn Kelley (Malden, MA: Blackwell, 2006), 129–45.

12. On the fluid national boundaries in *Moby-Dick,* see Edward W. Said, "Introduction to *Moby-Dick,*" in *Reflections on Exile and Other Essays* (Cambridge, MA: Harvard University Press, 2002), 358.

13. C. L. R. James, *Mariners, Renegades & Castaways: The Story of Herman Melville and the World We Live In* (Hanover, NH: University Press of New England, 1953, 1978), 18.

14. One notable example of an Ishmael-like character in *Clarel* is the turbaned Djalea, who leads the pilgrims by the Jordan, with a glare that conveys his affinity with Ishmael: "Elate he shot a brigand glare:/ I, Ishmael, have my desert mare!" (2.24.166–68). Note that the story of Ishmael also seeps in via Agar (Hagar), the mother of Clarel's beloved.

15. Timothy Marr, *The Cultural Roots of American Islamicism* (New York: Cambridge University Press, 2006).

16. In my rereading of form, I am indebted to George Levine, *Aesthetics and Ideology* (New Brunswick, NJ: Rutgers University Press, 1994); Susan J. Wolfson, "Reading for Form," *Modern Language Quarterly* 61, no. 1 (March 2000): 1–16; Frank Lentricchia and Andrew Dubois, eds., *Close Reading* (Durham, NC: Duke University Press, 2003); Christopher Castiglia and Russ Castronovo, "A 'Hive of Subtlety': Aesthetics and the End(s) of Cultural Studies," *American Literature* 76, no. 3 (September 2004): 423–35; Samuel Otter, "From *Typee* to *Clarel:* Across the Chasm" (forthcoming).

17. Stephens, *Incidents of Travel,* 174–75.

18. On the inextricable ties of travel literature, ethnography, and exegesis, see Michel de Certeau's classic work, primarily *Writing and History,* trans. Tom Conley (New York: Columbia University Press, 1988).

19. Alexander Keith, *Evidence of the Truth of the Christian Religion Derived from the Literal Fulfillment of Prophecy; Particularly as Illustrated by the History of the Jews, and by the Discoveries of Recent Travellers* (Edinburgh: Waugh and Innes, 1823), 352. The Jews too are construed by Kieth as a living prophecy, given that their wandering is compatible with prophetic warnings. Keith and his theories regarding Edom are ridiculed in *Clarel,* 2.29.99–107.

20. Keith, *Evidence of Prophecy,* 355.

21. This formulation appears in Keith's revised abridged version, titled *The Evidence of Prophecy: Historical Testimony to the Truth of the Bible* (London: The Religious Tract Society, 1830?), 111.

22. Stephens, *Incidents of Travel,* 175–76. For more on Stephens, see Davis, *Landscape of Belief,* 32–37; and Obenzinger, *American Palestine,* 46–49.

23. William C. Prime, *Tent Life in the Holy Land* [1857] (New York: Arno Press, 1977), 479.

24. Stephens, *Incidents of Travel,* 301.

25. Sarah Haight, *Letters from the Old World by a Lady of New York* (New York: Harper and Bros., 1840), 2:34.

26. Mark Twain (Samuel Clemens), *The Innocents Abroad* (New York: Signet Classic, 1966), 405–6.

27. Edward Robinson, *Biblical Researches in Palestine, Mount Sinai and Arabia Petraea* [1841] (New York: Arno Press, 1977), ix.

28. Ibid., 376.

29. Stephens, *Incidents of Travel*, 164. For more on nineteenth-century American travel to Palestine, see Yehoshua Ben Aryeh, *The Rediscovery of the Holy Land in the Nineteenth Century* (Jerusalem: Magnes Press, 1979); Robert T. Handy, ed., *The Holy Land in American Protestant Life, 1800–1948* (New York: Arno Press, 1981); Lester I. Vogel, *To See a Promised Land: Americans and the Holy Land in the Nineteenth Century* (University Park: Pennsylvania State University Press, 1993); Milette Shamir, "'Our Jerusalem': Americans in the Holy land and Protestant Narratives of National Entitlement," *American Quarterly* 55, no. 1 (2003): 29–60. Eitan Bar-Yosef's study on English Holy Land travel literature is relevant as well: *The Holy Land in English Culture, 1799–1917: Palestine and the Question of Orientalism* (Oxford: Oxford University Press, 2005). For a consideration of other modes of religious fiction on the Orient in nineteenth-century America, see David S. Reynolds, *Faith in Fiction: The Emergence of Religious Literature in America* (Cambridge, MA: Harvard University Press, 1981).

30. Edward W. Said, *Orientalism* (New York: Random House, 1978), 168.

31. Wearing Oriental costumes became common practice in nineteenth-century American Holy Land panoramas at World's Fairs. See Davis, *The Landscape of Belief*, 53–72; and Barbara Kirshenblatt-Gimblett, "Making a Place in the World: Jews and the Holy Land at World's Fairs," in *Encounters with the Holy Land: Place, Past and Future in American Jewish Culture*, ed. Jeffrey Shandler and Beth Wenger (Philadelphia: National Museum of American Jewish History, 1997), 60–82.

32. Note that Ishmael becomes a far more negative figure in Christian and Jewish exegesis after he is adopted as an ancestor of Islam; see Carol Bakhos, *Ishmael on the Border: Rabbinic Portrayals of the First Arab* (New York: State University of New York Press, 2006). Christian exegesis, one should bear in mind, relies not only on Genesis but also on Gal. 4:21–31. For more on the New Testament's version of the story of Hagar and Ishmael, see Elizabeth A. Castelli, "Allegories of Hagar: Reading Galatians 4:21–31 with Postmodern Feminist Eyes," in *The New Literary Criticism and the New Testament*, 228–250. On American perceptions of Islam, see Marr, *The Cultural Roots of American Islamicism*.

33. Marr regards Melville's ethnography as cosmopolitan. His observations are relevant to Melville's biblical ethnographies. See Timothy Marr, "Without the Pale: Melville and Ethnic Cosmopolitanism," in *A Historical Guide to Herman Melville*, ed. Giles Gunn (New York: Oxford University Press, 2005), 133–66.

34. Otter, *Melville's Anatomies*, 34.

35. In *The Sign of the Cannibal* (Durham, NC: Duke University Press, 1988), 136, Geoffrey Sanborn reads this passage as a point of transition in which Ishmael shifts away from the normative relation to savages, "governed by the logic of spectacle," and discovers the possibility of an "open dialogue." See also Geoffrey Sanborn, "Whence Come You, Queequeg?" *American Literature* 77, no. 2 (June 2005): 227–56.

36. Stephens, *Incidents of Travel,* 284. On the conflation of Arabs and Native Americans in Holy Land travel literature, see Vogel, *To See a Promised Land,* 77–85; and Obenzinger, *American Palestine.* On the identification of Native Americans as members of the lost tribes, see W. J. T. Mitchell, "Holy Landscapes: Israel, Palestine, and the American Wilderness," *Critical Inquiry* 26 (Winter 2000): 204.

37. The question of exegetical guidance is central in *Clarel* and is by no means confined to Oriental guides. The young divinity student, Clarel, follows several potential spiritual guides but finds no exemplary mentor. See Walter E. Bezanson, "Historical and Critical Note," in *Clarel: A Poem and Pilgrimage in the Holy Land* (Northwestern-Newberry Edition), 552–66.

38. Dorothee Metlitsky Finkelstein, *Melville's Orienda* (New Haven, CT: Yale University Press, 1961), 229.

39. Already in the Koran Ishmael is defined as a prophet. Ismailism offered a substantive elaboration on this title.

40. Fedallah's religious practices have been read in different ways. In addition to Ismailism, Fedallah has been associated with the religions of the Far East (India and Japan in particular). See James Baird, *Ishmael* (Baltimore, MD: Johns Hopkins University Press, 1956).

41. Peretz, *Literature, Disaster, and the Enigma of Power,* 72.

42. Agamben, *Potentialities,* 243–71.

43. Vargish, "Gnostic Mythos in *Moby-Dick,*" traces Gnostic beliefs in Ishmael's perception of whiteness.

44. The following passage from W. F. Lynch's *Narrative of the United States' Expedition to the River Jordan and the Dead Sea* (London: Richard Bentley, 1850) is but one example of the preoccupation with skeptical approaches in other sites, in this case, the lake (Sea) of the Galilee: "How could travellers describe the scenery of this lake as tame and uninteresting? . . . Away with such hard-hearted scepticism—so nearly allied to infidelity! What matters it, whether in this field or an adjoining one—on this mount, or another more or less contiguous to it, the Saviour exhorted, blessed, or fed his followers? The very stones, each a sermon, cry shame upon such a captious spirit" (152–53).

45. Haight, *Letters from the Old World,* 1:101–4.

46. Twain, *Innocents Abroad,* 426.

47. Ibid., 422.

48. Ibid., 427.

49. See Obenzinger, *American Palestine,* 161–76.

50. I am indebted to Basem L. Ra'ad's critique of Obenzinger's lack of attention to the distinctions between Melville and Twain, see Ra'ad, Review of *American Palestine, Leviathan* 5, no. 1 (March 2003): 94–98.

51. In associating Jaffa with Perseus and Andromeda, Melville relies on Kitto's entry, "Joppa" (*Cyclopædia,* 1:145–46). Kitto mentions the myth in his opening account of the traditions recorded by "Classical geographers" regarding Jaffa (among them Strabo). Melville found an account of Jaffa's pagan shrines in another entry of Kitto: "Whale" (II:947). For more on Melville's treatment of shrines, see Sanford E. Marovitz, "Melville's Temples," in *Savage Eye: Melville and the Visual Arts,* ed. Christopher Sten (Kent, OH: Kent State University Press, 1991), 77–103.

52. Johannes Leo (or Leo Africanus) was a sixteenth-century Moor. He is mentioned in the "Harris Collection," that is, in *Navigantium atque Itinerantium Biblioteca* (1705), which Melville quotes in "Extracts." In the Talmud, Rabbi B. Bar Hana, a renowned traveler and storyteller, offers a similar tale about the dead of the desert, who allegedly were so gigantic that even a rider on a camel with a spear in his hand could not reach the knee of one such giant on passing under it (Baba Bathra I, 73).

53. When Melville actually reached the Holy Sepulcher in 1857, he describes the site in these terms: "All is glitter & nothing is gold. A sickening cheat." *Journals,* 88.

54. I have focused on the Holy Land, but one should bear in mind that Melville is also concerned with the Egyptian Orient. The latter, like the former, does not lead to primary revelations. The "great Sperm Whale" was not known in the "young Orient World," claims Ishmael, where only the "crocodile of the Nile" was worshiped (347). Nor could any contemporary Orientalist shed light on the mysteries of the creature. Jean-Françoise Champollion (1790–1832), who deciphered the Egyptian hieroglyphs on the Rosetta stone, and Sir William Johns (1746–94), an Orientalist philologist "who read in thirty languages," were incapable of comprehending the hieroglyphic inscriptions on the Sperm Whale's "brow" or his "pyramidical silence" (347). The most captivating exegetical value of Egypt seems to lie in the sphere of language, embedded in the Oriental metaphors (hieroglyphs and pyramids) used to depict what remains unsolved: the riddle of the whale's face and silences.

55. The Pequots were not extinct but were nearly annihilated in 1637. Melville read about the war against the Pequot Indians in Benjamin Trumbull's *A Complete History of Connecticut.* See *Moby-Dick,* Norton Critical Edition (2002), 69. For more on the Pequot war and Melville's response to it, see Rogin, *Subversive Genealogies,* 122–24.

56. Rogin offers an illuminating discussion of Melville's critique of the use of the story of Ishmael to legitimate American dispossessions in the political discourse of his time. In 1851, he writes, a few months before the publication of *Moby-Dick,* the *Southern Literary Messenger* reminded its readers that God told Abraham that he must "cast out thy bondwoman and her son." Abraham loved his "child of nature," insisted the author of "Isaac and Ishmael," but Isaac was "the future patriarch of his chosen nation, with whom the covenant was to be established." "Is not our country the Isaac[,] . . . the child of promise given to [the world] in its old age? And shall any inferior nation stop us in our heaven-marked course?" he goes on to ask, preparing the

ground for a defense of slavery as a continuation of the act of the dispossession of the "red men" by the founding fathers of America. "If one must yield, are we not right in saying—the son of the bondwoman shall not be heir with the son of the free? And who will set themselves . . . against God and say let Ishmael be favored. . . . Those who dishonor the graves of their noble fathers by refusing to abide by the compact they made for themselves and their children . . . who would pull down with unhallowed hands the fair fabric of the Union" (quoted in Rogin, *Subversive Genealogy,* 141).

57. On the use of the American flag in Holy Land travels, see Davis, *Landscape of Belief,* 33.

58. Wai-Chee Dimock, in *Empire for Liberty* (Princeton, NJ: Princeton University Press, 1989), 109–39, points to the striking similarities between the representation of Ahab and the prevalent American ethnographic accounts of Native Americans in antebellum America. Both are depicted as savages, and both are doomed to extinction from the very outset: Ahab, as one who bears the name of a king whose body was dismembered; the Indians, due to what the American school of ethnography defined as an incapacity to change and adjust to modern civilization. Dimock sees the similarities as resulting from a shared antebellum discourse of Manifest Destiny in which fates are sealed by scriptural paradigms. However, she overlooks the fact that Melville's insistence on the fragility of the boundaries between the possessors and the dispossessed is indebted to the critical position of the Bible in this connection.

59. See Reuven Firestone, *Journeys in Holy Lands: The Evolution of the Abraham-Ishmael Legends in Islamic Exegesis* (New York: State University of New York Press, 1990), 148–51.

60. Phyllis Trible, *Texts of Terror: Literary Feminist Readings of Biblical Narratives* (Philadelphia: Fortress Press, 1984), 9–36; Yair Zakovitch, *"And You Shall Tell Your Son . . .": The Concept of the Exodus in the Bible* (Jerusalem: Magnes Press, 1991), 26–30. For more on the interrelations of the stories of Isaac and Ishmael, see Ronald Hendel, *Remembering Abraham: Culture, Memory, and History in the Hebrew Bible* (New York: Oxford University Press, 2005).

61. I provide an extensive consideration of the fragility of the biblical concept of chosenness in *The Biography of Ancient Israel: National Narratives in the Bible* (Berkeley: University of California Press, 2000). See also Regina Schwartz, *The Curse of Cain: The Violent Legacy of Monotheism* (Chicago: University of Chicago Press, 1997).

62. On the dark promises of Genesis, see Kronfeld, *On the Margins of Modernism,* 130–40.

63. Melville, *Billy Budd,* 346.

64. To complicate the typological reading of Billy even further, in the opening section the "Handsome Sailor" is represented as an idol, a sacred "grand sculptured Bull," calling to mind the Golden Calf. What is more, Melville, as many critics have noted, follows the normative Christian reading of the binding of Isaac as a prefiguration of the Crucifixion. Billy, in fact, is one of Melville's most prominent Christ figures.

65. Deleuze, "Bartleby; or, the Formula," 80–81.

4. AHAB, IDOLATRY, AND THE QUESTION OF POSSESSION

1. On the typological implications of the name "Ahab," see Wai-Chee Dimock, "Ahab's Manifest Destiny," in *Macropolitics of Nineteenth-Century Literature: Nationalism, Exoticism, Imperialism*, ed. Jonathan Arac and Harriet Ritvo (Philadelphia: University of Pennsylvania Press, 1991), 184–212.

2. Alan Heimert, "Moby-Dick and American Political Symbolism," *American Quarterly* 16 (April 1963): 503.

3. Ibid.

4. Theodore Parker, "The Sermon on the Mexico War—Preached at the Melodeon, on Sunday, June 25, 1848," in *Collected Works* [1863], 4:62. (The "Scripture Lesson" is not reprinted in Parker's *Collected Works*.)

5. Ibid., 74.

6. Theodore Parker, "The Chief Sins of the People" [1851], in *Collected Works*, 7:276. Rogin, *Subversive Genealogy*, 124, calls attention to the fact that "like Parker, and for the same purpose, Melville collects Ahab, Elijah, and Peleg" together in *Moby-Dick*. Parker also mentions Ahab in "The Hebrew Monarchy," where he reviews a book titled *A History of the Hebrew Monarchy from the Administration of Samuel to the Babylonish Captivity* (*Collected Works*, 10:1–18). Note that there is no reference in the biblical text itself to a law issued by Ahab regarding Baal, but in the days of his rule and that of Jezebel, the worship of Baal (and Ashera) had become one of the official modes of worship.

7. Quoted in J. Albert Harrill, "The Use of the New Testament in the American Slave Controversy: A Case History in the Hermeneutical Tension between Biblical Criticism and Christian Moral Debate," *Religion and America Culture: A Journal of Interpretation* 10, no. 2 (2000): 159.

8. In one of the most moving passages of his *Narrative*, Douglass recalls the following incident: "It was necessary to keep our religious masters at St. Michael's unacquainted with the fact, that, instead of spending the Sabbath wrestling, boxing, and drinking whisky, we were trying to read the will of God; for they had much rather see us engaged in those degrading sports, than to see us behaving like intellectual, moral, and accountable beings. My blood boils as I think of the bloody manner in which Messrs. Wright Fairbanks and Garrison West . . . rushed in upon us with sticks and stones, and broke up our virtuous little Sabbath school, at St. Michael's—all calling themselves Christians!" (*Narrative of the Life of Frederick Douglass, an American Slave Written by Himself* [New Haven, CT: Yale University Press, 2001], 59). For a consideration of the interrelations between Melville and Douglass, see Robert K. Wallace, *Douglass and Melville: Anchored Together in Neighborly Style* (New Bedford, CT: Spinner Publications, 2005).

9. Quoted in Harrill, "The Use of the New Testament in the American Slave Controversy," 160.

10. See Nathan O. Hatch and Mark A. Noll, eds., *The Bible in America: Essays in Cultural History* (New York: Oxford University Press, 1982); and James Turner Johnson, *The Bible in American Law, Politics, and Political Rhetoric* (Philadelphia: Chico Fortress Press and Scholars Press, 1985).

11. It is noteworthy that Melville refers to Ahab in two other works: *Clarel* (3.11.227) and between the lines in his critique of American expansionism in *Mardi*. See Heimert, "*Moby-Dick* and American Political Symbolism," 503–4.

12. Charles H. Foster, "Something in Emblems: A Reinterpretation of *Moby-Dick*," *New England Quarterly* 34 (March 1961): 20.

13. For more on the political implications of *Moby-Dick*, see Andrew Delbanco, Introduction to *Moby-Dick* (New York: Penguin Books, 1992), xxxi–xxiv.

14. Rogin, *Subversive Genealogy*, 108.

15. Robert Alter, *The Art of Biblical Narrative* (New York, Basic Books, 1981), 35.

16. Melville, *Correspondence*, vol. 14, *The Writings of Herman Melville*, ed. Lynn Horth (Evanston and Chicago: Northwestern University Press, 1993), 119.

17. The Bible, one should bear in mind, has been regarded as indispensable for political thought from the founding political writings of Hobbes and Lock onward. For modern considerations of the matter by scholars of political science, see Michael Walzer, *Exodus and Revolution* (New York: Basic Books, 1985); Michael Walzer, Menachem Lorberbaum, and Noam J. Zohar, eds., *The Jewish Political Tradition* (New Haven, CT: Yale University Press, 2000, 2004), vols. 1 and 2; and Aaron Wildavsky, *The Nursing Father: Moses as Political Leader* (Birmingham: University of Alabama Press, 1984). There are but a few studies of political imagination by literary critics. Two notable ones are Mieke Bal, *Death and Dissymmetry: The Politics of Coherence in the Book of Judges* (Chicago: University of Chicago Press, 1988); and Joel Rosenberg, *King and Kin: Political Allegory in the Hebrew Bible* (Bloomington: Indiana University Press, 1986).

18. See Robert Alter, *The David Story* (New York: Norton, 1999), 43.

19. For more on 1 Sam. 8, see Martin Buber, *Kingship of God*, trans. Richard Scheimann (London: G. Allen and Unwin, 1967); Semaryahu Talmon, "Mishpat ha-melekh," in *Ha-Melukha ha-Yisraelit bereshita* (Jerusalem: Mercaz Zalman Schazar, 1975), 16–27; Yair Zakovitch, "'al Dmut ha-Manhig ba-Mikra," in *The Real and Ideal Image of the Leader*, ed. Yair Zakovitch, Yonah Frenkel, and Aviezer Ravitzki (Jerusalem: Presidential Residence, 1994), 13–22 (in Hebrew).

20. Moshe Halbertal, "God's Kingship," in *Jewish Political Tradition*, 1:129. See also Moshe Halbertal and Avishai Margalit, *Idolatry* (Cambridge, MA: Harvard University Press, 1992), 214–35; and Carola Hilfrich, "'Making Writing Readable Again': Sign Praxis between the Discourse on Idolatry and Cultural Criticism," *Journal of Religion* 82, no. 2 (2005): 267–92. Whereas the likening of God to a king is the principal divine metaphor in Samuel and Kings, the guiding metaphor in the Pentateuch is God as Father (see my *Biography of Ancient Israel*), and the most resonant prophetic metaphor is that of God as Husband (discussed in the next chapter).

21. Martin Buber, "Biblical Leadership," in *On the Bible*, 144.

22. For more on Jezebel, see Phyllis Trible, "The Odd Couple: Elijah and Jezebel," in *Out of the Garden: Women Writers on the Bible*, ed. Christina Buchmann and Celina Spiegel (New York: Fawcett Columbine, 1994), 166–79.

23. There are many other intertextual links between the two stories. One notable parallel is the prophetic rebuke of Nathan vis-à-vis David in the well-known Parable of the Ewe.

24. Ahab and Elijah are by no means strangers. Other encounters between the two attest to the ambivalence that lies at the base of their relationship, most notably in 1 Kings 18:45–46, where Elijah runs before Ahab's carriage as both try to avoid being caught in the approaching storm. For more on the story of Naboth's Vineyard, see Binyamin Openheimer, *Ha-Nevu'a hakdumah beYisrael* (Jerusalem: Magnes Press, 1983), 206–36; Yair Zakovitch, "Kerem haya leNavot," *HaMikra kidmuto* (Jeruslaem: Mosad Bialik, 1987), 356–77; George Savran, "1 and 2 Kings," in *The Literary Guide to the Bible*, 146–64.

25. Chap. 34, "The Cabin Table," provides an elaborate depiction of Captain Ahab as king.

26. See Halbertal and Margalit, *Idolatry,* chap. 2.

27. Rogin, *Subversive Genealogy,* 116.

28. I am indebted to Otter's close reading of "The Doubloon" in *Melville's Anatomies,* 168–71.

29. The idol at the center of the Philistine temple was Dagon, the fish idol that Ishmael evokes in "The Honor and Glory of Whaling."

30. On Winthrop as Moses and Nehemiah, see Bercovitch, *The Puritan Origins of the American Self.*

31. Donald Pease, "Melville and Cultural Persuasion," in *Herman Melville—A Collection of Critical Essays,* ed. Myra Jehlen (Englewood Cliffs, NJ: Prentice Hall, 1994), 415.

32. Ibid., 413.

33. Note that Jeremiah (29:21) speaks of a false prophet named Ahab. Melville may be conflating the two biblical Ahabs. I am indebted to Batnadiv HaKarmi-Weinberg for calling my attention to this possibility.

34. On the "free space" of the aesthetic, see George Levine, "Reclaiming the Aesthetic," in *Aesthetics and Ideology,* 14–19.

35. For a consideration of "Benito Cereno" and New World politics, see Eric J. Sundquist, *To Wake the Nations: Race in the Making of American Literature* (Cambridge, MA: Belknap Press, 1993), 135–224. I am indebted to Francine Masiello for sharpening my understanding of the Spanish-American connection in Melville's ouevre.

36. Erich Auerbach, *Mimesis: The Representation of Reality in Western Literature,* trans. Willard R. Trask (Princeton, NJ: Princeton University Press, 1953), 15.

37. Melville, *Correspondence,* 192.

38. Wright, *Melville's Use of the Bible,* 65; Thompson, *Melville's Quarrel with God,* 200–201.

39. Martin Buber, "False Prophets," in *On the Bible,* 169–71. Henaniah is Jeremiah's version of a false prophet who lures his audience to wage an impossible war—in this case against Babylon.

40. For more on Hobbes and the political implications of divine kingship, see Menachem Lorberbaum, "Making Space for Leviathan: On Hobbes's

Political Theory," *Hebraic Political Studies* 2, no. 1 (Winter 2007): 78–100. On Hobbes's political imagination, see Yaron Ezrahi, "The Theatrics and Mechanics of Action: The Theater and the Machine as Political Metaphors," *Social Research* 62, no. 2 (Summer 1995): 299–320.

41. I am indebted to Stuart Schofman for calling my attention to the royal attributes of the "Whale Song" in the "Extracts."

42. P. Adams Sitney, "Ahab's Name: A Reading of the 'Symphony,'" in *Herman Melville's Moby-Dick: Modern Critical Interpretations,* ed. Harold Bloom (New York: Chelsea House, 1986), 135. On the circulation of the story of Samson and Delilah in Western culture, see David Fishelov, *Samson's Locks: The Transformations of Biblical Samson* (Tel Aviv: Zemora-Bitan, 2000) (in Hebrew).

43. See Henry A. Murray, "'In Nomine Diaboli': *Moby-Dick*," in Bloom, ed., *Herman Melville's Moby-Dick: Modern Critical Interpretations,* 45; Carolyn De Swarte Gifford, "American Women and the Bible: The Nature of Woman as a Hermeneutical Issue," in *Feminist Perspectives on Biblical Scholarship,* ed. Adela Yarbro Collins (Chico, CA: Scholars Press, 1985), 15.

44. Interestingly, the Hebrew text links Maachah's idol to the worship of the goddess Ashera. The King James Version, however, omits this detail in depicting the idol she had made.

45. On the mincer as "satirized minister," see New, "Bible Leaves! Bible Leaves!"

46. The dynamics between Macbeth and Lady Macbeth bears resemblance to the bond between Ahab and Jezebel. His affiliation with Saul is particularly noticeable in the scenes with the witches, with their echoes of Saul's tragic encounter with the witch of Ein Dor.

47. For more on Captain Ahab's madness, see Henry Nash Smith, "The Madness of Ahab," *Yale Review* 66 (Autumn 1976): 14–32.

48. Rogin, *Subversive Genealogy,* 150.

49. Melville may also be debunking the mad ramblings of the mad prophets of the religious revival. On the relevance of Elijah to Melville in this connection, see Paul E. Johnson and Sean Wilentz, *The Kingdom of Matthias: A Story of Sex and Salvation in 19th-Century America* (New York: Oxford University Press, 1994), 171.

50. Heimert, "*Moby-Dick* and American Political Symbolism," 514.

51. Alexis de Tocqueville, *Democracy in America,* trans. George Lawrence, ed. J. P. Mayer (New York: Perennial Classics, 1969), 293. See also 542.

5. RACHEL'S INCONSOLABLE CRY

1. I am indebted to Galit Hasan-Rokem's reading of Jeremiah's female dirge singers in the context of Midrash Eikha Rabba, *Web of Life: Folklore and Midrash in Rabbininc Literature,* trans. Batya Stein (Stanford, CA: Stanford University Press, 2000). On women's role as dirge singers in Greek tradition, see Margaret Alexiou, *The Ritual Lament in Greek Tradition* (Cambridge: Cambridge University Press, 1974).

2. On the destructive fantasy of absolute male power in *Moby-Dick,* see Gabriele Schwab, *Subjects without Selves: Transitional Texts in Modern Fiction* (Cambridge, MA: Harvard University Press, 1994).

3. Critics who did venture to contextualize Melville's relation to gender issues have focused primarily on sentimental literature. There is a certain overlap between women's Bibles and sentimental literature, but each realm, nonetheless, has distinct features. On Melville and sentimental literature, see Ann Douglas's groundbreaking book, *The Feminization of American Culture* (New York: Noonday Press, 1977); and the much-needed critiques of her definition of the sentimental: Jane Tompkins, *Sensational Designs: The Cultural Work of American Fiction, 1790–1860* (New York: Oxford University Press, 1985); Eve Kosofsky Sedgwick, *The Epistemology of the Closet* (New York: Harvester Wheatsheaf, 1991), 114–21; Otter, *Melville's Anatomies,* 210–13.

4. I would add African American religious practices to Stuckey's list: Ishmael's visit to the "negro church" in New Bedford, with its "weeping and wailing" (10), and Fleece's sermon are two notable examples.

5. Gifford, "American Women and the Bible," 11–33. The feminization of biblical exegesis is part of a broader phenomenon of the feminization of American religion. See the classical work of Barbara Welter, "The Feminization of American Religion: 1800–1860," in *Clio's Consciousness Raised: New Perspectives on the History of Women,* ed. Mary S. Hartman and Lois Banner (New York: Harper Torchbooks, 1974), 137–57.

6. Sarah M. Grimké, *Letters on the Equality of the Sexes and the Condition of Woman* [1838] (New York: Burt Franklin, 1970), 3–4.

7. Quoted in Gifford, "American Women and the Bible," 21. Margaret Fuller's *Woman in the Nineteenth Century* did not deal extensively with the question of women and religion, but it was vital to the formation of the exegetical rhetoric of the women's movement.

8. Thus Stanton hails the egalitarian Priestly account of the simultaneous creation of man and woman in Gen. 1:27 and rails against the Yahwist rendition of woman's creation out of Adam's rib in Gen. 2. For more on *The Woman's Bible,* see Barbara Welter, "Something Remains to Dare," introduction to *The Woman's Bible* (New York: Arno Press, 1974); and my *Countertraditions in the Bible,* chap. 2.

9. Shira Wolosky, "Women's Bibles: Biblical Interpretation in Nineteenth-Century American Women's Poetry," *Feminist Studies* 28, no. 1 (Spring 2002): 191–211. See also Shira Wolosky, *Major Voices: 19th-Century American Women's Poetry* (London: Toby Press, 2003).

10. See Welter, "The Feminization of American Religion," 14. For more on American missionary women, see Fiona Bowie, Deborah Kirkwood, and Shirley Ardener, eds., *Women and Missions Past and Present: Anthropological and Historical Perceptions* (Providence, RI: Berg, 1993); Dana L. Robert, "The Influence of American Missionary Women on the World Back Home," *Religion and American Culture* 12, no. 1 (Winter 2002): 59–80. Interestingly enough, even the writings of Elizabeth Cady Stanton were not innocent of colonial constructs, especially with respect to the definition of sovereignty;

see Lydia H. Liu, *The Clash of Empires: The Invention of China in Modern World Making* (Cambridge, MA: Harvard University Press, 2004), chap. 5.

11. In singling out Hawthorne and Parker, I follow Barbara Welter, "The Feminization of American Religion," 140.

12. Nathaniel Hawthorne, *The Scarlet Letter,* Norton Critical Edition, ed. Symour Gross, Sculley Bradely, Richmond Croom Beatty, and E. Hudson Long (New York: Norton, 1988), 177–78.

13. Elizabeth Cady Stanton, *The Woman's Bible* (Seattle, WA: Coalition Task Force on Women and Religion, 1974), chap. 10 and chap. 11, 59–64.

14. Gutjahr, *An American Bible,* 70–71. For more on *Harper's Illuminated Bible,* see also Danielle, *The Bible in English,* 656–58.

15. Stephens, *Incidents of Travel,* 339. For additional references to Rachel's tomb, see Prime, *Tent Life in the Holy Land,* 225.

16. *Clarel,* 4.29.110–14.

17. Harriet Beecher Stowe, *Woman in Sacred History* [1873] (New York: Portland House, 1990). See Janet B. Sommers, "Vision and Revision: The Midrashic Imagination in Harriet Beecher Stowe's *Woman in Sacred History,*" *Religion & Literature* 35, no. 1 (Spring 2003): 23–44; Gail K. Smith, "The Sentimental Novel: The Example of Harriet Beecher Stowe," in *The Cambridge Companion to Nineteenth-Century American Women's Writing,* ed. Dale M. Bauer and Philip Gould (New York: Cambridge University Press, 2001), 221–43.

18. Stowe, *Woman in Sacred History,* 56.

19. Harriet Beecher Stowe, *Uncle Tom's Cabin,* Norton Critical Edition, ed. Elizabeth Ammons (New York: Norton, 1994), 100.

20. Ibid., 102. In *Woman in Sacred History,* Stowe devotes an entire chapter to "Hagar, the Slave."

21. Ibid., 105.

22. Ibid., 113–15.

23. Ibid., 122.

24. Elizabeth Ammons, "Stowe's Dream of the Mother-Savior: *Uncle Tom's Cabin* and American Women Writers before the 1920s," in *New Essays on Uncle Tom's Cabin,* ed. Eric J. Sundquist (New York: Cambridge University Press, 1986), 159.

25. Quoted in Rogin, *Subversive Genealogy,* 140. For other uses of Jeremiah's Rachel beyond the context of abolition, see Heimert, "*Moby-Dick* and the American Political Symbolism," 531.

26. Camille Paglia, *Sexual Personae: Art and Decadence from Nefertiti to Emily Dickinson* (New Haven, CT: Yale University Press, 1990), 585. Wyn Kelley offers a much-needed complication of Melville's relation to gender in "Pierre's Domestic Ambiguities," in *The Cambridge Companion to Herman Melville,* 91–113.

27. Barbara Hochman examines *Uncle Tom's Cabin* in relation to other items in the *National Era* and suggests that Stowe was trying to radicalize the political line of the abolitionist press; see "*Uncle Tom's Cabin* in the National Era: An Essay in Generic Norms and the Contexts of Reading," *Book History* 7 (2004): 143–69. Whereas Melville's dialogue with Stowe in *Moby-Dick* is inadvertent, one can construe "Benito Cereno" as an actual

response to the representation of gender and race in *Uncle Tom's Cabin*. For a consideration of the interrelations of "Benito Cereno" and *Uncle Tom's Cabin,* see Emily Miller Budick, *Engendering Romance: Women Writers and the Hawthorne Tradition, 1850–1990* (New Haven, CT: Yale University Press, 1994), chap. 6.

28. For a comparison of the respective cultural-theological approaches of Melville and Stowe, see Buell, *New England Literary Culture,* 178–79.

29. On Uncle Tom as feminized Christ, see Ammons, "Stowe's Dream of the Mother-Savior."

30. Peretz, *Literature, Disaster, and the Enigma of Power,* 64.

31. Neal L. Tolchin reads Ahab's grief in light of Melville's biography, suggesting that it is a dramatization of Melville's own identification with his mother's mourning over the untimely death of his father; see *Mourning, Gender, and Creativity in the Art of Herman Melville* (New Haven, CT: Yale University Press, 1988), 117–37. Here too, then, Ahab's cry is associated with maternal mourning, though Tolchin overlooks the importance of the allusion to Jeremiah's Rachel in rendering Ahab's heightened bereavement. For more on Ahab's sense of orphanhood and quest for the maternal, see John Bryant, "*Moby-Dick* as Revolution," in *The Cambridge Companion to Herman Melville,* 76–79.

32. On Ahab's identity fissures, see Sitney, "Ahab's Name: A Reading of 'The Symphony,'" 131–46; Dimock, "Ahab's Manifest Destiny."

33. Ann Douglas overlooks the complexity of this tear and its biblical resonance in claiming that Ahab's weeping is a moment of sentimental weakness—which we, as readers, are asked to reject; *The Feminization of American Culture,* 304–5.

34. Leslie A. Fiedler regards Queequeg's embrace as the beginning of Ishmael's "sentimental reeducation" and "reconciliation with the 'tabooed mother'" that will end when he is picked up by the cruising *Rachel;* see *Love and Death in the American Novel* (New York: Stein and Day, 1966), 375.

35. Buell, *New England Literary Culture,* 178.

36. On Melville and the question of homosexuality, see Sedgwick, *The Epistemology of the Closet.*

37. The prophets were the first to imagine the relationship between God and the nation as a marital one. In doing so, they added a central resonant metaphor to the complex network of earlier metaphors for this relationship, the prominent ones being father-son and king-servant (the dominant metaphor in Samuel-Kings). Each prophet, however, imagined this metaphoric marriage in a different light. On the prophetic marital metaphor, see Halbertal and Margalit, *Idolatry,* 9–36; Julie Galambush, *Jerusalem in the Book of Ezekiel: The City as Yahweh's Wife* (Atlanta, GA: Scholars Press, 1992).

38. For a reading of the beloved's compassing of God as a continuation of Rachel's move, see Phyllis Trible, *God and the Rhetoric of Sexuality* (Philadelphia: Fortress Press, 1978), 38–50.

39. See Tikva Frymer-Kensky, *In the Wake of the Goddess: Women, Culture and the Biblical Transformation of Pagan Myth* (New York: Fawcett Columbine, 1992), 166–67.

40. I provide an extensive reading of Rachel as rebel in my *Countertraditions in the Bible,* chap. 4. For a discussion of the midrashic rendition of Rachel's audacity, see Hasan-Rokem, *The Web of Life,* chap. 6.

41. Rogin, *Subversive Genealogy,* 141.

42. Bercovitch, *The American Jeremiad,* 192.

43. Even in biblical times, consolation prophecies are never an easy task. It is not accidental that true prophets seldom deliver such prophecies.

44. In "Hawthorne and His Mosses," Melville depicts Hawthorne as having "that lasting temper of all true, candid men—a seeker, not a finder yet:—" (529). Seeking rather than finding is the predominant propelling force for Melville too, though finding is not discarded. The final "yet" with the colon and dash reminds us of the great value of struggling to maintain a potentiality of finding.

45. I am indebted to Sam Otter for calling my attention to the ambiguities of this term. I am also indebted to Leo Bersani's analysis in *The Culture of Redemption* (Cambridge, MA: Harvard University Press, 1990), 136–54. Let me add that while Bersani's complication of the question of redemption in *Moby-Dick* is much needed, he goes too far in eliminating every manifestation of a utopian order, overlooking the ways in which Melville (as "pilgrim-infidel") can endorse redemption and dismiss it at once. For more on Melville's treatment of redemption, see Michael Warner, "What Like a Bullet Can Undeceive?" *Public Culture* 15, no. 1 (2003): 41–54.

46. Melville, *Correspondence,* 212.

47. Natal imagery appears in Jeremiah's initiation scene as well: "Before I formed thee in the belly I knew thee; and before thou cameth forth out of the womb I sanctified thee, and I ordained thee a prophet unto the nations" (1:5). I am indebted to a seminar paper by Batnadiv HaKarmi-Weinberg on prophetic initiations for sharpening my understanding of Jeremiah 1. For more on Jeremiah's perception of his vocation, see Michael Fishbane, "'A Wretched Thing of Shame, A Mere Belly': An Interpretation of Jeremiah 29:7–12," in *The Biblical Mosaic: Changing Perspectives,* ed. Robert Polzin and Eugene Rothman (Philadelphia: Fortress Press, 1982), 162–95; Herbert Marks, "On Prophetic Stammering," *Yale Journal of Criticism* 1 (1987): 1–19 (reprinted in *The Book and the Text,* 60–80).

48. The stubborn vitality of the letter bolsters the sense of consolation in the gloomy ending of *The Scarlet Letter* as well. On the one tombstone that serves for both Hester and Dimmesdale there appeared a herald's wording, "so somber . . . and relieved only by one ever-glowing point of light gloomier than the shadow: 'On a black shield, the letter A in red.'" The letter *A,* which Hester is forced to bear, the letter that is reinterpreted time and again as it acquires different meanings—from "Adulterous" to "Abel" and "Angel"—mysteriously finds its way to this tombstone, engraving itself as a red letter on a black shield, as if refusing to relinquish the battle, unwilling to give up the possibility of delivering the tale.

49. Gilmore points out that such images of beasts of prey turning into peaceable creatures are common not only in the Bible but also in millennial writings; "Melville's Apocalypse: American Millennialism and *Moby-Dick,*" 159.

50. Deleuze, *Essays Critical and Clinical,* 84–90. Deleuze focuses on the ways in which Melville imagines American society as fatherless. Although he does not refer to the question of the mother, his comments on Melville's invention of "a society of orphans" are most illuminating in this connection.

EPILOGUE

1. There are numerous explicit and implicit allusions to Noah's ark throughout *Moby-Dick.* Of particular relevance are the lines leading to the "Epilogue," with their evocation of the time of Noah's flood: "Now small fowls flew screaming over the yet yawning gulf; a sullen white surf beat against its steep sides; then all collapsed, and the great shroud of the sea rolled on as it rolled five thousand years ago" (572). Moses is also evoked elsewhere, most notably in "The Affidavit," where Ishmael claims, "I had no more idea of being facetious than Moses, when he wrote the history of the plagues in Egypt," (206) and in "The Tail," where he bemoans not having the privilege of Moses who was at least granted the vision of God's back parts (379).

2. Interestingly, the link between the three arks is a choice of the King James translation. The arks of Noah and Moses are linked in the Bible through the use of the rare term *teva,* but the Hebrew term for the Holy Ark is different: *aron habrit.* This final scene calls to mind the myth of the birth of the hero. The hero, as Otto Rank argues, is often a foundling who is born against all odds and rescued against all odds after being cast away. Moses' birth story is one of his primary examples. See *The Myth of the Birth of a Hero,* trans. Mabel E. Moxon (New York: Vintage Books, 1932). I provide an extensive reading of Moses' birth story in *The Biography of Ancient Israel,* chap. 2. Note that in Ishmael's birth scene in the "Epilogue" the *Rachel* plays the role of Pharoah's daughter who finds the castaway Moses and adopts him as a son.

3. Herman Melville, *White-Jacket* (New York: Oxford University Press, 1990), 153.

4. The incident of the Holy Ark in the Temple of Dagon (1 Sam. 5) is mentioned in "The Honor and Glory of Whaling" (362).

5. I focus on Melville's dialogue with the biblical text, but his dialogue with the English literary canon in this passage, namely, with Coleridge's "The Rime of the Ancient Mariner," is equally important.

6. Drosnin applied a mathematical method for extracting equidistant letter sequence (ELS) to the Bible and claimed to have found predictions of the assassinations of various world leaders, from Gandhi to Rabin. His critics—Brendan McKay, together with the mathematicians Dror Bar-Natan and Gil Kalai and the philosopher Maya Bar-Hillel, refuted his claims by proving that such sequences could be found in many other texts. In light of Drosnin's remark, *Moby-Dick* was one of their primary test cases. For more on the controversy of *The Bible Code,* see Brendan McKay, Dror Bar-Natan, Maya Bar-Hillel, and Gil Kalai, "Solving the Bible Code Puzzle," *Statistical Science* 14, no. 2 (1999): 150–73.

7. Samuel Otter, "Blue Proteus: *Moby-Dick* and the World We Live In" (forthcoming).

8. Quoted in Otter, "Blue Proteus."

9. Andrew Delbanco's opening "Extracts" in *Melville: His World and Work,* playfully modeled after the opening "Extracts" of Ishmael in *Moby-Dick,* supplied as they are by a "Sub-Sub-Sub-Librarian," vividly underscore the cultural resonance of Melville's oeuvre. Delbanco opens with a selection of Melville citations by writers and critics as different as Joesph Conrad, Samuel Becket, Albert Camus, Howard P. Vincent, and Leslie Fiedler. From the literary realm, Delbanco moves to the political—Edward Said, BBC News, Richard Clark—and then to the popular realm via the caricatures of *MADD Magazine* and the Sopranos. Given the great resonance of Delbanco's own book, it too could be added to these extracts. For more on the popular reception of Melville's books, see Elizabeth Schultz, "Melville in Visual Media and Popular Culture," in *A Companion to Herman Melville,* ed. Wyn Kelley, 532–52.

10. Buell, "*Moby-Dick* as Sacred Text," 53.

11. James wrote this book while he was detained at Ellis Island. In his introduction to James's book, Donald Pease suggests that "James produced a fictive retroactivity whereby he represented the experience he underwent on Ellis Island as having 'realized' in historical time one of the national futures Melville had imagined a century earlier" (xxviii).

Index

Text: 10/13 Sabon
Display: Sabon
Compositor, printer, and binder: IBT Global

Made in the USA
Middletown, DE
03 March 2021

34672657R00123